✳   12, 772

818.5407 Kerr, Jean Collins.
KE   How I got to be perfect / Jean
         Kerr. -- 1st ed. -- Garden City,
         N.Y. : Doubleday, 1978.
              p.   cm.

         ISBN 0-385-13502-5

         I. Title.

PS3521.E7 44H6   818'.5'407
                                         78-1008
                                            CIP

Library of Congress
0 8654   538716   B   © THE BAKER & TAYLOR CO.   8234

HOW I GOT TO BE PERFECT

HOW I GOT
TO BE PERFECT

Jean Kerr

12,772

Doubleday & Company, Inc.   Garden City, New York
1978

ISBN: 0-385-13502-5
Library of Congress Catalog Card Number 78-1008
Copyright © 1954, 1955, 1956, 1957, 1958, 1959, 1960, 1976, 1977
by Jean Kerr
Copyright © 1966, 1967, 1968, 1969, 1970, 1978 by Collin Productions, Inc.

"The Highwayman" by Alfred Noyes, reprinted from the book *Collected Poems* by Alfred Noyes. Copyright, 1906, 1934, 1947 by Alfred Noyes. Reprinted by permission of J. B. Lippincott Company and John Murray (Publishers) Ltd. "Don Brown's Body," Copyright 1953 by Jean Kerr as a dramatic composition. "Dogs That Have Known Me," Copyright 1957 by The Condé Nast Publications, Inc. "The Kerr-Hilton," which appeared in *Ladies' Home Journal* as "Our Gingerbread Dream House," Copyright 1955 by The Curtis Publishing Company. "Where Did You Put the Aspirin?," *The Saturday Evening Post,* Copyright 1957 by The Curtis Publishing Company. "I Was a Sand Crab" appeared in *McCall's* as *Hand Me My Dark Glasses,* Copyright © 1958 by McCall Corporation. "Letters of Protest I Never Sent," *Good Housekeeping,* Copyright © 1958 by The Hearst Corporation. "The Only Way to Fly" appeared in *McCall's* as "Go, Josephine, in Your Flying Machine," *McCall's,* Copyright © 1960 by McCall Corporation. "A Child's Garden of Manners" appeared in *Ladies' Home Journal* as "Etiquette for Children," Copyright © 1959 by The Curtis Publishing Company. "As I Was Saying to Mrs. Rockefeller" appeared in *Suburbia Today Magazine* as "What Do I Do Now, Mr. Packard?," Copyright © 1960 by Suburbia Publishing Corporation. "Can This Romance Be Saved?," *Esquire, The Magazine for Men,* Copyright © 1959 by Esquire, Inc. "Tales Out of School . . . ," *Ladies' Home Journal,* Copyright © 1959 by The Curtis Publishing Company. "Out of Town with a Show" appeared in *Harper's Magazine* as "What Happens Out of Town," Copyright © 1960 by Jean Kerr. "The Ten Worst Things About a Man," *McCall's,* Copyright © 1959 by McCall Corporation. "Happy Motoring" appeared in *The American Weekly* as "My Dream Car," Copyright © 1958 by Hearst Publishing Company, Inc. "My Wild Irish Mother," *McCall's,* Copyright © 1960 by McCall Corporation. "When I Was Queen of the May" appeared in *Vogue* as "Mom, Were You Ever Miss Rheingold?," Copyright © 1959 by Jean Kerr. "Mirror, Mirror, on the Wall," I Don't Want to Hear One Word Out of

FOR JOAN FORD

Contents

Introduction to the Introduction

Kierkegaard—Sören Kierkegaard, of course—often spoke of "disoriented people." I think he meant *crazy*, but that's Kierkegaard for you, always putting the best face on things. What he said was: "A disoriented person is someone who is nostalgic about the future and hopeful about the past." Now isn't that a good description of a mixed-up person? It's also a good description of a collected book, especially when—as in this case—some of the pieces go back almost twenty years.

Actually, I suspected all along that I was hopeful about the past. Do you know that I honestly believe that someday I will be young and play three sets of tennis before an early breakfast and then, still in my swirly, pleated tennis skirt, make a perfect crème brûlée for the children's lunch? *That's* disoriented! However, I did not suppose that I was nostalgic about the future until I noticed I was still hanging onto the tiny tube of Tangee Natural Lipstick my mother allowed me to buy when I was thirteen. Crazy, crazy, crazy.

Anyway, what we have here—*now* I tell you—are pieces collected from three different books, plus some new pieces which indicate that the calamities continue. I have used the original introduction to my first book (unretouched) because it seems to prove that I was once on the very verge of being "liberated." God only knows what happened.

As for what's new with me—a lot, and not much. I've gained two children and twelve pounds, in that order. We still live in the same house. Our adopted dog, Frosty, has developed a passion for Old Dutch pretzels. The new rubber plant thrives. Walter is still going to plays and, as you can see, I'm still going to pieces.

Oh, I should add that I now have a quiet room to work in. Too quiet, maybe.

And what's new with you?

Introduction

I had the feeling all along that this book should have an Introduction, because it doesn't have an Index and it ought to have *something*. But I was getting nowhere until I received this dandy questionnaire from the publicity department at Doubleday.

Now, I'm an old hand at questionnaires, having successfully opened a charge account at The Tailored Woman. But this was a questionnaire with a difference. It had heart. Take the item: Why do you write? In less artful hands this might have been a touchy question, indicating—perhaps—a last-minute case of nerves at the head office. Instead, one felt that they cared. They just wanted to *know*, that's all.

Of course, there were a certain number of routine questions. List your pen name. (I just call it Ball-Point.) What do you do when you're not writing? (Buy geraniums.) Husband's name? (Honey.) List your previous addresses. (Funny, that's what The Tailored Woman was so curious about.)

But then we began to probe deeper. What is your life's ambition? What do you hope to accomplish ere dusk sets in? As far as this book is concerned, who should be notified in case of accident?

It was this next to last question that really yanked me to attention. It made me realize—and for the very first time—that in my scant twoscore minus seven years (all right, I'm the same age as Margaret Truman; let somebody check on *her*) I have already *achieved* my life ambition. That's something, you know. I feel it sets me apart, rather, like that nice convict who raises canaries in San Quentin.

To go back to the beginning, I was only eight years old, and clearly retarded for my age, when my goal in life dawned on me. I won't say there was a blinding flash, just a poignance, a suspension of time, a sweet recognition of the moment of truth not unlike that memorable instant in which Johnny Weissmuller first noticed that he was Tarzan and *not* Jane.

It was seven-thirty in the morning and my sister, who was six, was pulling my feet out from under the bedclothes and crying, "Oh, get up, get *up* you mean thing, Mother says I can't go downstairs until you're on the floor!" I withered her with one of my characteristically salty sayings—"Oh, you think you're so smart, Lady Jane Grey!"—but as I stumbled out of bed I realized then and there that all I wanted out of life was to be able to sleep until noon. In fact, I composed a poem right on the spot to celebrate the discovery. I remember the poem (unfortunately reprinted here in its entirety) because it is the only one I ever wrote, unless you want to include a two-line Valentine which said "Thee-whee." The poem:

> Dearer to me than the evening star
> A Packard car
> A Hershey bar
> Or a bride in her rich adorning
> Dearer than any of these by far
> Is to lie in bed in the morning.

Of course I realized even then that you can't sleep until noon with the proper élan unless you have some legitimate reason for staying up until three (parties don't count). But I was in high school before I grasped the fact that *I* was never going to do anything that would keep me up until three. I had been writing short stories which, in the first flush of failure, I sent to *Liberty* magazine on the innocent but quite mistaken theory that *Liberty* would buy them because everything in the magazine was so terrible. (The only story I can remember now was called "The Pursuit of Happiness" and I wince to report that Happiness was the heroine's name.)

The solution, for me, was obvious: I had to locate a husband who stayed up until three. With this in mind, I ruled out basketball players, who were the natural objects of my affection at the time (I was five feet nine). It had been my observation that all basketball players eventually joined their fathers in the construction business, an activity notorious for its chaste and early uprisings. Besides, I didn't want to marry a basketball player anyway. I really wanted to marry George S. Kaufman and was deterred only by the fact that (a) he had a wife, and (b) I never met him.

It may not seem very romantic, and I don't think Victor Herbert could have done a thing with it, but by the time I was eighteen Walter (my husband) was the only truly eligible man I had ever met. He was an assistant professor who began teaching his classes at three in the afternoon and who directed plays all night. Actually, he got up at *ten* o'clock in the morning, but that was close enough. It was something to build on. And, to be entirely fair, he had certain other endearing qualities. He could play "Ja-Da" on the piano, recite whole sections of *The Waste Land*, and make passable penuche. So we were married and I began each day bright and late at the stroke of the noon whistle, a splendid state of affairs which continued for two years or right up to the moment our first son was born.

Now the thing about having a baby—and I can't be the first person to have noticed this—is that thereafter you *have* it, and it's years before you can distract it from any elemental need by saying, "Oh, for heaven's sake, go look at television." At this point I was willing to renounce my master plan—so doth parenthood make cowards of us all—and go to bed at a decent hour like everybody else. Unfortunately, Walter was still staying up until three, busily engaged in making student actors look older by the ingenious device of keeping the stage lights very dim, and I was seeing *him* during the late hours, the children during the early hours, and double all the rest of the time.

It took me quite a while to come to grips with the situation, basically because I was thinking so slowly (from the lack of sleep) and because I had to spend so much time trying to remember to turn off the sterilized nipples before they melted. Eventually, after several years and several children, it came to me that the solution was to hire somebody *else* to get up in the morning.

At the university, we lived basically on a teacher's salary, which is the way you live on a teacher's salary; and this meant that if we were going to have a helpmate, I, Mommy, would have to make some money to pay her. But how? A job was out of the question: getting up in the morning was what I was trying to avoid. It had to be something I could do at home among the cans of Dextri-Maltose. But what? Could I sell little batches of my own special chicken creole soup, which I make by mixing together one can of Campbell's chicken soup with one can of Campbell's creole soup? No.

So I decided to write plays, spurred on by a chance compliment my father had paid me years earlier. "Look," he exploded one evening over the dinner table, "the only damn thing in this world you're good for is *talk*." By talk I assumed he meant dialogue—and I was off.

I won't say that my early efforts were crowned with glory. Oh, I'd say it, all right, but could I make it stick? When my first play was produced in New York, Louis Kronenberger wrote in *Time*, with a felicity it took me only ten years to appreciate, that "Leo G. Carroll brightens up Mrs. Kerr's play in much the same way that flowers brighten a sickroom." (I guess this is what they mean by the nick of *Time*.) I don't know why this and similar compliments for Leo G. Carroll didn't stay my hand forever. As someone pointed out recently, if you can keep your head when all about you are losing theirs, it's just possible you haven't grasped the situation. But what with one thing and another (the advance paid by the doomed producer, and the amateur rights) I was now paying the salary of a very nice girl who had insomnia anyway and who pretended to enjoy distributing pablum and crayons until I emerged, rosy and wrinkled, at eleven.

Thus, as the golden years rolled on, I typed my way through several maids. There was a brief, ghastly period, immediately after we left the university, when it looked as though Walter was going to take a civilian-type job and we might have to live, oh think of it, *normally*. But my fears were groundless and Walter became a drama critic. In many ways, a drama critic leads an ideal existence, or would if he didn't have to see so many plays.

Obviously, it's fun to share the opening-night excitement of a great big hit. And there are, every year, a certain number of plays that must be labeled failures (because they close, for one thing) which are nevertheless fascinating to watch. But then, alas, there are the dogs (the worst of these usually turn up in March or April, which is the origin of the phrase "the hounds of spring"). These are the plays that are so bad you sit there in stunned disbelief, fearing for your sanity while on all sides people are beating their way to the exits. It was after just such an evening that my husband commented, "This is the kind of play that gives failures a bad name."

I don't know what set of standards the critics themselves bring to these occasions. But *I* can sense the presence of a real disaster, where no one will be allowed to enter the area for twenty-four hours, by gauging the amount of incidental information I've picked up about the bit players. We sit so far front that it is possible to read by the light-spill from the stage. And through the years I have discovered that on a really grueling evening it helps me to keep alert—that is to say, *conscious*—if I study the program notes while the performance is going on. "Biff Nuthall," I read, "here making his debut in New York in the part of the elevator boy, hails from Princeton, New Jersey. He attended the University of Wisconsin, where he achieved notable success as Mosca in a student production of *Volpone*. Mr. Nuthall also plays the oboe."

As you can see, I now have something to chew over; my subconscious is now gainfully occupied. Biff Nuthall as Mosca. I'm sure that boy is loaded with talent, but he'd never be *my* idea of Mosca. Benvolio maybe, or Friar Laurence; but Mosca—with those freckles and that red hair? And if he hails from Princeton, New Jersey, what was he doing going to the University of Wisconsin? What's the matter with Princeton, for heaven's sake? But that's the way some boys are: just because a college is located in their home town, it's not good enough for them. I'm sure you had your reasons, Biff, but it doesn't seem loyal, somehow. And another thing: What do they mean by that curt statement "Mr. Nuthall also plays the oboe"? Do I imagine it, or is there a rebuke implied there somewhere? Doesn't he play it very well? Or does the press agent, who composed this little biography, not have a very high opinion of the oboe? For his information, the oboe is a noble instrument too much neglected by young people nowadays. What does he want, an entire orchestra composed of violins?

If the cast is long enough, one can while away a whole evening in this manner.

I do have a compulsion to read in out-of-the-way places, and it is often a blessing; on the other hand, it sometimes comes between me and what I tell the children is "*my* work." As a matter of fact, I will read *anything* rather than work. And I don't mean interesting things like the yellow section of the telephone book or the enclosures that come with the Bloomingdale bill about McKettrick classics in sizes twelve to twenty, blue, brown, or navy @ $12.95 (by the way, did you know that colored facial tissue is now on sale at the unbelievably low price of $7.85 a carton?). The truth is that, rather than put a word on paper, I will spend a whole half hour reading the label on a milk of magnesia bottle. "Phillips' Milk of Magnesia," I read with the absolute absorption of someone just stumbling on Congreve, "is prepared only by the Chas. H. Phillips Co., division of Sterling Drug, Inc. Not to be used when abdominal pain, nausea, vomiting, or other symptoms of appendicitis are present, etc."

For this reason, and because I have small boys, I do about half of my "work" in the family car, parked alongside a sign that says "Littering Is Punishable by a $50 Fine." So far as the boys are concerned, it's not the direct interruptions at home that are hard to adjust to. I don't mind when one of them rushes in to tell me something really important, like the Good Humor man said that banana-rum was going to be the flavor of the week next week. What really drives me frantic and leads to the use of such quantities of Tint-Hair is the business of overhearing a chance remark from another part of the house ("Listen, stupid, the water is supposed to go in the *top*"). Rather than investigate, and interrupt myself, I spend twenty minutes wondering: What water?

The top of what? I hope it's just a water gun and not, oh no, not the enema bag again.

Out in the car, where I freeze to death or roast to death depending on the season, all is serene. The few things there are to read in the front-seat area (Chevrolet, E-gasoline-F, 100-temp-200) I have long since committed to memory. So there is nothing to do but write, after I have the glove compartment tidied up.

Once in a while—perhaps every fifteen minutes or so—I ask myself: Why do I struggle, when I could be home painting the kitchen cupboards, *why?* And then I remember. Because I like to sleep in the morning, that's why.

Maybe we'd better have an Index.

HOW I GOT TO BE PERFECT

Partying
Is Such Sweet Sorrow

I always study reports on how the very rich entertain because I know I have a lot to learn. Actually, I could learn something from the way the poor entertain, like, for instance, where do *they* put the playpen when they have people in? But you never read about that.

I note, however and without any glee at all, that the rich make mistakes even as you and I. Just last week the Baroness Guy de Rothschild was confiding her problem to Thelma Sweetinburgh (actual name) in the Sunday *Times*. The Baroness was discussing a party she had given in Ferrières, her weekend château. Now that the ball was over, she had come to one definite conclusion. "Sixteen hundred people are just too many," she said.

See, I would have known that. In our weekend house (which we also use during the early part of the week) I have occasionally had as many as twenty-two people and I can't even keep *them* straight. I was once bidding good night to a rather quiet visitor and said—I still blush to think of it—"Oh, you did come, did you?"

But how would you say good night to sixteen hundred people? I suppose over a public-address system. And then, after the first thousand left, you could sit up and have a quiet nightcap with the six hundred that remained. That's always the best part of the evening.

Well, as even the Baroness now realizes, sixteen hundred people is not a party, it's an emerging new nation.

Another internationally famous hostess, Mrs. Fleur Cowles, had a close thing recently. It appears that Mrs. Cowles has an estate about an hour and a half from London. She also has an apartment in the city of London. Evidently it is Mrs. Cowles' wont to have the staff of the country house prepare a dinner and bring it in hampers to the apartment in London.

I had always supposed there were difficulties inherent in bringing the mountain to Mohammed, and so it proved. The guests had assembled one Sunday night in Mrs. Cowles' London apartment and were munching canapés when it was discovered that, due to some oversight (an inadequate hamper check, probably), the main course had been left in the country.

Naturally, the guests couldn't be allowed to drink for the three hours required to fetch the food. By that time they'd have required intravenous feeding. And no butcher shops were open.

Mrs. Cowles paled but did not panic. Nor did she make any kind of general statement, such as "I hope everybody here likes peanut butter." No, she drew a South American ambassador into a corner and told him all. He had the solution in a trice. One quick call to his staff and everything was arranged. Within the hour the guests were consuming a delicious entrée that had been sent over from the embassy and no one was the wiser—except, of course, the ambassador's staff.

Which brings me to my real question. What did the ambassador *say* when he called home? I try to imagine it. I presume he reached the butler. . . .

"Albert, this is the Ambassador. We are having dinner with Mrs. Cowles. Oh, you knew that. Well, here's the thing. Mrs. Cowles seems to have left the dinner in her other house. What? Yes, that is very tough luck indeed. Now, I was wondering if you and Cook could fix up thirty-two dinners. Albert, I never joke. Oh, anything, stuffed squab, perhaps some veal scaloppine. Now, Albert, that is a very big refrigerator and there surely must be something in it. Albert, I thought the British never cried. Just you put on your thinking-cap and the car will be there in half an hour to pick up the hampers."

You see that in my anxiety to improve as a hostess I do literally comb the society columns. I must learn how the *in* people entertain. Sometimes this can be very baffling. For instance, during her last visit to New York, Princess Margaret was entertained at dinner by a stage director and his beautiful wife. The menu, as reported in the papers the next day, included "creamed purée of mashed potatoes and chicken on a bed of tarragon."

I want to know more about this. What *is* creamed purée of mashed potatoes? Mashed potatoes? *Watery* mashed potatoes? And as for that chicken on a bed of tarragon, I just don't know. It's been my experience that a pinch, or a sprig, of tarragon goes a long way. Wouldn't a bed be too much? And how much *is* a bed? I know it isn't anything like a twin bed—but still. You can't get hold of recipes if they are going to be as vague as that.

Actually, the only reason *I* don't give chic, elegant dinner parties that are the talk of my whole set is that I get faint just thinking about it. In the first place, I don't know who to invite. In theory, I should invite the people who have already entertained us at dinner. In practice, it doesn't work out that way. We live in Larchmont, a small community about twenty miles from New York. Most of our friends live in New York City, and they invite us to dinner calm in the assumption that we will find our way to the great metropolis in less than forty minutes. To a reasonable person it would appear that the distance between New York and Larchmont is approximately the same as the distance between Larchmont and New York. However, when I invite people out here I am left with the feeling that I am inviting them to Ice Station Zebra and that I should offer to provide Sherpa guides for those last tortuous miles through the mountain passes. You understand that Larchmont is on Long Island Sound and flat as can be. The only place a guide will be required is to get them through our garage where, for reasons I couldn't explain under oath, our four children have stored sixteen battered bicycles.

From the time I have invited the first person, and am therefore committed to the affair, I sink into a state of catatonic torpor, rather as though I was waiting to undergo exploratory surgery. My ungracious and typical way of extending the invitation is to moan miserably into the telephone, "Oh, my God, Helen, we're having a party, do you want to come?"

I marvel that anybody comes. Other women have told me that at a time like this they become newly and painfully aware that the draperies are fading, the screens are full of holes, and all the slipcovers are frayed in the arms. I notice things like that, too, but I can put them out of my mind because I have learned if you get enough people in the living room you can hardly see the slipcovers. My anxieties lie elsewhere.

To me having a party is something like having a baby. The fact that you got through the last one alive is not somehow sufficiently reassuring now. My husband tries to penetrate my pre-party gloom by asking intelligent questions: "Good heavens, they're all old friends, what are you so worried about?" I'll tell you what I worry about. First, I worry that nobody will come. Nobody at all, and the family will have to eat chicken Kiev for a month. Then I worry that they *will* come but will simply refuse to talk to one another as they sit like so many birds on a telephone wire. Then if they do come and they *do* chatter, I worry that they won't touch a bite of food because it is undercooked or overcooked or just plain ghastly. After which there is the ultimate worry. Suppose they come, eat, drink, and make merry—and everybody leaves at a quarter after nine.

That actually happened to a woman I know. The poor thing hasn't been right since. Her husband has now sent her to a psychiatrist, even though, as I understand it, it was all his fault because he kept threatening to show movies of Debbie's confirmation.

But I see that I'm gliding past a real crisis area: what to serve. When I was very young I used to serve roast stuffed turkey and baked ham at *every* party. There were two reasons for this. First of all, I like turkey and ham. And secondly, I have (if I may say so) an excellent recipe for turkey dressing.

Down through the years I did notice that none of the people who invited us to dinner ever served turkey and ham. I never criticized them. I just thought they were too lazy to roast a turkey. Certainly I didn't dream I was placing myself in jeopardy socially.

Gradually the truth was borne in on me. In fact, it wasn't all that gradual. A chic friend of mine (you'll know how chic she is when I tell you she makes her own noodles) took me aside one evening and said, "Jean, turkey is traditional at Thanksgiving and Christmas. It is also suitable for sending to policemen who are snowbound. Otherwise—" And she shook her head sadly.

It's really awful to feel embarrassed retroactively. But, dammit, they used to eat that turkey. They even came back for seconds. However, I am easily intimidated. Wishy-washy, really. A twine would lead me. And so now I try to plan a main course that will be a "conversation piece" in spite of the fact that I *know* it's the conversation that should be the conversation piece.

With this in mind I go through all of the recipes I have torn out of magazines during the past six months—a fruitless enterprise, since the recipes turn out to be "New Tricks with Tuna," "A Wonderful Stew for Weight-Watchers," or "It's February, and It's Shad, Shad, Shad."

Obviously, truly well-adjusted people don't go into this sort of swivet over what they are going to serve as a main course. Last year I was actually invited to one of those parties I spend so much time reading about. This one was so grand that Governor Rockefeller was one of the guests. The host and hostess were perfectly charming, the house was exquisite, the art collection was fabulous, and the dinner was fried pork chops.

I hasten to add that the chops were absolutely succulent and delicious. The Governor ate both of his. And I think everybody there was as relieved as I was that we were not (once again) being served fillet of beef, roast of beef, loin of beef, or beef of beef.

The point is that I am not rich enough to serve fried pork chops to company. For that you have to have panache, a certain *élan,* and probably a special kind of pork chop.

As a matter of fact, even fried pork chops aren't all that simple to prepare. I mean, you can't slap them into a pan and just forget about them. An untended pork chop will look like and taste like a wet mitten.

Does anybody but me remember when President and Mrs.

Roosevelt entertained the King and Queen of England at Hyde Park and served them hot dogs? There, that's real class.

I have all these people coming to dinner next week. Do you suppose I could possibly—? No, no, no, of course not.

Marriage:
Unsafe at Any Speed

I know what I wish Ralph Nader would investigate next. Marriage. It's not safe, it's not safe at all.

Do you realize that every day the unwary and the unready leap into an arrangement that has no guarantee, no warranty, no money back? Even with the present divorce rate most people still marry with the conviction that they will remain together until death do them part. And, in this enlightened era, that could be one hell of a long time. During the Middle Ages, when whole villages expired early because of the prevalence of plague and the misuse of leeches, this was not such an awesome prospect. But nowadays people who marry in their early twenties have every reason to believe they'll still be kicking in their seventies. In other words, that marriage could last fifty years. What else in the world lasts fifty years—washers, cars, radios, governments?

Think of the innocents who make this staggering commitment for reasons no more coherent than that they feel icy fingers up and down their spine and, what is more curious, hear music when there's no one there. It is not enough to point out that the icy-fingers-down-the-spine stage of marriage is of limited duration. And that those husbands (married over two years) who look for that same old witchcraft when your lips meet mine will be told "Not now, for God's sake, can't you see I'm making din-

ner?" Actually, it's probably a mercy that these first, fine fevers
of romance do abate. I, for one, would not care to go fifty years
hearing music when there's no one there. You could get the reputation of being a little bit dotty.

But let's get beyond these rather elementary matters. Have
you faced up to the fact that it is harder to get a driver's license
than a marriage license? In most states, prospective drivers have
to take an eye test, a written test, and a road test. Now surely it
would be helpful if persons about to be married were required
to undergo an eye test. They should have to prove to some
qualified official that they really did see what they saw in each
other.

It would be harder, I know, to arrange a road test for marriage
which would duplicate the actual traffic conditions. But it could
be done. An engaged couple could be asked to live for one week
in a third-floor walk-up apartment with four children under ten
(two of whom have colds), a sink that was stopped up, and a
puppy that wasn't housebroken. This would prove an eye-opener
to the young couple. It would also provide a week's vacation for
the real parents of the four kiddies which would, of course, be
good for *their* marriage.

Lastly, there absolutely should be a written test. Not only do
we want to lower the divorce rate, we want to eliminate the
sorry spectacle of married couples who sit in public restaurants
for two hours without uttering eleven words between them and
then go outside and hiss at each other in the parking lot.

I know that psychiatrists say that the chief causes of trouble in
marriage are money, sex, and in-laws. But it has been my observation that it isn't what people *do* in these major areas that's so
important, it's what they *say*. (Do you know that there are no
recorded instances of divorce among deaf-mutes?) Let me give
you an example. My friend Helen had her mother from Arizona
visiting for three weeks. Helen's husband, Ralph, could not have
been more saintly. He met Mother at La Guardia. He took her to
Radio City Music Hall. He played gin rummy with her. He
watched "The Lawrence Welk Show." Twice he took her to a
restaurant where the only thing served as salad was a sliced
pineapple filled with tinted cottage cheese. He allowed her to

talk to him all the time he was trying to read the morning *Times*. He was, as I say, saintly.

Then he blew it. Two days after the old lady went back to Arizona he turned to his wife and said, "Helen, I wish you'd lay off that fudge, you're going to be fat and waddle just like your mother."

Helen says she is never going to speak to him again, though of course she will—in time. Ralph, however, is going to have a rough twenty-four hours, at least. And it all could have been avoided. If the specter of Helen turning into Mother really unnerved Ralph, he might have said, "Honey, why don't we both go on a diet and buy some new clothes?" There is a right way to put things and a wrong way. Alas, most people rush like lemmings to make the very remark that is bound to lead to dropped forks, slammed doors, and a Bad Day at Black Rock.

Here is where a written test would help. Just as potential drivers go on record indicating that they are aware that one never parks in front of a fire hydrant, the about-to-be-married ought to show that they are aware that one never asks, "How did you ever get out of high school without learning to add?" or "Is this the same lamb we had three nights ago?"

Now I don't know every wrong statement that can be made in a marriage (my husband would dispute this), but I know some of them. And I have made up my own little multiple-choice test to weed out the unmarriageable.

Since it is barely out of the blueprint stage, I am making things easier by placing the one correct answer *last* in every case. This way you can't cheat by looking up the answers on another page.

FOR MEN

What is the proper answer when the little woman asks the following questions:

How is the roast beef?
  (a) Roast beef? I thought it was pot roast.
  (b) Honey, do we have any ketchup?
  (c) Great.

*My best friend from college is coming for a couple of days. Is that
all right?*

    (a) Okay, but don't expect me to steer her through the
Guggenheim again.

    (b) Do you mean Grace, who twitters like a parakeet and
leaves squashed Kleenex all over the house because of
her sinus condition?

    (c) Of all your friends, honey, I think Grace is the one most
like you.

Can you tell I've lost weight?

    (a) Not really. I'd say you'd have to lose another ten pounds
before it begins to show.

    (b) If you say so.

    (c) Wow.

I suppose you wish I was as good a cook as Emmy?

    (a) Or even half as good.

    (b) I'm sure you could cook as well as Emily if you were
willing to put the same amount of time into it.

    (c) Oh, I'd get pretty sick of all that rich food day after
day. And they say Bill's getting a liver condition.

Do you love me as much as the day we were married?

    (a) Yeah, yeah, yeah, I love you as much as the day we
were married.

    (b) Oh, God, not again.

    (c) If you have to ask that question, honey, it must be my
fault. I mustn't be showing all the love I really feel.

Will you lower that damn ball game?

    (a) If I lower that ball game, all I'll hear is you screaming
at the kids.

    (b) When *you're* listening to your darling Walter Cronkite
I can hear him as I step off the New Haven.

    (c) Oh, is it bothering you? Why don't I go up to the bed-
room and watch it on the portable? You'll be coming
up, won't you?

Would you say that I have been a help to you in your work?

    (a) Honey, don't make dumb jokes.

    (b) Undoubtedly, undoubtedly. If I didn't have you and
the kids I'd be a beachcomber today. And very happy.

(c) Honey! Could I ever have got to teach third grade without you right here beside me?

You never talk to me.

(a) I don't talk to you because the only topics in the world that interest you are Billy's rotten report card, your rotten dishwasher, and that rotten milkman who keeps tracking up your linoleum.

(b) Of course I talk to you. What am I doing now, pantomime?

(c) And here I was, sitting here and thinking how beautiful you are and how lucky I am and how peaceful it was.

FOR WOMEN

What is the proper answer when hubby makes the following observations:

What happens to all my clean handkerchiefs?

(a) I eat them.

(b) You don't have clean handkerchiefs because you don't put them in the wash. You leave them all scrunched up in your slacks which are on the floor of the closet.

(c) Here's a clean one of mine. We'll fold it so the lace doesn't show.

Hey, Abe's new wife is attractive as hell, don't you think?

(a) Everybody's new wife is attractive. Your problem is that you're stuck with your old one.

(b) Yes, but I think she might do something about that little mustache.

(c) I think *all* Abe's new wives are attractive.

When you write a check, will you for God's sake, please, please, write down the amount somewhere, anywhere?

(a) Why do you carry on like a madman? Nothing ever ever happens, the checks never bounce.

(b) Okay, you're Paul Getty, *you* make out the checks.

(c) Yes.

Ye gods, does that kid have to eat that way?

(a) No, I coach him to eat that way because I know it drives you absolutely crazy.

(b) That kid just also happens to be your kid, and any time you want to give him your famous lecture on table manners, I'll be rooting for you all the way.

(c) Darling, I *want* to reprimand him but he's so exactly like you I just melt.

Oh, Lord, you're crying again. What is it this time?

(a) I spent three hours stuffing the veal and you never even said it was good. I had my hair done and you didn't notice. It rained all day and the kids were like maniacs. And after I sewed all the buttons back on Billy's sweater he lost it in the park. And you never, never, never offer to do anything to help me.

(b) Because I want to be an Anchorperson and make a million dollars a year and have my picture on the cover of the *Ladies' Home Journal*.

(c) Oh, because I'm silly and I don't count my blessings. Come on, give me a little squeeze and take out the garbage and I'll be through here in no time.

There. Of course I don't mean to suggest that this test is either foolproof or definitive. I mean only to be the first pebble in the avalanche that must surely come. But perhaps I should add just one final cautionary note. Those persons who found themselves anticipating the correct answer *in each instance* are probably so perfect that they would drive any other human being bonkers. I suggest that they remain single.

Dogs That Have Known Me

I never meant to say anything about this, but the fact is that I have never met a dog that didn't have it in for me. You take Kelly, for instance. He's a wire-haired fox terrier and he's had us for three years now. I wouldn't say that he was terribly handsome but he does have a very nice smile. What he *doesn't* have is any sense of fitness. All the other dogs in the neighborhood spend their afternoons yapping at each other's heels or chasing cats. Kelly spends his whole day, every day, chasing swans on the millpond. I don't actually worry because he will never catch one. For one thing, he can't swim. Instead of settling for a simple dog-paddle like everybody else, he has to show off and try some complicated overhand stroke, with the result that he always sinks and has to be fished out. Naturally, people talk, and I never take him for a walk that somebody doesn't point him out and say, "There's that crazy dog that chases swans."

Another thing about that dog is that he absolutely refuses to put himself in the other fellow's position. We have a pencil sharpener in the kitchen and Kelly used to enjoy having an occasional munch on the plastic cover. As long as it was just a nip now and then, I didn't mind. But one day he simply lost his head and ate the whole thing. Then I had to put it up high out of Kelly's reach. Well, the scenes we were treated to—and the sulking! In fact, ever since he has been eating things I know he doesn't like just to get even. I don't mean things like socks and mittens and paper napkins, which of course are delicious. Lately he's been eating plastic airplanes, suede brushes, and light bulbs. Well, if he wants to sit under the piano and make low and loving growls over a suede brush just to show me, okay. But frankly I think he's lowering himself.

Time and again I have pointed out to Kelly that with discriminating dogs, dogs who are looking for a finer, lighter chew—it's bedroom slippers two to one. I have even dropped old, dilapidated bedroom slippers here and there behind the furniture, hoping to tempt him. But the fact is, that dog wouldn't touch a bedroom slipper if he was starving.

Although we knew that, as a gourmet, he was a washout, we did keep saying one thing about Kelly. We kept saying, "He's a good little old watchdog." Heaven knows why we thought so, except that he barks at the drop of a soufflé. In fact, when he's in the basement a stiff toothbrush on the third floor is enough to set him off into a concerto of deep, murderous growls followed by loud hysterical yappings. I used to take real pleasure in imagining the chagrin of some poor intruder who'd bring that cacophony upon himself. Last month we had an intruder. He got in the porch window and took twenty-two dollars and my wrist watch while Kelly, that good little old watchdog, was as silent as a cathedral. But that's the way it's been.

The first dog I remember well was a large black and white mutt that was part German shepherd, part English sheepdog, and part collie—the wrong part in each case. With what strikes me now as unforgivable whimsy, we called him Ladadog from the title by Albert Payson Terhune. He was a splendid dog in many respects but, in the last analysis, I'm afraid he was a bit of a social climber. He used to pretend that he was just crazy about us. I mean, if you just left the room to comb your hair he would greet you on your return with passionate lickings, pawings, and convulsive tail-waggings. And a longer separation—let's say you had to go out on the front porch to pick up the mail—would set Ladadog off into such a demonstration of rapture and thanksgiving that we used to worry for his heart.

However, all this mawkish, slobbering sentiment disappeared the moment he stepped over the threshold. I remember we kids used to spot him on our way home from school, chasing around the Parkers' lawn with a cocker friend of his, and we'd rush over to him with happy squeals of "Laddy, oleboy, oleboy, oleboy," and Ladadog would just stand there looking slightly pained and distinctly cool. It wasn't that he cut us dead. He nodded, but it was with the remote air of a celebrity at a cocktail party saying, "Of *course* I remember you, and how's Ed?"

We kept making excuses for him and even worked out an elaborate explanation for his behavior. We decided that Ladadog didn't see very well, that he could only recognize us by smell and that he couldn't smell very well in the open air. However, the day came when my mother met Ladadog in front of the A & P. She was wearing her new brown coat with the beaver collar, and, lo and behold, Ladadog greeted her with joy and rapture. After that we just had to face the truth—that dog was a snob.

He also had other peculiarities. For instance, he saved lettuce. He used to beg for lettuce and then he would store it away in the cellar behind the coalbin. I don't know whether he was saving up to make a salad or what, but every so often we'd have to clean away a small, soggy lump of decayed vegetation.

And every time the phone rang he would run from wherever he was and sit there beside the phone chair, his tail thumping and his ears bristling, until you'd make some sort of an announcement like "It's just the Hoover man" or "Eileen, it's for you." Then he would immediately disappear. Clearly, this dog had put a call in to someone, but we never did figure out who.

Come to think of it, the dog that gave us the most trouble was a beagle named Murphy. As far as I'm concerned, the first thing he did wrong was to turn into a beagle. I had seen him bounding around in the excelsior of a pet-shop window, and I went in and asked the man, "How much is that adorable fox terrier in the window?" Did he say, "That adorable fox terrier is a beagle"? No, he said, "Ten dollars, lady." Now, I don't mean to say one word against beagles. They have rights just like other people. But it is a bit of a shock when you bring home a small ball of fluff in a shoebox, and three weeks later it's as long as the sofa.

Murphy was the first dog I ever trained personally, and I was delighted at the alacrity with which he took to the newspaper. It was sometime later that we discovered, to our horror, that—like so many dogs—he had grasped the letter but not the spirit of the thing. Until the very end of his days he felt a real sense of obligation whenever he saw a newspaper—*any* newspaper—and it didn't matter where it was. I can't bring myself to go into the sordid details, except to mention that we were finally compelled to keep all the papers in the bottom of the icebox.

He had another habit that used to leave us open to a certain amount of criticism from our friends who were not dogophiles. He never climbed up on beds or chairs or sofas. But he always sat on top of the piano. In the beginning we used to try to pull him off of there. But after a few noisy scuffles in which he knocked a picture off the wall, scratched the piano, and smashed a lamp, we just gave in—only to discover that, left to his own devices, he hopped up and down as delicately as a ballet dancer. We became quite accustomed to it, but at parties at our house it was not unusual to hear a guest remark, "I don't know what I'm drinking but I think I see a big dog on the piano."

It's not just our own dogs that bother me. The dogs I meet at parties are even worse. I don't know what I've got that attracts them; it just doesn't bear thought. My husband swears I rub chopped meat on my ankles. But at every party it's the same thing. I am sitting in happy conviviality with a group in front of the fire when all of a sudden the large mutt of mine host appears in the archway. Then, without a single bark of warning, he hurls himself upon me. It always makes me think of that line from *A Streetcar Named Desire*—"Baby, we've had this date right from the beginning." My martini flies into space and my stockings are torn before he finally settles down peacefully in the lap of my new black faille. I blow out such quantities of hair as I haven't swallowed and glance at my host, expecting to be rescued. He murmurs, "Isn't that wonderful? You know, Brucie is usually so distant with strangers."

At a dinner party on Long Island last week, after I had been mugged by a large sheepdog, I announced quite piteously, "Oh dear, he seems to have swallowed one of my earrings." The hostess looked really distressed for a moment, until she examined the remaining earring. Then she said, "Oh, I think it will be all right. It's small and it's round."

Nowadays if I go anywhere I just ask if they have a dog. If they do, I say, "Maybe I'd better keep away from him—I have this bad allergy." This does not really charm the lady of the house. In fact, she behaves rather as though she'd just discovered that I was back in analysis for my kleptomania. But it is safer. It really is.

Mirror, Mirror, On the Wall, I Don't Want to Hear One Word Out of You

I'm tired of all this nonsense about beauty being only skin deep. That's deep enough. What do you want—an adorable pancreas? Personally, I find that it's work, work, work just trying to keep this top half inch in shape.

And while I'm on the subject, the first rumor I want to scotch is that I don't *care* how I look. Care? Why, I haven't even read *Robert Frost: The Years of Triumph*, I've been so busy reading every single one of those articles which insist that I can be a younger, lovelier me this summer. Actually I intended to be a lovelier, younger me last winter, but what with one thing and another (we had to put in new formica around the kitchen sink, and the oil burner broke down) I never got around to it. But from now on there will be no more excuses. I am going to mend my fences and learn the trick of artful make-up.

I think I ought to make it clear that I am not primarily concerned with my social appearance. If I turn up at dinner parties with that tousled, straight-from-the-haystack look that is so unaccountably attractive in Italian movie actresses I don't think it matters, because I happen to have this little trick which always endears me to hostesses. I invariably ask the young children who pass the stuffed celery what grade they are in. In fact I keep the conversational ball aloft a moment longer by musing reflectively,

"Fifth grade—just imagine that." Of course one does have to look right at the children or, at the very least, keep in mind that they push on and age just like the rest of us. Imagine my surprise last week when I asked a young man who was urging a sixth deviled egg upon me, "And what grade are you in, dear?"—only to learn that he was in Harvard Law.

Nevertheless I feel I am rather sweet at dinner parties; let other women be trim and gorgeous. The one place I have simply got to look better is Bloomingdale's, when I go in there to buy face powder. It has been my practice in the past to double-park the car and dash into the store with the air of one arriving at Radio City Music Hall two minutes before the prices change. (I always leave the motor running so the policeman can feel pretty sure I'm going to be right back.)

Now it's a curious fact that I can go into Housewares and stand among the pots for thirty-five minutes without attracting the attention of a single salesgirl, all of whom appear to be working out logarithms on their little pads. But in Cosmetics I get attention, immediate attention. The salesgirls as far away as Perfume drop everything and gather about me, making little clucking sounds. They really respond with the amiable ferocity and instinctive good will of a bevy of well-trained St. Bernards coming upon a stiffened form in an Alpine pass. At last—here is someone they can *help*.

May they suggest a blossom-pink make-up base? Do I need a herbal facial mask? What about a rich skin food for those fine lines? It is fruitless in these circumstances to explain that I already have enough cosmetics in my bathroom to make up every single extra in *The Ten Commandments*. They see what they see. And what they see is a pale-beige face that blends, in a way that is almost uncanny, with the raincoat I'm wearing, which happens to belong to my husband. Before I left the house I did apply a quick smudge of that purple lipstick somebody left in the guest room two years ago, but there is only my word for that. Right now, as I can plainly see for myself in the large mirror on the counter, I look exactly like a peeled grape—a condition which is not really appetizing even in a grape.

Of *course* I need a herbal facial mask and a cream to give new life and luxuriance to my eyelashes and a lotion to remove those telltale signs of age. And it's nice that I'm going to have something for those signs of age, because I have definitely aged in the last five minutes, and those fine lines are now becoming furrows as I realize—with mounting panic—that I have just spent twenty-eight dollars on assorted cosmetics when what I really need is a box of face powder and a raincoat of my own.

As I tear myself away from these ministering maidens (I know they think I am returning to my coal barge) I keep wishing I could somehow convey to them that, all appearances to the contrary, I do have a conscience—style and beauty-wise. If they but knew that before the discovery of the hydrogen bomb I used to spend *all* my time worrying about my dry skin. Anyway, the next time I go into that store I will be wearing three layers of make-up, all exquisitely applied. And the salesgirl will no more think of urging an extra product on me than an art-supply dealer would dream of pressing Picasso into trying a new burnt umber.

Left to my own devices, I will buy only sensible, useful cosmetics. Unlike some women, I can tell whether a cream is an absolute necessity merely by reading the advertising. I can also tell whether it's intended for me. For instance, if the ad begins "*At last*—an entirely new concept of skin care intended for you who are tired of trying every new skin cream that comes on the market" it has to mean me because I *am* tired of trying every new skin cream that comes on the market.

Now, fully alerted, I read on to discover that "After four years of careful laboratory experimentation, Mildred Rosnick announces 'Formula 22,' a cream made exclusively from the lungs of young goldfish."

There, don't you just know that will help? I mean, you have only to pause and consider how clear-eyed and spruce even a middle-aged goldfish looks to realize that Mildred Rosnick has stumbled onto something pretty important. And I will have to act fast, because they make it pretty clear that their special introductory offer of a one-ounce jar for $12.98 will be good for a limited time only. While $12.98 does seem a little high, I want no one to tell me that Mildred Rosnick can whip up her Formula 22 for a mere nine cents a jar. Listen, she has that whole laboratory full of technicians and goldfish and you don't feed them on peanuts.

Speaking of wet-blanket attitudes, my husband has a different angle altogether. He is always trying to explain to me that dermatologists have proven that lard, or even bacon drippings, will do just as much or just as little to lubricate the human skin as any cosmetic ever invented. Now I ask you, if dermatologists had really proven anything as ridiculous as that, wouldn't we all know about it? And another thing. When I consider the dreadful samples of lumbering humor I am subjected to when I apply the merest dab of Formula 22 ("Oh, you're coming to bed? With all that grease, I thought you were getting ready to swim the Channel") I can't bring myself even to contemplate the low-comedy scenes we'd have if I came to bed covered with bacon fat.

Of course the thing about my husband is that he is not really on this planet. He's the kind of man who will come home from a cocktail party and tell you about the fascinating conversation he had with a new editor at Simon and Schuster who feels that all these new beat-generation authors are merely a reflection of the mass protest against the thermonuclear potential. I mean, that's his idea of a gossipy tidbit. Later, I will hear that *she* was one of the guests, and I will fly at him accusingly. "Listen, Peggy said that Ingrid Bergman was at that party." And he will say, "That's right, I guess she was." And a man like that will presume to give advice.

I'm sure it would be a help in any program of beauty to set oneself a simple goal. Personally, I concentrate on keeping myself in a state of repair just sufficient to stop people asking me if I remember how charming Ethel Barrymore was on the opening night of *Captain Jinks of the Horse Marines*.

But one can set one's sights too high. Just last week in the beauty parlor I witnessed a poignant example of this very thing. A rather mousy matron handed the hairdresser a picture of Candice Bergen, her lovely Edwardian profile glimmering beneath a mass of tossed-salad curls. "See," the lady explained rather ingenuously, "this is the way I want to look." Honey, we all do. But a mountaineer doesn't *start* with Everest.

I try to pick a model closer at hand, like any one of those young women who appear on the society pages handing each other checks for the Milk Fund. What an elegant crew they are— so svelte in black, so chaste in that solitary strand of pearls.

"Lovely Mrs. Philip van Rensselaer Skylark III," I read, quite consumed with envy, "is celebrated for her candlelight suppers. Though Mrs. Skylark is the proud possessor of two young daughters, three whippets, and a myna bird, she still finds time to help the North Shore Hospital." Well, that's the way I'm going to look even if it means that I have to help the North Shore Hospital.

Looking back over these paragraphs, I sense the absence of that one piece of constructive advice that might save this from being simply another self-reproaching sermon entitled "Once I Was Considered Plain—Today I Am a Mess." Luckily I have just remembered not one, but two definite rituals for beauty that have been *known to work.*

1. *How to Be Adorable, Though Pregnant.* Actually this is much simpler than it seems. The mother-to-be should get her hair set, apply a rosy-pink make-up, put on her most becoming maternity frock, and—here we get to the important part—climb into bed and pull the covers up under her arms. In this position she will feel chic. Overheated, perhaps, but chic.

As a matter of fact I have never been able to follow this prescription to the letter because I wear a size eighteen, and, as you may know, it is practically impossible to buy a maternity dress, becoming or otherwise, in size eighteen. The manufacturers seem to operate on the unquestionably sound premise that a woman who takes a size eighteen is already in sufficient trouble and has no business getting pregnant. Having made this mistake, she ought to have the simple decency to remain indoors in her bathrobe, where she will not depress the entire community with the spectacle of her bulky contours.

2. *How to Keep Your Husband Believing That You Are Still the Same Enchanting Girl He Married.* First you set aside a half hour in the late afternoon to put your hair up in pin curls and—no, this is ridiculous. I don't believe one word of it. Of course you're not the enchanting girl he married. How could you be—with those kids, and that dog racing through the house, and practically no help, and a washer that's always on the blink? And don't tell me about Mrs. Skylark; that woman probably *lives* at Elizabeth Arden's.

Besides, why should *you* be all that enchanting? How does *he* look these days? Is *he* still the lean and handsome athlete who first caught your girlish fancy? And was he even embarrassed when you had to bring back all those size forty shorts and get size forty-two? Do you catch him poring over articles instructing him how to look younger and sprucer so he can make your little heart palpitate? Boy, that'll be the day!

Frankly, I'm weary of the whole business. It's true: beauty *is* only skin deep. From now on I'm going to stop struggling. I'm just going to develop my character and let it shine through my fine eyes.

Please Don't Eat the Daisies

We are being very careful with our children. They'll never have to pay a psychiatrist forty-five dollars an hour to find out why we rejected them. We'll tell them why we rejected them. Because they're impossible, that's why.

It seems to me, looking back on it, that everything was all right when there were two of them and two of us. We felt loved, protected, secure. But now that there are four of them and two of us, things have changed. We're in the minority, we're not as vigorous as we used to be, and it's clear that we cannot compete with these younger men.

You take Christopher—and you *may*; he's a slightly used eight-year-old. The source of our difficulty with him lies in the fact that he is interested in the precise value of words whereas we are only interested in having him pick his clothes up off the floor. I say, "Christopher, you take a bath and put all your things in the wash," and he says, "Okay, but it will break the Bendix." Now at this point the shrewd rejoinder would be, "That's all right, let it break the Bendix." But years of experience have washed over me in vain and I, perennial patsy, inquire, "Why will it break the Bendix?" So he explains, "Well, if I put *all* my things in the wash, I'll have to put my shoes in and they will certainly break the machinery."

"Very well," I say, all sweetness and control, "put everything but the shoes in the wash." He picks up my agreeable tone at once, announcing cheerily, "Then you *do* want me to put my belt in the wash." I don't know what I say at this point, but my husband says, "Honey, you mustn't scream at him that way."

Another version of this battle of semantics would be:

"Don't kick the table leg with your foot."

"I'm not kicking, I'm tapping."

"Well, don't tap with your foot."

"It's not my foot, it's a fork."

"Well, don't tap with the fork."

"It's not a *good* fork . . ." et cetera, et cetera.

Christopher is an unusual child in other respects. I watch him from the kitchen window. With a garden rake in one hand he scampers up a tree, out across a long branch, and down over the stone wall—as graceful and as deft as a squirrel. On the other hand, he is unable to get from the living room to the front hall without bumping into at least two pieces of furniture. (I've seen him hit as many as five, but that's championship stuff and he can't do it every time.)

He has another trick which defies analysis, and also the laws of gravity. He can walk out into the middle of a perfectly empty kitchen and trip on the linoleum. I *guess* it's the linoleum. There isn't anything else there.

My friends who have children are always reporting the quaint and agreeable utterances of their little ones. For example, the mother of one five-year-old philosopher told me that when she appeared at breakfast in a new nine-dollar pink wrap-around, her little boy chirped, in a tone giddy with wonder, "Oh, look, our Miss Mommy must be going to a wedding!" Now I don't think any one of my children would say a thing like that. (What do I mean I don't *think;* there are some things about which you can be positive.) Of course, in a nine-dollar wrap-around I wouldn't look as if I were going to a wedding. I'd look as if I were going to paint the garage. But that's not the point. The point is: where is that babbling, idiotic loyalty that other mothers get?

A while back I spoke of a time when there were two of them and two of us. In my affinity for round numbers I'm falsifying the whole picture. Actually, there never were two of them. There was one of them, and all of a sudden there were three of them.

The twins are four now, and for several years we have had galvanized iron fencing lashed onto the outside of their bedroom windows. This gives the front of the house a rather institutional look and contributes to unnecessary rumors about my mental health, but it does keep them off the roof, which is what we had in mind.

For twins they are very dissimilar. Colin is tall and active and Johnny is short and middle-aged. Johnny doesn't kick off his shoes, he doesn't swallow beer caps or tear pages out of the telephone book. I don't think he ever draws pictures with my best lipstick. In fact, he has none of the charming, lighthearted "boy" qualities that precipitate so many scenes of violence in the home. On the other hand, he has a feeling for order and a passion for system that would be trying in a head nurse. If his pajamas are hung on the third hook in the closet instead of on the second hook, it causes him real pain. If one slat in a Venetian blind is tipped in the wrong direction he can't have a moment's peace until somebody fixes it. Indeed, if one of the beans on his plate is slightly longer than the others he can scarcely bear to eat it. It's hard for him to live with the rest of us. And vice versa.

Colin is completely different. He has a lightness of touch and a dexterity that will certainly put him on top of the heap if he ever takes up safecracking. Equipped with only a spoon and an old emery board, he can take a door off its hinges in seven minutes and remove all of the towel racks from the bathroom in five.

Gilbert is only seventeen months old, and it's too early to tell about him. (As a matter of fact, we can tell, all right, but we're just not ready to face it.) Once upon a time we might have been taken in by smiles and gurgles and round blue eyes, but no more. We know he is just biding his time. Today he can't do much more than eat his shoelaces and suck off an occasional button. Tomorrow, the world.

My real problem with children is that I haven't any imagination. I'm always warning them against the commonplace defections while they are planning the bizarre and unusual. Christopher gets up ahead of the rest of us on Sunday mornings and he has long since been given a list of clear directives: "Don't wake the baby," "Don't go outside in your pajamas," "Don't eat cookies before breakfast." But I never told him, "Don't make flour paste and glue together all the pages of the magazine section of the Sunday *Times*." Now I tell him, of course.

And then last week I had a dinner party and told the twins and Christopher not to go in the living room, not to use the guest towels in the bathroom, and not to leave the bicycles on the front steps. However, I neglected to tell them not to eat the daisies on the dining-room table. This was a serious omission, as I discovered when I came upon my centerpiece—a charming three-point arrangement of green stems.

The thing is, I'm going to a psychiatrist and find out why I have this feeling of persecution . . . this sense of being continually surrounded . . .

The Ten Worst Things
About a Man

Actually I feel a bit of a fraud to be picking on men when I always pretend to be so crazy about them. And, deep down inside, I am crazy about them. They are sweet, you know, and so helpful. At parties, men you've barely met will go back to the buffet to get you a muffin and they will leap to their feet to tell you that you've got the wrong end of the cigarette in your mouth. Notice that when you are trying to squeeze into a tight parking place there will always be some nice man driving by who will stick his head out of the window and shout, "Lady, you've got a whole *mile* back there!"

But, charming as men are, we can't sit here and pretend they're perfect. It wouldn't be good for them, and it wouldn't be true. Marrying a man is like buying something you've been admiring for a long time in a shop window. You may love it when you get it home, but it doesn't always go with everything else in the house. One reason for this is that most men insist on behaving as though this were an orderly, sensible universe, which naturally makes them hard to live with. The other reason they're hard to live with (and I know this sounds illogical) is that they're so *good*. Perhaps I can clarify that last statement by listing a few of their more intolerable virtues.

1. *A Man Will Not Meddle in What He Considers His Wife's Affairs*

He may interfere at the office, driving secretaries to drink and premature marriage by snooping into file drawers and tinkering with the mimeograph machine. Back home in the nest he is the very model of patience and *laissez-faire*. He will stare at you across the dining-room table (as you simultaneously carve the lamb and feed the baby) and announce, in tones so piteous as to suggest that all his dreams have become ashes, "There's no salt in this shaker."

What a wife objects to in this situation is not just the notion that Daddy has lived in this house for thirteen years without ever discovering where the salt is kept. It's more the implication that only she has the necessary fortitude, stamina, and simple animal cunning necessary to pour the salt into that little hole in the back of the shaker.

2. *A Man Remembers Important Things*

It really is remarkable the fund of information he keeps at his finger tips: the date of the Battle of Hastings, the name of the man who invented the printing press, the formula for water, the Preamble to the Constitution, and every lyric Larry Hart ever wrote. It is obviously unreasonable to expect one so weighted down with relevant data to remember a simple fact like what size shirt he takes, or what grade Gilbert is in, or even that you told him fifteen times that the Bentleys were coming to dinner. A woman just has to go through life remembering for two. As an example of this, I was recently told about a wife who, from time to time, pinned a tag on her husband's overcoat. The tag read, "Please don't give me a ride home from the station. I have my own car today." However, this technique wouldn't work with my husband because he usually forgets and leaves his overcoat on the train.

3. *A Man Will Try to Improve Your Mind*

Working on the suspicion that women read nothing in the newspapers except bulletins from Macy's and Liz Smith, the average man takes considerable pains to keep his scatterbrained wife *au courant* with the contemporary political situation. And we get the following dialogue:

"Did you read James Reston today on the shake-up in the Defense Department?"

"No, what did he have to say?"

"You should have read it. It was a damn good piece."

"Well, what was the gist of it?"

"Where is that paper? It should be around here someplace."

"It's not around here someplace. It went out with the garbage."

"That's too bad, because it would have clarified the whole situation for you."

"I'm sure. But what was he saying?"

"Oh, he was talking about the shake-up in the Defense Department."

"I know that, but what did he *say?*"

"He was against it."

4. *A Man Allows You to Make the Important Decisions*

Because he has such respect for your superior wisdom and technical know-how, he is constantly asking questions like "Does this kid need a sweater?" or "Is that baby wet?" Personally, I am willing to go down through life being the court of last appeal on such crucial issues as bedtime (is it?), cookies (can they have another?), rubbers (do they have to wear them?), and baths (tonight? but they took one last night). But, just between us, I have no confidence in a man who wanders out to the kitchen, peers into the icebox, and asks plaintively, "Do I want a sandwich?"

5. *A Man Will Give You an Honest Answer*

If you say, "Honey, do you think this dress is too tight for me to wear?" he'll say, "Yes."

6. *A Man Takes Pride in His Personal Possessions*

A woman will go all her days in the wistful belief that her husband would give her the shirt off his back. Thus she is in no way prepared for the cries of outrage that will go up should she ever be rash enough to take the shirt off his back. It doesn't matter that the shirt in question has a torn pocket, a frayed collar, and has, in any case, been at the bottom of the clothes hamper for three years. It's his, and you wear it at your risk.

My husband will say to me, "What are you doing in that shirt, for heaven's sake?" Now he doesn't really want to know what I'm doing. He can see what I'm doing. I'm painting the garage doors. He just wants me to know that that shirt was near and dear to him, and now, as a result of my vandalism, it's totally ruined.

There are two possible solutions to this problem. You can hire a painter to paint the garage doors, or you can dye the shirt purple so he won't be able to recognize it.

7. A Man Believes in Sharing

Men are all advocates of togetherness, up to a point. They will agree that it is "our house," "our mortgage," and, of course, "our song." It is interesting, however, to observe the circumstances under which items that once were "our" joint concern suddenly become your exclusive possession. For instance, a man will return from a stroll through "our back yard" to tell you, "Honey, I think your daffodils are getting clump-bound." Or, on another occasion, "I see that the hinge is off your medicine chest." In my opinion, this policy of dissociating from anything that is temporarily out of order reaches its ultimate confusion with statements like "Hey, your man is here to fix the chimney." My man? I never saw him before in my life.

8. A Man Doesn't Want You to Worry

Since he supposes, and quite correctly, that you worry a great deal about his health, he will go to any lengths to spare you the least alarm about his physical condition. He will say, as though it were the most casual thing in the world, "Well, I almost keeled over in Grand Central today."

"Good Lord," you will say, "what happened?"

"Nothing, nothing. I leaned against a pillar and I didn't actually fall down."

"But honey, what happened? Did you feel faint? You didn't have a terribly sharp pain in your chest, did you?"

"Oh, no. No, nothing like that."

"Well, what do you mean you almost keeled over?"

"I almost keeled over, that's all."

"But there must have been some *reason*."

"Oh, I guess it's that foot again."

"What foot again? Which foot?"

"Oh, I told you about my foot."

"You most certainly did not tell me anything about your foot."

"The one that's been numb since last summer."

"Your foot has been numb since last summer?"

"Now it's more like the whole leg."

"Good heavens, let's call the doctor. Let's call this minute!"

"Why?"

"Why? Are you out of your mind? Because there's something the matter with your leg, that's why!"

"See, there you go, flying off again. I'm sorry I mentioned it; and there's nothing the matter with my leg, nothing."

9. *A Man Is Reasonable*

Actually there is nothing wrong with a man's being reasonable so long as he doesn't insist on your being reasonable along with him. "Let's be *reasonable*," he keeps saying with about the same frequency that he says, "Go ask your mother," and "What's for dinner?" The occasions on which he thinks you should be reasonable vary, but on the whole it's safe to say that it's any time you're driven past your endurance and out of your mind by shiftless department stores (who promised faithfully to deliver that crib three weeks ago) and irresponsible cleaning women (who simply don't show up on the day you're having sixteen people to dinner). At times like these, a woman wishes only a word of sympathy, like "Yes, yes, they're all a bad lot." And any man who urges his wife to be reasonable and to consider the possibility that Hattie may really *have* "the virus" deserves to wax all the floors himself.

10. *A Man Idealizes His Wife*

This is another way of saying that he hasn't really looked at her in fourteen years. To get me a housecoat for my birthday, my husband will make the unthinkable sacrifice of entering Lord & Taylor's and even penetrating the awesome portals of the lingerie department. There, as I reconstruct the scene later, he selects the slimmest, trimmest little salesgirl on the floor and announces, "She's about your size." Naturally I have to take the thing back and get one four sizes larger.

On second thought, I shouldn't complain about that. If you stop and think, it's really rather charming of him.

The Kerr-Hilton

Ever since Gilbert was born we had been looking for a larger house, and we knew what we wanted. I wanted a house that would have four bedrooms for the boys, all of them located some distance from the living room—say in the next county somewhere.

I also yearned for space near the kitchen for a washer, a dishwasher, a freezer, a dryer, and a large couch where I could lie on sunny days and listen to them all vibrate.

Walter, on the other hand, was looking for a place where the eggs would be near the range and the range would be near the telephone so that he could fry his eggs and perhaps even eat them while he answered the thirty-eight phone calls he always gets during breakfast. The calls are never important, but they make up in quantity what they lack in quality. Mostly, it's somebody from one of the broadcasting companies who wants him to appear on a television show at five-thirty in the morning or it's a young man named Eugene Klepman who wants Walter's advice about making a musical based on the first three books of the Old Testament. One way or another he hasn't had breakfast in seven years. This might have had the salutary effect of causing him to lose weight, except that he munches peanut brittle all morning in an effort—he says—to gain enough strength to cope with the people who will call while he's eating lunch.

I don't know that the twins had any very concrete picture of their dream house. One thing they *didn't* want was a playroom, since they really prefer to cut up the new magazines in the middle of the kitchen floor while I'm trying to serve dinner. I have tried to explain to them about playrooms, but I can see that the mere notion of a room in which there is nothing to break fills them with panic and frustration.

Gilbert may have had strong preferences, but at seventeen months he was a boy of few words. In fact, they were so few I can list them. He could say, with ringing clarity: cookie, ice keem, no, kolly-pop, *no*, Cokee-Cola, NO, and take-a-walk. Of course this taciturnity has certain real advantages. It means, for one thing, that he cannot report his personal impression of the folk wisdom of "Captain Kangaroo."

Christopher, now that he is eight and quite sophisticated, has at one time or another expressed a desire for a house that would have no sinks or bathtubs. But as I keep telling him, such a sanctuary would be hard to come by these days.

In the beginning we made the usual mistake of looking at houses we could afford. I am working on a proposition, hereafter to be known as Kerr's law, which states in essence: all the houses you can afford to buy are depressing. For months and months we followed happy, burbling real estate agents through a succession of ruins which, as the agents modestly conceded, "needed a little paint and paper to make them happy." These houses invariably had two small dark living rooms and one large turn-of-the-century kitchen—and I don't mean the nineteenth century. At my various feeble protests that I would like to get away from a pump in the kitchen, the agent was usually very stern. "If you want six bedrooms in your price range," he'd say, "you must expect an older house." Well, I did expect an older house, but not any older, say, than the battle at Harpers Ferry. I remember one house in Larchmont. No one knew when it had been built, but it had two cells in the basement and a tunnel going down to the Sound for the protection of runaway slaves. Looking back, it seems to me that we should have snapped up that place. With four boys, you never know when you're going to need an escape hatch.

By this time we had been looking for nearly a year, and I had just about decided to wait until the boys were married and buy a *smaller* place. Then one afternoon we had an appointment to go back and see a house in which we had been mildly interested. There was some little mix-up on time and we found ourselves with half an hour to kill. At this point the real estate agent, Mrs. McDermott, suggested, "Look, there's a crazy house down on the water. It's nothing you'd be interested in, but would you like to see it just for the laughs?" We said, "Oh, sure—if it's that funny."

Well, we got our laugh, starting the minute we pulled up at the front door. It was a huge brick castle in which clock towers and cupolas and tilted chimneys all blended in a style that Walter was later to describe as neo-gingerbread.

The front door itself was a tremendous carved-oak affair that looked like the door of St. Gabriel's Church—not unreasonably, since it turned out that it *was* the door of St. Gabriel's Church. Hanging on the door was a large, hideous lion's head. This seemed to be a knocker, but when Walter went to knock it, it fell off into his arms. (It's since been put back.) Eventually someone on the inside heard our halloos, and the door swung slowly open on its great hinges with a whistle and a creak like the gate on that old radio show "Inner Sanctum." We stepped inside. I jumped back suddenly to avoid colliding with two cannon and fell into a gun rack. As we were picking up the guns, we noticed the courtyard.

Though it hadn't been apparent from the outside, the house was actually built on four sides around a large open court. Tudor-ranch, you might call it. Many of the walls bordering on the court were of glass, so that the great outdoors seemed constantly to be coming indoors. Normally, I wouldn't have minded a bit, except that this particular courtyard strongly resembled an M-G-M set for *Quo Vadis*. There were Persian idols and towering stone cats and Chinese bells and gargoyles, and I expected Peter Ustinov to step out of the fish pool any minute. The fish pool, by the way, drained into a smaller fish pool through a diving helmet which then lighted up. It took us some time to tear ourselves away from this bit of Old Baghdad, particularly as Walter had got his foot caught in the diving helmet.

Working our way back through a room that had been completely assembled from an old Hudson River steamboat, we saw the living room—or, rather, we saw the fireplace, which was all you could see in the living room. It was a monster rising two stories high. At the base there were two large stone arches over which loomed layers and layers of brick, interrupted by occasional layers of fieldstone, and in the center of which reposed a series of Dutch tiles depicting, I am told, Death and the Knight. Hovering over this was more brick in a variety of colors, leading the eye to a vast blue panel, quite near the ceiling, onto which had been glued thirteen ceramic angels. (They may be muses; we've never climbed high enough to see.) Somehow or other the final effect was so like the grotto at Lourdes that you felt there ought to be crutches hanging on it.

At one moment Walter was leaning against a section of oak paneling in order to get a better view of the ceiling, the ceiling being composed entirely of carved pink and gold plaques representing the Vanderbilt coat of arms (it had come from the old Vanderbilt place in New York City). I called to him to notice the selection of gilt semi-Byzantine pillars, some of which supported the balcony while others were just standing there, only to discover that he had quietly vanished. The section of paneling had swung back into an old secret closet, and so had he.

The next thing we knew we were exploring a winding staircase, at the foot of which gleamed a glass box containing the works of a clock. "Oh, I forgot to tell you about that clock," remarked Mrs. McDermott. "It plays the duet from *Carmen* at noon." . . . "Of course," I agreed, "and how about Beethoven's Fifth at six?" As it turned out, though, she was merely stating the facts. The clock was connected electrically to a thirty-two-bell carillon in the courtyard which—what with one thing and another—I hadn't even noticed.

After that, we passed through a number of conventional rooms. That is to say, except for the Venetian paneling and the iron gates and the portholes and the stained-glass windows, they might have looked just like any other rooms.

Not the dining room, though. Even in this house it was something special. It was entirely lined with mirrors, not only the walls and the ceiling but the top of the dining-room table as well. I was sure that if you glanced down while you were eating, you could see your inlays reflected all over the room. Walter was fascinated. He kept trying to calculate the number of possible reflections. Obviously he was imagining an infinity of images like the boy on the Cliquot Club bottle who is carrying a bottle, etc., etc. He'd say, "Now, let's imagine you're here at breakfast in your old pajamas with your hair in curlers—how many times?" It was staggering, all right. And we were staggering as we got back out on the sidewalk.

Mrs. McDermott turned to us and asked playfully, "Well, what did you think of all that?" Walter and I replied in the perfect unison of a Greek chorus, "It's the nuttiest house we ever saw, we'll buy it." Whereupon she, faithless to every real estate code, screamed, "You're not serious, you're out of your minds!" Walter said, "We're out of our minds, but we're serious."

As we drove home in a trance, Walter finally broke the silence by asking fearfully, "What do you suppose we like about it?" But by this time I knew. Somewhere among the bells and the gargoyles I had become aware of the fact that it was just the house for us. For one thing, the master bedroom was completely isolated in a wing by itself. Then there was a room off the garage that would make a wonderful playroom, and another one off the living room that would make a perfect den. Nearly every room in the house had a glorious, sweeping view of the Sound, and the dining room—miracle of miracles—had a heavy oak floor which obviously would never require a rug.

Now one of the problems of my life is trying to keep the dining-room rug clean. A friend of mine solved a similar problem in the living room by buying a rug the color of Coca-Cola. But it's not really possible to find a rug the color of mashed potatoes, Russian dressing, and butter-pecan ice cream. (Though this is a project I do wish some enterprising rug company would mull over.)

When we're at home we always eat dinner with the boys. Heaven knows why. It will eventually give us ulcers, and even in my most optimistic moments I can't honestly believe that their childhood is being enriched by the warm and tender memory of those family meals accompanied by a steady stream of directives: "No, you can't make a sandwich with your potato chips"; "Yes, you have to eat the tassels on the broccoli"; "Don't put your finger in the plate—all right, don't put your *thumb* in the plate"; "No, we don't have carrots *all* the time," and so on and on.

In dealing with our children, we don't lean on any of the more advanced methods of child psychology. I tend to remember the immortal words of that philosopher and father Moss Hart, who once announced that in dealing with *his* children he kept one thing in mind: "We're bigger than they are, and it's *our* house."

I do read in the textbooks that even an occasional spanking tends to make a child feel insecure. This may be so. On the other hand, if a child really needs a whacking and doesn't get it, *I* feel very insecure. Normally, our boys accept discipline with resignation, even detachment. There was a night, though, when the twins had been sent to their room for some infraction (they had removed the caps from a whole case of beer, as I recall) and we could hear revolt brewing. Johnny muttered, "Well, I'm not going to give *her* any more kisses. Col, you tell her you won't give her any more kisses either." And then I heard Col say, in his croaky little voice, "I couldn't do that. It would break her heart."

We didn't consult the twins about the house, but we did take Chris over on one of our subsequent tours of inspection. He wandered over the whole place in utter silence, and even on the way home couldn't be prodded into venturing an opinion. Some hours later a single sentence escaped him:

"Compared to that house, Camelot was mod*ren*."

But then, Chris's avowed goal in life is to become a comedian. I don't know what's happened to the youth of America. I can remember when boys wanted to be policemen or firemen or something respectable. Lately, Chris rattles off everything in a quick, flat patter, obviously trying to approximate the cadences of his idol, Bob Hope. I say to him, "Christopher, don't you dare lie on that new bedspread," and he snaps back with, "I will always tell the truth on this bedspread." I say, "Christopher, you're filthy!" and he remarks, "I resent that. I don't deny it, but I resent it."

Any lingering doubts we may have had about buying the house quickly disappeared when we discovered that nobody really wanted to sell it. It belonged to Charles B. King, a charming old gentleman who had been an inventor and an early associate of Henry Ford (he got out just *before* the nick of time, as I understand it) and who had taken over the property in the early twenties, when it was still the stable and coach house of an estate that has since become the Larchmont Shore Club. King was a collector and world traveler, and he clearly never passed a junk shop or a cathedral without picking up something for his fairy-tale house. He built it up piece by piece, whim by whim. His affairs were now being handled by a committee, and, through negotiations that lasted as long as the San Francisco Conference, we discovered that on Mondays and Wednesdays the committee was willing to sell the house but couldn't agree on a price. The rest of the time it was agreed on a price but wouldn't sell.

It seemed as though we were permanently stalemated when a friend of ours called on the phone one morning to say, "You know that house you were trying to buy? Well, it burned down last night."

We were stricken (particularly as we had just sold our own house), and we rushed right over. At first glance it looked as though Nuremberg had been bombed all over again, but we finally realized that only one side of the quadrangle, plus portions of two other sides, had really been destroyed, and that the living quarters proper had barely been touched. Faced with the problem of rebuilding, the committee turned around and agreed to sell us the house, charred timbers and all.

Having made up our minds that we were going to go ahead no matter what anybody said, we began to ask the opinions of our friends and relations. My father, who is a contractor, marched glumly around the house muttering darkly about stresses and strains, so I cheerfully pointed to the water and said, "But, Dad —look at the view you get." He contented himself with observing that during hurricanes we'd get the view right in the basement.

Most of our friends agreed that, like New York, it was a great place to visit but you wouldn't want to live there. "Maybe you could charge a shilling and show people through," one said. Someone else had a really bleak thought. He walked up and down the echoing living room and announced, "Obviously the only people you'll ever be able to entertain here are actors. Nobody else could be heard."

I have a friend who is a decorator, and I was sure he'd be fascinated by the place. I showed him through, and then waited for him to exclaim and extoll. "Well?" I asked brightly. "Well?" He paused with the air of a man being torn between the demands of friendship and of honesty. "I will say this," he at last said, "you have a lot of interesting horizontals."

After that I stopped asking for opinions, but I didn't stop getting them. We began to bring contractors in to get bids on the reconstruction. Without exception, they all burst into peals of hilarity the minute they set foot inside the door. I'd say, "Now, we want to eliminate this door and put in linoleum," and they'd shout, "Holy fright, take a gander at that ceiling." I'd say, "Now, about the linoleum," and they'd say, "My brother-in-law is a junk dealer. Would *he* get a bang out of this!" Some days we never got back to the linoleum at all.

Eventually, we worked out a system. To this day, when somebody comes to the door—a new milkman or a boy from the delivery service—we take the milk or sign for the parcel and then stop everything while we show him right through the house. It's much simpler than having him hover around the kitchen asking questions for twenty minutes.

We knew we were moving on May the first and I had planned to take a whole week off so that I could pack, and perhaps discover what was in those boxes in the attic marked "Sloms, drinds, and blue jeans." On the first of the week, however, I came down with a sodden cold which quickly developed into bronchitis. I piteously begged the doctor for pleurocillin or peneomyacin, or one of those things that cost eight dollars for six tablets and cure you overnight. The doctor just shrugged his shoulders and murmured sympathetically, "Now if you only had pneumonia—" Unfortunately, I didn't have pneumonia, so I was sick all week and we had to have the moving men do all the packing. And a conscientious crew they turned out to be. When we arrived at the new house, I discovered that at eight dollars a carton they had carefully packed, in excelsior, a fine assortment of broken crayons, three wheels from an old tractor, the back covers of fourteen coloring books, odd slats from an old Venetian blind, and a number of empty tins left over from Birdseye frozen chicken pies.

My mother came to help us move. This was a great boon, except that there is something wrong with her metabolism. She is not able to work for more than nineteen hours without stopping. During this period she is sustained by nothing more than several gallons of hot tea, which she consumes while on the top rungs of ladders or deep inside crates. By midnight, when I was ready to sob with fatigue, it was nothing for Mother to announce cheerfully, "Well, what do you say we clean out the garage?" She was a little disconcerted, though, when she discovered she wasn't able to pick up a television set, and I heard her moaning softly, "Jean, I'm afraid I'm beginning to slow down." I don't know whether it's true, but we can hope.

On the whole, moving day was like a scene from an old Mack Sennett comedy, with the four men moving our stuff in and the three men moving *their* stuff out plus the contractors and the plumber who was installing the washer and the little boy from next door who came to show us where the birds' nests were and the men from Macy's who brought the wrong beds. Not to mention the engineers who came to fix the furnace and spent an hour and a half looking for it. I had one man bring four loads up to the attic before I discovered that he was there to install the television set.

Walter had a show to review that night, so at six o'clock we just dropped everything and went into New York, leaving Mabel —our combination maid, housekeeper, nurse, companion, and friend—to find the children and find the food and find the beds. She also had to find the fuse box since only one light was working and that was out in the burned-out section of the garage. She, talented girl, found it too. By the time we returned home at one o'clock in a most unseasonable hailstorm, every light in the house was blazing away cheerfully. We were in our new home.

That was some time ago. Since then we've learned quite a few things. We've learned about the master bedroom, for instance. To get to it, you climb a short flight of stairs, then a longer flight of stairs, take a detour through a balcony, and then muster your strength for the last upward pull. To get down, you reverse the process. Nowadays whenever we come down in the morning and discover we've forgotten something, we either do without it or go out and buy a new one.

We've learned what happens to young boys. Everybody warned us that we could expect a lot of broken bones the moment the lads started to clamber over the balcony and out among the gargoyles. As it happened, we weren't in the house a week when Johnny broke his arm. It didn't happen here, though —it happened in nursery school. A four-and-a-half-year-old blonde named Cleo had had her eye on Johnny. On Monday she gave him a penny. On Tuesday she gave him a Davy Crockett button. On Wednesday she pushed him into a box and broke his arm in two places. Clearly this girl means business, and I think Johnny should keep the hell away from her. I asked him recently what ever happened to Cleo and he replied solemnly, "I don't know, but I hear she's going to have to sit in a corner for the rest of her life." And good enough for her, too.

Other things have happened. Two dogwood trees and one lilac bush that we didn't even know were there have bloomed and faded. The squirrels in the bell tower have had more squirrels. Sometimes I think the carpenters have had more carpenters. There were three or four to start with and today there are six.

But the roof is finally on, the garage has been restored, and most of the charred timber has been carted away—much to the dismay of the children, who used to make forts with it and emerge after ten minutes looking like Welsh coal miners. Oh, things are progressing. Even Gilbert notices it. This morning he pointed at the peacocks on the new wallpaper in the breakfast room and murmured, "Nice doggies, nice doggies."

Of course the playroom isn't finished and the den isn't even begun and all the bricking and painting remain to be done. By my own private calculations (I multiply the number of carpenters by the number of days in a week and divide by the cost of one panel of wallboard) I figure that the workmen will be here for seven years, give or take a few quarantines. On the one hand, I do get just a shade weary of seeing old tarpaulins over all the floors all the time, not to mention little piles of sand in the pantry and big piles of lumber under the piano. On the other hand, when I consider what gentle, personable people carpenters are, and what splendid companions they will be for the children as they are growing up, I begin to see a plan and a purpose in it all.

The Only Way to Fly

I feel about airplanes the way I feel about diets. It seems to me that they are wonderful things for other people to go on. When a friend of mine decides to fly to Milwaukee, I drive her out to La Guardia with marvelous calm and equanimity. I am positively lighthearted in the knowledge that she will receive loving, tender care and arrive with every curl intact. Lightning may be cracking around us, but I am calm.

"Nonsense, Martha," I say, clasping her perspiring palm. "It's the *only* way to go." Whereupon I deliver a brisk lecture on the statistics of safety in air travel. Indeed, if my figures are correct the only possible way you could be injured in an airplane is by inadvertently strangling yourself with the seat belt.

If my departing friend continues to be pessimistic about the lowering sky and the leaden clouds, I get just a wee bit impatient. "Honestly," I say, supported by the facts and good common sense, "you *are* a fuddy-duddy. This is the twentieth century, for heaven's sake. You'll get there right on time." And I'm right, of course. She always gets there, frequently before I get back home from the airport, what with the tie-up of traffic on the Whitestone Bridge.

When I fly, it's a different story altogether. In the first place, I am a rational human being and I'm not the least bit interested in statistics. I happen to know that planes do crash. *You* see those pictures in the paper—the smoking ruins, the dazed survivors, the pilot (when he is able to answer questions at St. Vincent's Hospital) reporting, "All I know is that two of the engines conked out." And please don't tell me a lot of irrelevant stories about train wrecks and auto collisions. The fact remains that I have been driving in cars and riding on trains all my life and nothing has ever happened to me. And you can't say as much for planes. All kinds of things have happened to me on planes.

So the day before a flight I always revise my will and write short notes of maternal guidance to each of my children. (These will be found in the top bureau drawer after my demise.) My husband drives me to the airport full of random remarks about what a beautiful day it is for flying and be sure to tell my mother he enjoyed the candy. I, on the other hand, try to seize these precious moments to make it clear to him that "after I'm gone" I expect him to remarry, really *expect* him to. How *could* he manage —a widower with *those* children? He makes a completely unsuccessful attempt to choke back his laughter and then pats me on the shoulder. "Honey, you're nuts," he says without a trace of sympathy. "But think of Will Rogers," I say plaintively, "and Wiley Post. And remember the Hindenburg." "Good heavens, that was a Zeppelin," he says. Yeah, and a lot of difference that made.

By the time the plane is ready to depart I have been fortified with tranquilizers, Dramamine, and intoxicating beverages. Nevertheless I creep up the entrance ramp a craven creature, escorted usually by the copilot, who recognizes a case of nerves when he sees one. "I suppose you've checked all the engines," I say, laughing wildly—giving a performance like James Cagney being led to the chair in one of those old Warner Brothers movies. The only reason I don't change my mind and make a break for it right down the ramp is because they have by this time absconded with my luggage, which is now, I presume, locked away in the hold.

I never bring reading material aboard a plane because I am convinced that if I'm not right there, alert every minute, keeping my eye on things, heaven knows what might happen to us. When it comes to selecting a seat I am torn between my wish to sit well back in the tail (surely the safest place to be when we crash) and the feeling that it is my civic duty to take a place next to the window where I can keep a constant watch over the engines. You have no idea how heedless and selfish some passengers are— reading magazines and munching sandwiches the while that I, alone, am keeping that plane aloft by tugging upward on the arms of my chair and concentrating intensely, sometimes for hours. And when it becomes absolutely clear that something is amiss, who has to ask that simple, straightforward question that will clarify things? I do. Honestly, I don't think these people care whether they live or die.

On a recent daylight flight to Washington, D.C., I was quick to notice that in spite of the fact that the weather was brilliantly clear our plane kept losing altitude. By which I mean it was dropping and dropping and dropping. "Stewardess," I said, raising my voice to a whisper, "is something the matter?" She flashed me a wide, Cinemascope smile and said, "I'll ask the captain, if you wish." By this time my stomach was in such a precarious condition that I didn't trust myself to vocalize, so I merely made a little gesture meaning "That would be very nice." She disappeared into the cockpit, where, evidently, the intercom between pilot and passengers had been left open. Presently we were all able to hear the stewardess reporting, "The passengers want to know if something is the matter." The next thing we heard was a short oath and a hoarse male voice saying, "The hell with the passengers, I'm up to my ass in trouble."

Well, talk about a conversation stopper. Even the jaunty junior executives who, a moment before, had been exchanging noisy jokes about an extremely co-operative girl named Mildred re- treated into silence behind their copies of *The Wall Street Jour- nal*, which could be seen to flap and rustle in their trembling hands. Mercifully, there were no more bulletins from the cabin and we landed uneventfully, none the worse for wear. Well, I can't speak for the other passengers, of course. But after five days' bed rest I felt fine.

I know perfectly well that people who talk about "their flights" are on a par, conversationally, with people who talk about their operations. Consequently at social gatherings I al- ways try to find a subject that is genuinely interesting, like, for instance, my dishwasher. (The man was here *three* times and still the water pours out all over the kitchen floor.) However I barely get started when someone interrupts me to say, "Listen, do you want to hear a really hair-raising story?" And I know we are off on another saga of the perils of this age of flight. A songwriter recently told me that his plane from the Coast was barely aloft when he overheard the following exchange between a dear old lady across the aisle from him and the stewardess:

Dear Old Lady: I hate to mention this, stewardess, but I think one of the engines is on fire.

Stewardess: No, indeed, madam, those little sparks you see are a part of the normal functioning. May I ask, is this your first flight?

Dear Old Lady: That's right. My children gave me this trip as a present for my eighty-sixth birthday.

Stewardess: I thought so. Many of our first-time passengers are a little nervous, but there is nothing to worry about. Not one member of the crew has had less than two thousand hours in the air.

Dear Old Lady: Thank you, my dear. I felt I was being a little silly. But before you go would you mind taking a look out of my window here?

Stewardess: Why, certainly. If it will make you feel a little better I'll be glad to—*oh my God!*

The engine, needless to say, was on fire, but I won't wear you out with all the details—except to say that all landed safely, including the little old lady, who was heard remarking to her son-in-law, "You won't believe this, Henry, but *I* had to tell them the plane was on fire."

In every tale of airborne trouble one hears the same recurring phrase: "The passengers behaved so well." They do, too. They are brave, considerate, prompt, reverent, and, I sometimes think, just plain lacking in common sense. A friend of mine who is a theatrical agent told me that when her plane stopped at Gander an announcement came over the loudspeaker to the effect that there would be a six-hour delay for repairs. Twenty minutes later, to everybody's surprise, there was a second announcement asking the passengers to reboard the plane. Several of them buttonholed the pilot on the way up the ramp and said, "I thought we were stopping for repairs." He smiled winningly and replied, "We've changed our minds. We've decided to go on." And would you believe it, every single one of those passengers went back onto that plane. If it had been me, I'd have hitchhiked my way home, or taken a canoe. Listen, before I'd have put one foot on that plane I would have stayed right there and begun life anew in Gander.

Even in the very best weather I find it advisable to take Dramamine, if for no other reason than it helps one to cope with the smiles of the personnel. Another thing that has to be coped with is the handy leaflet of information provided so thoughtfully by every airline.

A year ago my husband and I made our first overseas flight. During the endless delay in the London airport it became clear that we had been assigned to the fifth section of what was originally intended as a three-section flight. Obviously they were out combing the hangars for something that would fly. I could imagine the arguments: "Oh, don't be such a worrywart. You put a little 3-in-1 Oil in her and she'll go up." I'll say this: they made no hurried, spot decisions, because it was seven hours later that we assembled on the runway to inspect the craft that was to be our home away from home on the North Atlantic. My husband took one look and said, "Good Lord, it's *The Spirit of St. Louis!*" Of course he was exaggerating, but there was no doubt it was an extremely elderly plane. A little paint and paper would have done wonders, though not, I feared, enough.

As we were poking our way to our seats, I heard the stewardess ask the pilot, "Did you ever see one like this, Bill?" I was spared his answer, because there was a loud *flap!* caused by two upper berths which had suddenly, and for no apparent reason, dropped down over our heads. These berths were never occupied (for what I'm sure were good and sufficient reasons) and, since they resisted the efforts of every single member of the crew to lock them, they kept appearing and disappearing with about the same frequency as the commercials on "The Late, Late Show."

Eventually, or in a lot more time than it takes to tell about it, we were over the ocean. It was two o'clock in the morning, *my* time, but we were all eating scrambled eggs because, I gathered, it was now breakfast time in Scranton, Pennsylvania. I had become accustomed to the rhythm of this particular plane: it went shlumn-blip, shlumn-blip, which seemed perfectly reasonable to me. Soon, however, I began to detect what I assumed was an alien note in this refrain. Now it went shlumn-blip, shlumn-blip, *pickety*. It got worse in a moment when the upper berths began once more to flop open, and with the addition of this new leitmotiv we had what sounded like a full chorale: shlumn-blip, shlumn-blip, pickety, *flap!* Feeling that I must distract myself, I hunted through the seat pocket for something to read. Imagine my horror when I fished out a pamphlet entitled "Your Role in a Water Landing." The minutes flew by like hours as I read on and on. Clearly the world lost a great humorist when the author of this piece went to write for the airlines. In his jaunty phrase, the great North Atlantic—now looming menacingly below us— became "the drink." "Should we go into the drink," he wrote, blithe as a skylark, "you should be none the worse for the dunking." I was already the worse, just contemplating the prospect. But let's get back to that title: "Your Role in a Water Landing." Put it that way and I'm simply not interested. I know my role in a water landing. I'm going to splash around and sob. What I want to know, what I am really and truly curious about, is *their* role in a water landing. But the author kept pretty mum about that part of it. As for me, I kept entirely mum until the moment, ten hours later, when I was able to kiss the sweet soil of Kennedy Airport.

Of course you don't have to go your whole life being a scairdy-cat. Bob Newhart got over his fear of flying through hypnosis. I read that in some responsible publication. And he really had something to get over if you can believe those records he used to make. As he tells it, he was once sitting in the cabin of a small plane when the pilot called to the passengers, "Hey, listen, does anybody in there know what Hawaii looks like? It *is* a kidney-shaped island, isn't it?"

Oh that Newhart! I do love him but I think he's always exaggerating.

As I Was Saying
to Mrs. Rockefeller

The Confessions of a Status Finder

I have just finished reading *The Status Seekers* and now I'm really upset. Here I've been, all these years, supposing that I was a perfect example of a low-status type. Oh, I just *knew*, that's all. In fact, there didn't seem to be any other possibility. Here we were: Democrats, driving around in a ten-year-old Chevy, eating meat loaf, and going to see *American* movies. Little things, you say, but they add up—particularly when you now have five children and not one of them can spell.

But I wasn't really worried. I was bearing up nicely until I read Vance Packard's book. And the reason I am at sixes and sevens now is because it seems, and you won't believe this, it seems that I am really a high-status type. But here's the terrible thing: nobody knows it. My friends (a low-status group if I ever saw one) don't know it. The salesgirls in Saks Fifth Avenue clearly don't know it. My very own mother doesn't know it or she wouldn't keep saying to me, "For heaven's sake, buy yourself a decent set of dishes." This is simply not the remark one makes to a high-status person.

Oh, I am surrounded by skeptics, but I refer them all to Mr. Packard. He says very plainly that "women who are really secure in their upper-class status may become fond of a good outfit and wear it for years." You'll know how secure I am when I tell you that I still have this suit I bought before I was married. (It's a little tight now, so I just don't button the last three buttons.) But fond of it? If I weren't afraid of sounding mawkish, I'd come right out and say that I'm just plain crazy about that brown tweed suit. It may be fifteen years old this month, but it's just as baggy as the day I bought it. And it's suitable for so many occasions. Whether I am taking two sick cats to the vet, spreading peat moss on the rose bushes, or merely staining the front door, I know I'm dressed correctly when I'm wearing that suit.

There are those who may scoff to read Mr. Packard's report that "the fabulously well-dressed Mrs. Winston Guest recently took with her to Europe a suit she has been wearing for eight years." Now it seems perfectly clear to me why Mrs. Guest took that suit to Europe. It's probably been hanging there getting on her nerves for seven years. By this time she's ashamed to give it to the help and reluctant to burn it. So what could be simpler than shoving it through a porthole? If I ever go to Europe again, that's exactly what I mean to do with this horrible brown tweed suit. Okay, I lied when I said I was crazy about it.

But let's get back to the facts. Another dead giveaway of my high social status is the way I entertain. Mr. Packard insists that at the upper-class level people "tend to prefer relaxed informality. Food typically is offered casually. There may be amiable and fairly open flirting and talking. Weaving figures may offer toasts." Honestly, if I didn't know better I'd swear that Packard was here one night last week. But then I imagine he has his spies, don't you?

As for this business about food being offered casually, I've actually been known to say, "Bill, I think you'll find pretzels on the second shelf." How could you be more upper-status than that? Mr. Packard concludes his summary of entertaining among the elect by stating flatly that "the people having the party at the upper level usually are not trying to prove anything. Publicity in the newspapers is not sought." Well, I should think not. With those weaving figures offering toasts, it seems to me the less said about the whole thing the better. But isn't it nice to know that when you are not trying to prove anything with a party you are *really* proving that you are a high-status person?

Reading further (you notice how this is all adding up, don't you?), we learn that "the slim figure is more of a preoccupation with women of the upper classes. As you go down the scale, married women take plumpness more calmly." Observe that there is nowhere the suggestion that the upper-class female may not be plump. No, the implication is clear. It's all right to be plump as long as you're not calm about it.

Well, as far as that goes, you should have seen me trying on bathing suits in Lane Bryant's last summer. Not that there was any chance you'd have seen me, since I wouldn't even allow the motherly saleswoman to witness the struggles of that dreadful half hour. I tried on suit after suit, all of them designed by some shut-in in California who, it seems to me, would benefit from a beginner's course in anatomy. But at each succeeding glimpse of myself in the rearview mirror I burst into wild outcries and muffled sobs. Indeed, I was anything but calm as I went off to soothe myself with a butterscotch sundae.

And don't worry about the quality of your conversation. Once you begin to get the hang of it you will find yourself just naturally making statements that are irreproachably upper-status. For instance, should the occasion arise, you might say, "Gimme a hunk ['the high-status person uses unpretentious language'] of that pumpernickel" ['only the upper classes like firm, hard bread']. If you want to be really on the safe side, you might add, parenthetically, "But make it a small hunk," which would indicate that you were not taking plumpness calmly. As I say, it's a technique that can be learned. What's nice for me is that I was *born* liking pumpernickel bread.

Now that I've laid out the evidence and proved beyond question that I am a true high-status type, there is one statement in the book that comes back to haunt me. It says, "Medical investigators have noticed as you get near the bottom of the social scale, there is an abrupt rise in a disorder called anomie—feeling isolated, loosely attached to the world, and convinced that things are tough all over."

Feeling isolated? Loosely attached to the world? Convinced that things are tough all over? But that's the way *I* feel. That's the way I feel all the time. Now what do I do, Mr. Packard?

Where Did You Put the Aspirin?

I'd be the last one to say a word against our modern child psychologists. They try, they really try. I know that. So I am prepared to swallow a number of their curious notions, including even the thought-provoking statement that "children are our friends." This premise may be open to question, or even to hysterical laughter, but it probably does contain a germ of truth.

What I have no patience with is the growing tendency among psychologists to insist that children are really *people*, little adults —just like the rest of us, only smaller. Really, the impression you get in some quarters is that the only difference between children and grownups is that children don't drink, smoke, or play bridge.

Come, come, men. We all know better than that. Children are different—mentally, physically, spiritually, quantitatively, qualitatively, and furthermore they're all a little bit nuts.

Take a simple matter like going to bed. An adult will say, "If *you* want to sit up all night watching an old George Raft movie, okay, but I'm turning in." And he turns in, and that's the end of him until tomorrow morning.

Getting a child to bed is a different proposition altogether. First you locate your child and make a simple announcement to the effect that it is now bedtime. This leads to a spirited debate in which you have to listen to a passionate defense of the many

mothers of character and vision who live just up the block and
who *always* allow their seven-year-old boys to stay up and watch
"Starsky and Hutch." (Indeed, if my informant is correct, ours
are the only children in Larchmont who don't habitually sit up
to catch "The Tomorrow Show.")

You gently and gracefully present your side of the picture.
"Listen," you say, "I don't want to hear one more word about
Rory Killilea's mother. You're going to bed right now, do you
hear, *now,* this minute!" These persuasive remarks, declaimed in
clear, ringing tones with perhaps an additional "this *minute!*"
thrown in for good measure, are usually sufficient to get a boy
up into the bedroom. Theoretically, the matter is closed. Actually, you've just begun to fight.

Now begins a series of protracted farewell appearances. He
comes back on the landing to say that his pajamas are wet and
he has a neat idea: he's going to sleep in his snow pants. You say
it's impossible, how could those pajamas be wet? And he says he
doesn't know unless it's because he used them to mop up the
floor when he tipped over the fish tank.

It shouldn't take you more than fifteen minutes to find his
other pajamas—the ones that haven't got any buttons, the ones
that are supposed to be in the clean-clothes hamper but aren't.
When you've finally got him pinned into that dry pair, you can
go back and glare at your husband, who has found the whole incident rather amusing (well, dammit, he's a *boy*). Your husband's hilarity, however, will be somewhat quenched in a moment when he hears that one of the fish has perished in the
disaster and will require an immediate burial outside by flashlight.

But soft! That boy is back again, and we are into the following
dialogue:

"I suppose you want me to brush my teeth."

"Of course I want you to brush your teeth."

"Okay, but I won't be going to school tomorrow."

"Why not, for heaven's sake?"

"Because I'll be poisoned to death."

"What *are* you talking about?"

"Chris used my toothbrush to paint his model car."

This necessitates a brief but painful interview with Chris, who declares, "He never used that toothbrush anyway, he always used mine."

Normally, along about here, you can count on a seven-minute *Luftpause* during which you can cut out a recipe for Baked Alaska which you will make as soon as you lose ten pounds, which will be never.

But we're about ready for that third appearance. "Mommy"— this time the voice is dripping with tragedy—"Mommy, it's raining."

You leap out of your chair.

"Do you mean to tell me that you got up just to tell me it's raining? I *know* it's raining. Go back to bed!"

He goes back, but presently the sound of muffled sobs comes flooding down the stairwell. Naturally, you have to go upstairs and turn on the light and find out what's the matter with the poor little thing. What's the matter, it turns out, is that he has left his bicycle over on the Slezaks' lawn. Not that he is at all concerned about the bicycle, which he has just got for Christmas and which cost sixty-nine dollars and ninety-five cents, but he has tied a keen foxtail to the handle bar and it will be ruined, just absolutely ruined. So you can go over and get the bicycle and if you hurry you'll be back in time to catch his fourth and final appearance.

This time, noticing the edge of hysteria in your voice (he's been around for seven years; he knows when you are going to crack), he keeps his message brief.

"Mommy, this is important. Can I take our telephone to school? We're doing a report on communications."

If children and adults differ in their approach to bedtime, there is even greater discrepancy in the separate ways they greet the morn. To begin with, the average, healthy, well-adjusted adult gets up at seven-thirty in the morning feeling just plain terrible. He stumbles through the physical motions of dressing, staring glassily at the shirt button that has just come off in his hand. His mind, oddly enough, is razor-sharp, probing, questioning: why was he born, why are there never any clean handkerchiefs, where will all this end? He's moody, morose, and above all else— silent. (This is a desirable situation, since it makes it easier for him to live with that other healthy, normal adult who isn't feeling so top-of-the-morning either.) He walks with a slight list, holding his hands out in front of him—presumably to catch his head should it fall off. During the entire breakfast period he will break the silence only once, to mutter hoarsely, "*I* don't call this *half* the paper, this is nothing but real estate ads."

Now we come to the little ones, who rise from their beds like a swarm of helicopters buzzing and sawing the air around them. Although it's only seven-thirty, they haven't been idle. One of them has written "I am a pig" on the bathroom mirror with toothpaste—and won't that be a cool joke on Gilbert when he is old enough to read? Somebody else has found a good secret hiding place for his pirate knife: he just cut a little corner off the pillow and stuffed it inside, and *that* clears up the mystery of where all those feathers came from. Even so, it's not the mayhem that eats away at the nerve ends of the adult; it is the riotous good humor and wild, gay chatter that spills like a Kansas twister out of the bedroom, down the stairs, and over the breakfast table.

If the matutinal conversation of children and grownups differs in volume and velocity, it also differs in essence. An adult, if he speaks at all, makes statements ("Well, I see William Safire is after Carter again"), a remark that not only doesn't require an answer, it practically precludes one.

The child, on the other hand, makes questions. Even when he is only trying to impart information, he will phrase it as a query: "Did you know that the Egyptians invented marshmallow?" "Did you know that Billy said if his turtle has a turtle he's going to give me a turtle?"

Now most of these questions can be answered by a simple "yep." (This is clearly not the time to give your reasons for supposing that the output of a solitary turtle will be necessarily limited.) There is a danger, though, that you will "yep" your way into trouble by missing the ghastly implications of a trick question like, "Do you want to see me drink my milk without touching the glass with my hands?"

There are other important ways in which children differ from their elders. For instance, it is perfectly possible to have a really satisfactory quarrel with an adult. You say to the beloved, "Do you mean to tell me that you met Mrs. Gordon and you didn't ask her about her operation? Of *course* I told you, you just don't *listen.* Oh, never mind—you're obtuse, that's all, just plain *thick!*" This should lead to a spirited exchange and result in a good, two-day sulk.

Conversely, you can tell a child that he's the worst boy ever born into the world, follow up this sweeping statement with a smart thump on the behind, and in two and one half minutes he will come back, look you straight in the eye, and say, "Wanna hear a neat riddle?"

Of course we haven't time here to discuss the more obvious and basic differences, such as the fact that adults believe in Santa Claus and children don't. But we must get in a word about the Sweater Fetish that is so peculiar to the young. Adults, many of them, don't *have* sweaters, and those who do find that the mere possession of a sweater in no way detracts from their enjoyment of a rich, full life. Children, however, regard the Sweater primarily as something to take off. More than that. They see in the Sweater a symbol of all that is plainly idiotic and unreasonable about the adult world. I'm sure that even in Alaska, when the temperature thuds to fifty below zero, little Eskimo children plead, "Do I *have* to wear it? It's not cold." To me, there is something almost touching about the way children fight the daily, doomed battle of the Sweater. It's as though they were saying to themselves, "Okay, I have to wear this, but someday, somewhere, some kid who is bigger than me and better than me is going to make it out that back door without one." There are, to be sure, some lucky children who *don't* have sweaters, having left them in school, or in the park, or in a drawer wrapped around a pair of ice skates.

Psychologists tell us that the things we *want*, the things we ask for most often, provide us with a vital clue to our personalities. Children, having linear minds and no grasp of the great intangibles, spend most of their energy yapping about trifles: "Can I have a Coke?" "Can I have an apple?" "Can I have a Good Humor?" "Can I see *Last Tango in Paris?* Dickie says it's a keen picture."

In contrast, notice the maturity and breadth of vision that is revealed in this sampling of a typical adult's daily demands: "Where did you put the aspirin?" "Did anybody call the

plumber about that faucet?" Don't you *ever* put cigarettes out?"
"Tell them we can't come, tell them I'm sick, tell them I'm dead,
tell them anything you want!" "Who the hell took my fountain
pen?"

Let's have no more of this nonsense about children being Little Adults. They are a breed apart, and you can tell it just by
looking at them. How many of them have gray hair? How many
do you see taking Gelusil? How many of them prefer Jack Daniels?

Okay, we've settled that.

Toujours Tristesse

After reading A Certain Smile *by Francoise Sagan:*

I was waiting for Banal. I was feeling rather bored. It was a summer day like any other, except for the hail. I crossed the street.

Suddenly I was wildly happy. I had an overwhelming intuition that one day I would be dead. These large eyes, this bony child's body would be consigned to the sweet earth. Everything spoke of it: the lonely cooing of a solitary pigeon overhead, the stately *bong bong bong* of the cathedral chimes, the loud horn of the motorbus that grazed my thigh.

I slipped into the cafe, but Banal was late. I was pleased to notice that that simple fact annoyed me.

Banal and I were classmates. Our eyes had met, our bodies had met, and then someone introduced us. Now he was my property, and I knew every inch of that brown body the way you know your own driveway.

A stranger across the booth spoke.

"Monique, what are you staring at, silly girl?"

It was Banal. Curious that I hadn't recognized him. Suddenly I knew why. A revolting look of cheerfulness had twisted and distorted those clear young features until he seemed actually to be smiling.

I couldn't look. I turned my head, but his voice followed me, humbly and at a distance, like a spaniel.

"Monique, why did you skip class? We were studying the *Critique of Pure Reason*. It was interesting, but I think Kant offers a false dichotomy. The only viable solution is to provide a synthesis in which experience is impregnated with rationality and reason is ordained to empirical data."

How like Banal to say the obvious. Sometimes as I sat and listened to Banal and his companions trade flippancies, I could feel the boredom grow and swell within me almost as if I had swallowed a beach ball.

Why must we chatter fruitlessly and endlessly about philosophy and politics? I confess that I am only interested in questions that touch the heart of another human being—"Who are you sleeping with?"; "What do you take for quick relief from acid indigestion?"

Banal's voice droned on like a chorus of cicadas on a hot day until finally there was a statement I couldn't ignore.

"Monique, I want you to meet my grandfather, Anatole. My rich grandfather."

A slight, stooped man came toward me. He was no longer middle-aged, but I liked that. I was so tired of these eager boys of fifty. His hair, which was greenish white, might have been unpleasant had there been more of it. As he smiled gently, showing his small, even, ecru teeth, I thought, "Ah, he's the type that's mad for little girls." In fact, hadn't I read that he'd had some trouble with the police?

But now, as his dull eyes looked directly into mine and I noticed him idly striking a match on the tablecloth, I realized with a sudden stab of joy that finally I had met a man who was as bored as I was.

And yet, I reminded myself firmly as my heart slid back to earth, this won't last. It can't last. He won't *always* be this bored.

Now Banal was speaking in his infantile way.

"Do you know Monique has never seen the sea?"

Then a woman spoke, Anatole's wife. She was sitting beside him but I hadn't noticed her because she was wearing a brown dress and blended into the back of the booth. Her voice was warm, like a caress.

"Why, that's awful that this poor child has never seen the sea. Anatole, darling, you must take her to our little château by the ocean. I won't be able to come because I'm redecorating the town house. But there is plenty of food in the Frigidaire, and Monique will be able to see the ocean from the bedroom. Here are the keys."

I liked her for that.

Then they were leaving. Dorette, for that was Anatole's wife's name, had forgotten her gloves, and I admit I felt a pang of jealousy as I noticed the intimate way that Anatole threw them to her.

Now Banal and I were alone. As I suspected, Banal was stormy and full of suspicion. How I hated him when he got this way. He kept asking me, again and again, "Are you sure, Monique, are you really sure that you have never seen the sea?"

But when I assured him, what was the truth, that I never had, he seemed comforted and became once more the sunny, smiling, handsome young man I found so repellent.

We were in Anatole's open car. Overhead the sky was blue as a bruise.

The gleaming white road slipping under our wheels seemed like a ribbon of cotton candy. As I realized we were nearing the château, my heart turned over once, quickly and neatly, like a pancake on a griddle.

Anatole's voice seemed to come from a great distance.

"Bored, darling?"

I turned to him.

"Of course—and you?"

His answering smile told me that he was.

And now we were running up the long flight of steps to the château hand in hand like two happy children, stopping only when Anatole had to recover his wind.

At the doorway he paused and gathered me into his arms. His voice, when he spoke, was like a melody played sweetly and in tune.

"My darling," he said, "I hope I have made it perfectly clear that so far as I am concerned you are just another pickup."

"Of course," I whispered. How adult he was, and how indescribably dear.

So the golden days passed. Mostly we were silent, but occasionally we sat in the twilight and spoke wistfully of Dorette and Banal and what suckers they were.

And who could describe those nights? Never in my relationship with Banal had I felt anything like this. Ah, how rewarding it is to share the bed of a really mature man. For one thing, there was the clatter and the excitement four times a night as he leaped to the floor and stamped on his feet in an effort to get the circulation going. My little pet name for him, now, was Thumper.

The last day dawned cold and bright as a star. Anatole was waiting for me out in the car, so I packed my few belongings, ran a nail file through my curls, and joined him.

What shall I say of the pain of that ride back to Paris? In one sense, we were, both of us, precisely as weary as ever. Yet for the first time it wasn't a shared weariness.

We pulled up to my front door, and then the blow fell.

"Monique," he said, "little one. I *have* been bored with you. Nobody can take that away from us. But the truth is, and I know how this will hurt you, I am even more bored with my wife. I'm going back to her."

He was gone. I was alone. Alone, alone, alone. I was a woman who had loved a man. It was a simple story, prosaic even. And yet somehow I knew I could get a novel out of it.

Can This Romance Be Saved?

Lolita and Humbert Consult a Marriage Counselor

It was a mistake to read Vladimir Nabokov's *Lolita* and the "Can This Marriage Be Saved?" column in the *Ladies' Home Journal* on the same evening. The total effect was a little confusing.

The counselor interviews Humbert, and reports his side of the story:

Humbert was a tall, graying man. The natural pallor of his skin was perhaps accentuated by the drabness of his present garb. With his quiet, old-world charm he made me welcome in the cell and spoke quite readily of his broken romance.

"Doctor, picture—if you will—my darling, my nymphet, my Lolita, her scrawny, brown, twelve-year-old legs splashed all over with daubs of Mercurochrome, which spread like roses under the little white wings of Band-Aids.

"To watch her sit at the kitchen table and play jacks was to know what Aristotle meant by pity and terror and to feel with Oedipus, arriving blind and gutted at Colonus. The jacks in her grubby paws flew into the air like little prisms of silver, like stars. And when sometimes it happened, as often it did, that the small rubber ball dropped from her hands into the butter dish (my darling was not very well co-ordinated), the stream of four-letter words that poured from her adorable mouth would have dazzled a fishmonger.

"Ah, Lolita—the snap, snap, splat of her bubble gum (she chewed twelve hours a day, my lamb did) will echo down the corridors of all my dreams. Even in hell (*is* there a hell, shall we talk theology, Doctor?) I will be bedeviled (forgive the pun; it was intended) by visions of the precious one who curled up so sweetly in my lap after I gave her five dollars.

"My conscience, that wary censor, that watchdog of memory, permits me to recall only the happy hours, when Lolita lay at my feet poring over movie magazines and munching candied apples (alas, she often brought these—the apples—to bed). Her bright eyes sparkled as she gorged herself on pictures of pulchritudinous Rock or Tab or Guy (surely I invent these names) here photographed in a limed-oak study, there caught spread-armed and godlike on a surfboard.

"It has been suggested that after her mother's most timely demise I forced my attentions on this angel-nymphet. (Idle roomers beget idle rumors.) But I swear to you that I did no more than kidnap her from that summer camp, right under the toothy smiles of the lady counselors (fat, middle-aged sows, all of them, twenty-two or older). It was little Lolita, accomplished beyond her years, who seduced poor old Humbert. It was the fly, if you will, who gobbled up the spider. You must remember that I was worn down from poring over scholarly journals (did you know, dear Doctor, that Dante's Beatrice was a nymphet of thirteen?) and weakened by the atrociously poor food provided by the series of mental institutions to which I was periodically committed. On the other hand, my little lamb chop was in fighting trim, lean and lithe from playing hopscotch. Oh, Lolita, oh those nights, *mon Dieu!* (that's French, Doctor; I'm a very educated fellow).

"Imagine my horror when my darling, who—what is the vulgar phrase?—who had it made, who had handsome, hairy Humbert in the palm of her tiny hand, left, scrammed, vamoosed, ran off. And ran off, would you believe it, with the first fat, balding slob who promised her a glimpse of Hamburger Heaven. And I, all alone, bewailed my outcast state and troubled the deaf deities with my burping, noisy grief. Ah, laugh if you will, but hath not a pervert eyes, hands, senses, passions, and affections? Do you wonder that I killed him?

"And here I am, behind bars which contain me and enclose me like my own parentheses. Yesterday and yesterday and yesterday I was always her victim, Doctor. An unlikely story, you say, and yet you may have observed how it sells."

The counselor interviews Lolita, and reports her *side of the story:*

I would not say that my first interview with twelve-year-old Lolita was entirely successful. In the first place, she was busy manipulating her Yo-Yo and seemed reluctant to talk. After I had gained her confidence, she opened up a little.

"Look, Doc, it was a nightmare from the beginning. The night he swiped me from that camp and took me to the motel, do you know what he did to me? First of all, you've gotta get the picture that there's nothing in this room but the double bed and one bureau. So what happens? Humbert takes the three big drawers for his stuff and leaves me with those two little tiny drawers on top. I couldn't even get all my hair ribbons in. Was I burned up!

"I'll say this. He could be sweet enough when he wanted to. But as soon as we got out of bed in the morning, my troubles began. Boy did he overwork the togetherness bit. All this jazz about 'sharing' nearly drove me out of my little pink mind. If I went out on the front sidewalk to skip rope, *he* had to skip rope. We had to cut down the clothesline to get a rope big enough for him. Boy, you should have seen him, huffing and puffing and getting his big clodhoppers all tangled up in the rope. If I had an onion sandwich, you bet your life Big Daddy had to have an onion sandwich. He'd pile on the onions and then, as soon as he got it all down, he'd turn absolutely green and have to drink *gallons* of Bromo-Seltzer. All this time he'd be groaning and saying, 'You see, mah puhteet, I'd do anything for you—anything.' I'd come right out and tell him, 'Look, Pops, if you wanna do me a real favor, go to the movies and leave me alone for two hours.' Then he'd start to cry and say I was just trying to get rid of him. That guy cried so much he should have had windshield wipers for those glasses.

"But the worst of all was the way he hogged things. On Sunday morning, who used to toddle out in his pajamas and grab all the funnies first? Mr. Geritol. Of course by the time I got hold of them, they were an absolute mess. He used to pretend that he just wanted to know what I was reading. But he didn't fool me. A forty-year-old yakking it up over Moon Mullins—I ask you. If you want the inside story, Doc, I'm looking for a more mature man."

The counselor gives his advice:

At first glance it seemed as though these two people were poles apart. To begin with, there was the vast difference in their ages. Obviously it was difficult for an experienced girl like Lolita to put up with Humbert's childishness.

However, as our interviews continued, I was quick to notice that they had a number of important things in common. For instance, Humbert, as a child, suffered from an "absent" mother. That is to say, his mother died when he was eighteen months old, and so, quite naturally, he hated her. As a counselor, I was able to show Humbert that his rebellious attitude stemmed in large part from the fact that, as a child, he lacked that symbol of sensual pleasure, the cookie jar. Resentful at being abandoned by his mother, he was trying to penalize all other women who, in his fantasies, became "cookies." Humbert was quick to acknowledge the truth of my diagnosis. "Doctor," he said, "that's a new one on me."

Lolita, on the other hand, had a "present" mother who danced attendance on her night and day. Naturally she hated her. The mother, with that obtuseness so often found among females of the lower middle classes, made a fetish of propriety. Consequently, she was unsympathetic to twelve-year-old Lolita's valiant efforts to form a sexual alliance with an older man. And, what was worse, she constantly interfered with Lolita's natural development by saying things like "Don't leave the soap in the bathtub" or "Get your fingers out of the plate." Is it any wonder that Lolita has spent her whole life trying to get her fingers in the plate?

The solution for this pair did not come all at once. But as our sessions drew to a close I felt that the future looked brighter for both of them. Lolita has agreed to stop bringing candied apples to bed. (The onion sandwiches are no longer a problem; since Lolita's gall bladder operation she is no longer able to tolerate raw onions.)

On his side, Humbert has agreed to stay in prison. With time off for good behavior, he can look forward to a parole in forty-five years. At this time he will be eighty-five and should be sufficiently mature to shoulder his responsibilities. Lolita will wait. (I have decided to take her into my home as a ward.) In the meantime, she is optimistic. As she herself expressed it, "With my luck, he'll get out of the clink."

Good luck to you both, Lolita and Humbert.

Snowflaketime

I've been hearing that overproduction and high costs are killing the theater, but I don't know that I actually worried about such things until I saw *Snowflaketime*, the third-grade Christmas play at a school in Larchmont. Then it all came clear to me.

Here was a dazzling production with a chorus of sixty angels in pink gauze, who sang "The First Noel" three times. There was, in addition, a chorus of sixty angels in white gauze, who handed tinsel stars to the angels in pink gauze. There were twenty toy soldiers in red felt uniforms with gold rifles, of whom nineteen were able to march backward. There were 120 dancers "from every land" but mostly from the Balkan countries. There were two scarecrows who had taken tap-dancing and twelve jack-in-the-boxes.

Oh, the whole thing was a "triumph," "a visual delight," and a "stunning success." But of course it will never pay off. Even with a thirty-five-cent top and a capacity house (the house seats six hundred, with each mother seating one or two extra depending on the width of the mother), they're going to have trouble getting their money back.

Our eight-year-old, who was wrapped in tissue paper and red ribbons and was supposed to be a present, was very distressed because two of the toy soldiers waved at the audience. As my husband remarked, that's the kind of thing they could have cleaned up if they had taken the show to New Rochelle for a couple of weeks. But I imagine they were afraid of those out-of-town losses.

When I was in third grade we didn't gear our productions to the tired business boy. We eschewed extravaganzas. Well, it wasn't so much that we eschewed them; we'd never heard of them. We did the "great" plays—*Nahaliel, The Shepherd, The Shepherd's Gift,* and *The Young Shepherd Boy.* We did them on a shoestring, but with the sense of doom and dedication of some movie actors doing a revival of Ibsen.

I always played the tallest shepherd. I wore my father's old dressing gown and I said, "Full many a moon have I watched on yon hill, and ne'er saw I such a star as this." In an effort to suggest great age, I used to make my voice creak and crackle like a short-wave receiver. All the shepherds were very, very old (the mystery is how they were ever able to watch any sheep), except for one shepherd boy whose characterization changed from year to year.

Sometimes he brought his flute, his only possession, and laid it in the manger. Other years he was lame and brought his crutch. He never came empty-handed and he always had a big scene in which he sobbed and said, "I, Nahaliel, have naught, naught save only this flute [or crook or crutch or whatever it was that year], but freely do I give it to THEE." Then he threw himself down in the straw.

There was a part for an actress. I finally did play Nahaliel, but I started at the bottom. Actually, the first thing I played was part of the scenery. No one was allowed to nail anything to our stage floor, so all the scenery had to be held up by the students. On this occasion I stood behind a large balsam tree and with my free hand shook Lux flakes on Mary and Joseph as they passed, the while making low humming sounds to indicate the inclement state of the weather. My family regarded this triple accomplishment with mixed emotions. As a matter of fact, I don't think my father's were too mixed. I recall his inquiring bleakly, as the evening of my debut approached, "My God, do you mean we're going to have to get dressed and go all the way up there to see her stand behind a tree?"

Our audiences, generally, came prepared for a profound emotional experience, which may explain why certain locations, directly behind pillars, were in great demand. We always had standees at the rear of the house, even when the auditorium was half empty. But we were proud, and the overhead was low.

Nowadays you hardly see a shepherd at all. As far as the school in Larchmont is concerned, I sensed a shift away from the serious theater even before Christmas. Some weeks ago our oldest boy came home with the information that he was appearing in a Safety Play. His costume was to be very simple. He was playing a back tire. I asked him what his part consisted of, and he said, "Oh, mostly I just blow out." What I want to know is, will this equip him to play the great parts like Lear or even a front tire? At that, I can scarcely wait for him to play Lear. It'll be so much easier to make the costume.

I suppose that, for the untalented, all costumes are hard. John (age four) came home recently with a yellow slip pinned to his sleeve announcing that his nursery school was going to present *Frosty, the Snowman,* and John was playing—oh, the wonder of it! and why wasn't there a phone call from *Variety—Frosty.*

"You can make the costume out of a worn sheet and an old top hat from the attic," wrote his teacher. The note concluded with the inexplicable statement: "In the first scene Frosty is supposed to be half melted." (Why tell me? As I explained to Johnny, it's the actor's job to characterize. I just make costumes.)

Johnny plowed upstairs ahead of me to find an old sheet in the linen closet, and the next thing I heard was a sob of anguish. "Mommy"—it was the cry of Oedipus on the heights of Colonus —"our sheets are GREEN!" And so they were. In a burst of whimsy some years ago I had purchased all colored sheets. When I think of those Pepperell people, so full of loud talk about the myriad wonders that can be wrought with colored sheets! I'd like to see them try to make a snowman costume sometime.

But never mind the sheet. What old top hat? What attic? We don't keep old top hats in our attic. We keep academic gowns, white Palm Beach suits that are bound to come back in style, and three storm windows that evidently belong to another house.

When it came right down to it, though, there was nothing to

making that costume. By giving up lunch I whipped the whole thing up in less than a month. And finally the day arrived. Johnny was a superb Frosty. His was an exquisitely conceived, finely wrought performance—limpid, luminous, tender. When he took his bows there was tremendous applause, in which he enthusiastically joined. I could just hear him in Congress, forty years from now, referring to himself as "the able senator from New York."

This production ended, however, in a short tableau that said to me that the day of economy and sincerity was not wholly past. A small red-headed boy in a brown toga, with dirty sneakers showing briefly beneath, escorted a tiny girl in white dress and blue veil across the stage. He stopped suddenly and said, in a voice of piercing sweetness:

"Oh, Mary, 'tis a cold, cold night."

Mary turned and said simply, " 'Tis."

It won't make a nickel, but it's a great audience show.

One Half of Two On the Aisle

In my short and merry life in the theater, I have discovered that there are two sharply contrasting opinions about the place of the drama critic. While in some quarters it is felt that the critic is just a necessary evil, most serious-minded, decent, talented theater people agree that the critic is an unnecessary evil. However, if there is some room for argument about the value of the critic, there is none whatever about the value of the critic's wife. To the producer, in particular, it is painful enough that the reviewer must bring his own glum presence to the theater, but the thought that he will also bring his wife and that she, too, will occupy a free seat is enough to cool the cockles of his heart and send him back on a soft diet. "What if a doctor had to bring his wife along when he performed an operation?" he will ask you. "Can't you see her sitting there murmuring, 'Here's a nice suture, dear, and why don't you try this clamp?'"

In their innermost souls, the producer and the press agent are convinced that the wife has a bad effect on the critic and consequently a bad effect on the notice. Of course, not all critics have wives; some of them habitually attend the theater in the company of pretty actresses, a practice which is thought to be not only suitable but even, on occasion, inspiring.

It isn't that anyone believes a wife's influence is direct or intentional. Presumably no one has suggested that it is her practice to tuck her spouse into a cab at eleven o'clock with the stern admonition, "Now you hurry right back to that little office and say what a bad play this was, hear?" No, the whole thing is much more intangible than that, and I'm afraid it boils down to the sobering fact that the producer feels that the mere physical presence of a wife depresses the critic, lowers his spirits, clogs his areas of good will, and leaves his head rattling with phrases like "witless," "tasteless," and "below the level of the professional theater."

On the other hand, just let some wife absent herself from the happy revelers at an opening and you will see consternation settle like a fine dew upon producer and press agent alike. Souls are searched. Old wounds are probed. Is the jig up? Have runners been coming in from Philadelphia with the bad word? Have those preview audiences been squealing? Clearly somebody talked. The lady has had fair warning and is at home with a good book.

It is my impression that my own attendance record is rather higher than the average. This can be explained by the fact that I have those children and naturally have to get out a lot. When my husband first went on a newspaper, and for several years thereafter, I brought my larklike disposition and gooey good will to every single solitary show that opened. Lately, however, I've begun to develop a small, cowardly instinct for self-preservation, and I find that there are two kinds of plays I can bear not to see: plays about troubled adolescents who can't find themselves, and plays about the Merchant of Venice.

During this past summer we paid a visit to Stratford, England, and saw a number of plays not including *The Merchant of Venice*. It seemed to make the whole trip worth while. I have friends, old-time theatergoers who have seen every Hamlet since Forbes-Robertson, and they love to sit around and reminisce about the way Leslie Howard played the ghost scene and how Gielgud read the speech to the players. Now, I hope to spend my twilight years reminiscing about the Shylocks I haven't seen. Donald Wolfit, Luther Adler, Clarence Derwent, Morris Carnovsky, Hume Cronyn—oh, it's a splendid gallery already and I expect to add to it before I'm through.

As everyone knows, one of the chief problems of going to the theater with a critic is getting out of there a split second after the curtain comes down or, if the show is a very long one, a split second before. Lately I've become very adept at judging the precise line of dialogue on which to start pulling the sleeves of my coat out from under the lady next to me. This might be when an actress says, "In future years, when you speak of me, be kind," or when an actor says, "Now that I've got you, darling, I'll never let you go," although I have known shows in which he let her go for another ten minutes after that.

Then follows a wild scramble down a dark and crowded aisle. I used to forge stolidly ahead, having developed a technique for this sort of thing in Ohrbach's basement, but one night, when I felt I had Walter firmly by the hand and was propelling him out into the traffic, I heard a plaintive voice muttering, "Hey, lady, gee, lady, please!" I looked up to discover that I had Farley Granger firmly by the hand. It's things like that that make one pause and reconsider.

After the show, most wives go out with their friends or go home to their peaceful apartments. I tag along to the office because we live in Larchmont and neither one of us wants to make the trip back alone. Obviously, if I were planning to influence my husband, my golden opportunity would come during the cab ride over to the office. The only trouble is that he immediately assumes the yogi-like silence and the glazed manner of a sandhog in a decompression chamber.

I used to think he was going into shock, but I have gradually gleaned that he is just trying to think of an opening sentence. I wouldn't dream of breaking the cathedral hush that surrounds us. However, if there is one thing a cab driver does not seem to recognize, it is a cathedral hush. All the cab drivers we get at ten forty-five in the evening are sports, bon vivants, and raconteurs. One man the other night had a really tantalizing story about how he had to drive a burro to Riverdale. My only question is, where are all these gay blades during the six-o'clock rush hour in front of the Biltmore?

Once my husband is at his desk, he sets to work immediately, furiously consulting the dozens of penciled notes he makes during the show on intricately folded yellow paper. I glanced at the notes one evening and the first one said, "Why he shedelepp so often, especially in the speckeldiff?" I only hope he doesn't lose them some night. They might be found, and how would he prove they're not atomic secrets?

Anyway, while he's working, I'm not idle. I sit at an empty desk and read back copies of *The Hollywood Reporter* and draw horses. Sometimes I chat with bright young copyboys, who, it would appear, are serious students of the theater. The only difficulty is that they want to discuss Toller and Strindberg, whereas, at that hour of the night, I want to discuss Lindsay and Crouse. Occasionally someone wants to know why Kafka's *The Trial* is never done. Of course I have no figures here, but I have this feeling that it is done all the time. Maybe not.

Then, too, my husband sometimes consults me while he's writing a review. A hoarse shout will come over the partition, "Hey, how do you spell desiccate?" But this is patently ridiculous. If I could spell desiccate I would long since have assumed my rightful place in the world of letters.

An interesting aspect of dramatic criticism is that an actor can remember his briefest notice well into senescence and long after he has forgotten his phone number and where he lives. Thus it is quite a common occurrence for a critic to meet a nice young thing at a party and have her say, "Oh, don't you remember me? You saw me in *The Squared Circle* four years ago and you said I was 'earnest, effortful, and inane.'" Well, that's what makes cocktail parties so interesting.

On the other hand, most people who read more than one drama critic quickly forget who said what. We had an interesting demonstration of this one summer in London when we met a film actress who was chatting wisely and wittily about the theater until she reached the subject of a certain musical comedy. Then she declared with some heat, "I don't know what gets into Brooks Atkinson sometimes. Do you know what he said about that show?"

Whereupon she proceeded to recite from memory two paragraphs, word for word, semicolon for semicolon, of Walter's review. After the brief hush that followed this recital, I murmured, "Did Brooks really say that? Well, there you are—even Homer nods," the while my husband made little clicking sounds indicating that he was too shocked even to comment.

In common with the wives of other critics, I am so anxious to indicate that I in no way influence or attempt to influence my husband's opinions that I rather overstate the case and perhaps give the impression that we never discuss the theater at all—that our conversation is exclusively concerned with stories about our adorable children and the cute way they spilled 3-in-1 oil all over the living-room rug, interspersed occasionally with highlights from the world of sport.

The fact is that we have many an intelligent discussion of the play coming home on the train, at which time I have a carbon copy of the review to read. A typical opening gambit in such a conversation would be: "Boy! If *that* was a magical, memorable performance . . . !"

Don Brown's Body

After one of those evenings in the theater, an evening that happened to be devoted to a staged reading of Stephen Vincent Benet's *John Brown's Body*, I worked out my own little entertainment:

The curtain—if there is one—rises on a vast blue sky, relieved only by a chaste white balustrade in the foreground. A chorus of pretty girls and pretty boys is seated on folding chairs at one side. Before them, and menacingly near us, stand four lecterns on which scripts that no one will ever look at have been placed. The readers enter, with a dignity that will be theirs to the very end. The first reader begins, however, with a shy, boyish smile.

FIRST READER

In recent years there has been a marked revival of interest in the art of dramatic reading. We have dipped into the treasures of Charles Dickens, George Bernard Shaw, and Stephen Vincent Benet, among others. Yet there is an entire facet of our culture that has never been tapped. I am speaking now of that special genre known as detective fiction, where, as some authorities have pointed out, the interest has lately shifted from "who done it" to "wit what." There has also been an increasing emphasis on violence and—the woman across the hall has an awfully good word for it—

He glances at a note in his hand

—sex.

As every schoolboy knows, many of these works were written not to be read, but to be inhaled. With this in mind, we offer you *Don Brown's Body*—by Mickey Spillane.

WOMAN READER

Mike Hammer's tune.

FIRST READER

I'm Mike Hammer. I don't take slop from nobody. Like this guy. He ankles up to me on the street. He opens his big ugly yap, and says—

THIRD READER

Pardon me. Have you the correct time?

MIKE

So I kicked him in the mouth and his teeth dropped all over the sidewalk like marbles. Like I say—I don't take slop from nobody.

THIRD READER

Sally Dupre's tune.

WOMAN READER

I know I'm just a broad, Mike. I'm a round-heeled babe with a dirty record. My type comes two thousand dollars a dozen. But I'm clean inside, Mike.

MIKE

I picked her up in Jimmy's bar. She was lying there, so I picked her up. She was in pretty bad shape.

CHORUS

Chanting in unison
Sally Dupre, Sally Dupre,
Her eyes were neither black nor gray,
They were black and blue.

MIKE

I was on a case. When I'm on a case nobody or nothin' takes my mind off it for a minute.

We went up to her place.

She lives on the St. Regis roof. Sooner or later some wise guy of a cop is gonna find her up there and make her come down. But tonight was ours. She opened her good eye. There was no mistaking that invitation. Her lips were like fresh ketchup on a white tablecloth. My heart was throbbing like a stubbed toe.

She was waiting for me, a hungry thing. Now there was nothing between us but us. I spoke:

"You were a member of the Carney gang at the time that One-Finger Matthews put the finger on Soft-Spot Sullivan, who was at that time going under the name of Samuel X. Sullivan and who knifed Maurie Magnusson in the back of the Easy-Way Garage. The *QE 2* docked at eleven forty-six on the twenty-third, and Joey Jacobson was found in an abandoned milk truck two years later. What do you know about Don Brown?"

Her eyes found mine. Down below, the great idiot city went its old familiar way: birth and death, love and lust, Sonny and Cher. A long time afterwards she spoke:

WOMAN READER

Don *Who* Brown?

MIKE

That took me back. The first time I saw Don Brown was in the locker room at the "Y." He was in my locker.

CHORUS

Not in the good green fields, Don Brown.
Not in the loamy earth, Don Brown,
Under the spike-eared corn—
But in a locker, a long green locker, a lonely long green
locker
At the "Y."

MIKE

He'd been dead about three weeks then, judging from the condition of my tennis racket. I reached for a butt. I was pretty cut up.

CHORUS

Ah, yes, Mike Hammer—ah, yes.
But you were not as cut up as Don Brown was cut up.

MIKE

Who'd be next? I wondered. I looked in the next locker. Bill Brown was in that one. One thing was clear. Somebody was going to have to clean out those lockers.

I went out to the street.

CHORUS

Tramp . . . tramp . . . tramp . . .

MIKE

I passed this kid sucking a lollipop. Don Brown dead, and him sucking a lollipop. I rammed it down his throat. I hate injustice.

I walked for hours.

CHORUS

Don Brown's body lies a molderin' at the "Y"—

WOMAN READER

Don Brown's song.

THIRD READER

Wish you were here, wish you were here, wish you were here . . .

MIKE

I went back to the place I call home.

CHORUS

Tramp . . . tramp . . . tramp . . .

MIKE

The Hairy Arms, Apartment 3-D. I put the key in the lock. I opened the door. A gun smashed into my skull. Heavy boots ground into my spine. A pair of fists tore into my throat.

I saw something coming towards me. It was a fly swatter. This was no ordinary killer.

I knew then they were after me. And I knew one other thing, as they threw me over the third-floor railing: they were afraid of me.

I hit the second-floor landing.

I hit the first-floor landing.

I hit the cigar counter.

The girl behind the cigar counter looked up. There was no mistaking that invitation. She was naked beneath that reversible. She reversed the reversible. She was still naked. A long time later she spoke:

WOMAN READER

Bring me your tired, your poor, your huddled masses . . .

MIKE

I went to the office.

CHORUS

Tramp . . . tramp . . . tramp . . .

MIKE

My secretary, Josephine, was there. She looked up.

She was mad for me. I tried to be good to Josephine. I used to let her kiss my fingertips every once in a while. But now I carefully put my fingers in my pockets. Josephine would have to wait. There was only one thing on my mind these days.

"What's new on the Don Brown case?"

JOSEPHINE

I checked this morning. He's still there.

CHORUS

Nothing is changed, Don Brown. Nothing is changed.

But men are beginning to notice.

In the locker room at the "Y," they're beginning to notice.

It will grow stronger, Don Brown!

MIKE

We went outside.

CHORUS

Tramp . . . tramp . . . tramp . . .

MIKE

My heap was parked at the curb. I had a strong feeling it was wired. I asked Josephine to get in first. She put her foot on the starter.

Boy!

CHORUS

Come Josephine in my flying machine
As *up* we go, *up* we go . . .

MIKE

A long time afterward, she came down. I didn't wait. I knew Josephine. She'd pull herself together.

The patrol wagon went by. I thought of Sally. I called her up.

"Sally?"

WOMAN READER

Mike?

MIKE

I'm sweatin' for you, Sally.

WOMAN READER

I'm clean inside, Mike.
Both hang up.

MIKE

We could talk forever and never get it all said. I was still in the booth when the phone rang. On a hunch, I answered it. It was the killer. He laughed at me. That was all. Laughed at me.

I was no longer a man, I was an ugly thing. I wanted to get his skull between my hands and crack it like a cantaloupe. I wanted to scramble that face like a plate of eggs. I wanted to work him over till his blood ran the color of coffee. That's when it came to me: I hadn't had any breakfast.

I was going into Schrafft's when this tomato waltzes by. She was a tomato surprise. A round white face with yellow hair poured over it like chicken gravy on mashed potatoes. Her raccoon coat was tight in all the right places.

I watched her as she disappeared into a doorway. She shut the door. There was no mistaking that invitation.

I followed her in. Inside it was inky darkness. I groped my way across the room. Her lips were warm. Her nose was warm. She barked.

I spoke.

"Down, dammit, down!"

I went back to my place, good old 3-D. I no sooner opened the door than they were at me again. This time I was ready. I smashed my eye into his fist, I forced my ribs into his boot, and the first thing he knew I was flat on my back in the hall. He was standing above me now. He spoke.

THIRD READER

Look, buddy. You do this every night. This is *not* your apartment. You're in 3-D. This is 3-A.

MIKE

After that, everything was like a nightmare. I was sitting in this bar with Sally

"What'll you have?"

WOMAN READER

Straight Clorox. I'm clean inside, Mike.

MIKE

Then I was in this strange room with this strange blonde. How did I get here? What kind of a girl was she?

CHORUS

Tramp . . . tramp . . . tramp . . .

MIKE

Then I was in another strange room with another strange blonde. She had just stepped from the tub. There she was as God made her, a mess.

Our eyes were riveted together. I took a step towards her. I took another. I fell over the coffee table.

The next thing I knew they had me surrounded. Blondes, brunettes, redheads . . .

THIRD READER

There was no mistaking that invitation.

WOMAN READER

Mike Hammer was a man in a million.

Mike Hammer had the strength of ten.

Mike Hammer spoke.

MIKE

No, girls—*no!*

CHORUS

Astonished and exultant

"Glory, glory, hallelujah! . . ."

With a swell in the music, the lights fade.

How to Talk to a Baby

Celebrities don't intimidate me. It's babies that intimidate me. Or at least it's with babies that I make such a fool of myself. I'm so afraid I won't make a good impression on them, I'm so afraid they won't be able to place me the next time we meet that I talk too much—and with the frenzied animation of a nervous guest on "The Tonight Show." I also rattle bracelets to get the baby's attention, and wave small objects in the air, and burst into snatches of song. This is naturally very boring to the baby, who fastens me with a glance of such unblinking, such crystalline intensity that I know perfectly well what he's thinking. He's thinking "What *is* the matter with that poor soul?"

I find that I have more success when I affect indifference, because babies, like some men, seem to like you better if you are unattainable. I remember a time when I marched into Katharine Josephine's room and pretended to be surprised to discover that somebody was occupying the bassinet. "Don't tell me *you're* still here!" I exclaimed. "Listen, kid, do you know what day it is? It's the ninth, you're four months old, and you're not getting any younger, let me tell you. These are your best months and what are you doing with them? Nothing. For your information, babies a lot smaller than you are already out advertising North Star Blankets and you just lie here fluttering your fingers!"

She seemed to hang fascinated on my every word, and then

broke out a battery of smiles, oh, a waterfall of smiles—crinkles, wrinkles, dimples, and little gurgling sounds. Naturally, I went to pieces and said the wrong thing. "Oh, goodness!" I said. "You really are the dearest little creature, the sweetest little thing, Mommy's little lamb chop." That did it. All smiles stopped, and it was clear to me our revels now were ended. Immediately she assumed that pained and aloof expression that makes her look like Queen Elizabeth I bidding farewell to the troops. I had to snub her for an entire hour before she'd speak to me again.

It's an interesting fact that babies who won't smile for love or money will smile for vegetables. And the messier the vegetable the more they will smile. A baby with a mouth full of strained spinach is almost guaranteed to smile from ear to ear, while green rivulets ooze down into his neck and all over his wrapper. Now most people make the foolish mistake of trying to scoop the spinach back into the baby's still-open mouth. They also try to reason with the baby: "No, no, honey, don't laugh anymore, Mommy's got spinach all over her stockings and—no, oh *no,* not on the rug!"

The best procedure at this moment is to be silent. You are not going to get the baby to see things your way. And anything you do say will merely indicate how completely you have lost your grip on the situation. For instance, to say "Okay, I hope you're satisfied, it's just five minutes since you had a bath and now you're a mess, a complete mess!" will cause you to lose dignity. And since the baby will find that remark pretty hilarious it will cause him to lose more spinach.

Some adults who find themselves uneasy in the silence have discovered that it is helpful to intone, rhythmically, the names of the entire family: "Here's a bite for Grandma, here's a bite for Daddy, here's a bite for Christopher." If the family should be small and the dish of Pablum large, the list can be padded by adding the names of all the deliverymen. A friend of mine has worked out a variant of this for her little boy. With the first bite of food she says, "Open up the garage doors, here comes the Chevy, here comes the Cadillac," and so forth. That child took the game so seriously that eventually he would eat only foreign cars.

But any method is better than the method I used on our first baby. In those days I believed in enthusiasm and the hard sell. I also believed that if a baby missed a single meal it died or something. And I tried to conceal my panic with spurious cheer. "Oooh, yummy, yummy," I would say, sounding like some manic commercial. "Oooh, what have we got *here?* Tasty, tasty Pablum. Oooh, I wish *I* could have some of this delicious Pablum." Then, to indicate that all was on the level, I would actually eat a spoonful or two. Even when I didn't gag, my expression would give the whole show away. In due time that baby found out who was in charge. He was in charge.

Now, light-years later, I find I get better results with total candor. I put the cards on the table with the Pablum. "That's right, honey," I say, "it tastes just like library paste. But remember this —it's full of niacin, thiamin, and riboflavins. Furthermore, you really don't have any taste buds yet, so what's the difference? Come on, let's get it right down the hatch!" This seems to work just fine, and you have the satisfaction of knowing that you are building a relationship that is not based on a tissue of lies.

By the way, many people make the false assumption that because a baby can't speak he can't hear. As a result, when confronted with an infant, any infant, they raise their voices and speak very distinctly, as though they were ordering a meal in a foreign language. "Oh, is this the baby?" they ask. (Who else would be sitting in the middle of that playpen—George C. Scott?) "Well, she doesn't look like any of the others, does she?"

A baby will put up with a certain amount of this, but sometimes the remarks get too personal. We once had a visitor who stared at Katharine Josephine (by that time Kitty, a ripe sixteen months) and, after a minute, said, "Walter, I think she's going to have your nose." Kitty was quite properly irate. She immediately stopped winding her musical egg. And she wouldn't smile. And she wouldn't say "Hi!" on her pink plastic telephone. She wouldn't do anything, and who could blame her?

By contrast, her godfather dropped in that same night. He noticed that she was wearing her Bavarian dress with the white ruffled blouse and all the petticoats, and he said, "Hey, didn't I see you in *The Sound of Music?*" Well, we couldn't shut her up. She let loose a volley of pear-shaped vowel sounds, with a few

consonants here and there. And, while I don't pretend to understand her exactly, I'm sure she was explaining that they really
wanted her for the part and that it was all a matter of conflicting
schedules. The point is that little girls of sixteen months appreciate compliments just as much as great big girls of forty.

Another thing: since a conversation between an infant and a
grown person is hardly likely to be memorable, most adults don't
remember what they have said to the children. But sometimes
children remember. When our Gregory was about two years old,
he had the power and the velocity of a torpedo. So the simple
business of taking off his clothes and putting on his pajamas
turned into a chore roughly equivalent to the landing of a two-
hundred-pound marlin. It wasn't just that he wouldn't lie down
or sit down or even that he always pulled his arms out of the
tops of his pajamas at the precise moment you were sticking his
feet into the bottoms of his pajamas. The real problem was that
when you tried to put your arms around him in order to snap the
various snappers, he shot into the air like a fountain, tumbling
over lamps and spilling baby oil all over the wallpaper.

It wasn't to be expected that I would remain silent during this
ordeal. But I honestly didn't know what I had been saying until
I listened to Gregory one night after he *had* gone to bed. He was
muttering something over and over to himself. What he was
muttering was "Oh, my God—your poor *mother!*" We can't have
that. I mean I guess we can't have that.

While admitting that adults frequently make unfortunate remarks to babies, it has to be said that babies, too, can make mistakes. Last week Kitty made a real whopper. Her vocabulary is,
of course, limited. But she can pronounce the names of all her
brothers as well as the name of the man who comes to fix the
dishwasher. Also the name of the nice girl who comes on Friday
to clean. "Bessie there," she says with winning clarity. She can
also say "Mommy" and "Daddy," of course. The only problem is
that sometimes she calls me "Mommy" and sometimes she calls
me "Daddy." And there is no excuse for this because my husband
and I don't look the least bit alike. Personally, I have never let
myself get touchy about the matter because I figured that down
the years it would be cleared up. But not everybody is so high-
minded. My husband, for instance, reacts to being called

"Mommy" by making unworthy remarks like "Okay, wait'll she comes to *me* for an allowance."

As I say, I was philosophical until last Thursday. I went to pick her up after her nap. She smiled the kind of smile that would give you hope even in February. Then she held up her arms and said, very distinctly, "Hi, little fella."

Now, honestly.

My Twenty-one Minute Shape-up Program

I am one of those tiresome people who *will* accept a fifth canapé while protesting to the empty air "I've got to stop eating these things, I'm too fat now." Usually, when my mutterings are overheard, there is some loyal soul at hand to console me. "It's all right," this philosopher says. "You're tall, you can carry it."

I don't know why I have ever allowed myself to be soothed by this observation. When you come to think of it, it doesn't make any sense at all. Carry it *where?* I can't carry it in my two hands in front of me. And all the other places are unsuitable and unbecoming.

However, the day came when a True Friend placed herself between me and a platter of stuffed eggs and said, pleasantly but firmly, "You *are* too fat and I am sending you a copy of *Miss Craig's Twenty-one Day Shape-up Program.*" Actually, I knew all about this book because two ladies in my neighborhood who have applied themselves to the text have, in just a couple of months, become so slender and so supple that I'm not sure I quite like them anymore.

In any case, my copy arrived last week and the reason I didn't start then is because we had a lot of leftover potato salad to use up. Subsequently we have had houseguests. I can't exercise when I have houseguests. I can't even read the morning paper in the evening when I have houseguests. And since I believe that others may find themselves in this same boat (rocking, rocking, and beginning to sink), I have devised my own twenty-one minute shape-up program:

1. *Exercise for the Nose. 2 minutes.* Stand in front of a good mirror. Press your upper teeth down over your lower lip until the entire lower lip is covered with teeth. Lift your nose in the air and wrinkle it until you look rather like a rabbit. Stare at this image for a minute. Now allow your face to relax. You will be forcibly struck with the improvement in your appearance now that you no longer look like a rabbit.

2. *Exercise for Scruffy Elbows. 3 to 5 minutes.* (If you can't tell whether or not your elbows are scruffy, ask somebody.) Cut a lemon in half. Scoop out most of the pulp. Heat a little olive oil in a small saucepan. Pour the oil into the lemon cups. Then rest your elbows in the lemon cups. The whole point of this procedure is to give you a little rest. For, while you are actually in the lemon cups, you can't do anything else whatsoever. You can't even file your nails because the least little jiggling will cause the oil to ooze out all over the table. If one of the children comes in and asks you what you are doing, refuse to answer. For those who worry about such things, I have been assured that this exercise is in no way injurious to the elbows.

3. *Facial Mask for Toning Up the Complexion. 4 minutes, 30 seconds.* Make a facial mask with one cup of butterscotch ice cream and three tablespoons of baby oil. (The purpose of the baby oil is to keep you from licking the ice cream.) Apply this liberally all over the face. (You may wish to use rubber gloves because it's pretty cold.) Stand close over a sink, because it does drip. After the ice cream has completely melted off your face (the time varies with the heat of the bathroom), rinse your face with lukewarm water and clean up the floor. This should be very beneficial for your circulation. And, what is more to the point, after several applications you will find that you no longer wish to eat ice cream in any flavor, which certainly is a step in the right direction.

4. *Exercise for Abdomen and Upper Arms. Time: I'll just have to give you some leeway here, it could take all day if you're unlucky.* Find an old bathing suit that is a size too small for you. If it should turn out that your new, or current, bathing suit is a size too small for you, you will of course save the time it takes to hunt all over the attic for an old one. Put on the bathing suit. And—this is important—do not get any help in closing the zipper. There is no exercise so efficacious for the upper arms as the effort involved in closing the back zipper of a tight bathing suit. Many women report that before they complete the last five inches of the zipper they are gasping heavily. This is understandable and also very good for the upper abdomen muscles. If you have any doubt about this, just place your hand gently on your upper abdomen and give a loud gasp. You will sense that the abdomen is definitely doing something.

5. *Exercise for the Upper Thigh. 4 minutes and not a second longer.* Holding firmly to the two sides of the refrigerator, raise your right leg behind you until it forms a right angle with your body. Now raise it higher still until the whole leg throbs. Repeat, using left leg. Continue this exercise until you have reached the state of mind where it is perfectly clear to you that you would prefer to have flabby legs rather than put yourself through this kind of thing. Now, open the refrigerator and make yourself a small snack, which you are certainly entitled to. And, speaking of snacks, do you find it heartening as I do to know that even chocolate milk shakes are not so high in calories or so fattening as an equal amount of cod-liver oil? Once you have grasped that fact, you will not keep loose bottles of cod-liver oil lying about the house.

6. *10-minute Reading Interval.* Early in the week tear out of newspapers and magazines articles which you judge to have a special interest for you. *I* gravitate to those pieces which remind me that I am not the only person in this world who has problems. For instance, a piece that made me more willing to hoe my own lonely row came from a British weekly. It was captioned "Liz and Burton Plagued with Problems as They Refurbish Yacht." Now those who have never tried to decorate a yacht will

make light of the difficulties, but I assure you it was hell. The paneling, brought over piece by piece from Florence, didn't fit. Workmen dropped a large onyx table on the gangplank and it was badly chipped. (The table; God knows what happened to the gangplank.) Worst of all, the inlaid carpeting had been entirely installed when it was discovered that the manufacturer had forgotten to have it Scotch-guarded or Welsh-guarded or whatever it is you do to make the world safe from irresponsible terriers.

This last oversight was discovered, or—to be more explicit—revealed, by one of the Burton dogs short minutes after the last carpet tack was nailed down. I am eagerly awaiting the follow-up story. Did the Burtons get rid of the carpeting or the dogs? (One supposes they made the usual compromise and simply rearranged the furniture.)

Another item that brought me cheer was a short piece that appeared in our local newspaper. "Heart Attacks Rare Among the Mentally Ill," the headline ran. Reading on eagerly, I learned that mentally ill persons are not sufficiently well organized to react to stress. Being unable to grasp what a mess we're all in, they do not worry. And it is this lack of worry that reduces heart strain. You didn't know that, did you? However, the mentally ill *are* subject to respiratory ailments. The article doesn't say why, but I assume that mentally ill persons just don't have sense enough to come in out of the rain. Now you will wonder why I take heart from this theory, or why, indeed, I identify with mental cases. I'll tell you. The simplest definition of a mentally ill person is—to me—the most acceptable: i.e., a person who does not function properly in the environment, "one who does not cope." I do not cope. Of course, I cope every so often, but there are whole days, even weeks, when my behavior is, to put the best face on things, eccentric. Last Monday it took me two hours to find my car in the parking lot in front of Korvette's in Scarsdale. One reason for this is that Korvette's has an enormous lot. Another is that I was looking for a beat-up white Chevy, whereas, it turned out, I was that day driving a beat-up brown Buick. This became clear as the store closed and the other cars drove away.

I also got very wet, as a sharp rain started up during my

search. Knowing myself to be subject to respiratory ailments, I decided to take a hot bath and hot toddy when I returned home. But first I set the oven to 325 and put in the leg of lamb for dinner. I returned to the kitchen two hours later, feeling much restored, and found that I had neglected to turn the oven On to Bake. Do you see why I feel so certain that I will never have a heart attack?

End of Reading Interval. It's good to stretch the mind as well as the body once in a while.

7. *Exercise for the Will Power. Time: 1 minute for every 10 pounds you are overweight, considering 4 minutes as an absolute ceiling.* Still wearing that tight bathing suit, stand in front of a full-length mirror. Turn so that you are in profile. Lower your chin until it almost reaches your collarbone. Let your arms dangle. Allow the stomach muscles to sag completely. (Your average stomach muscle is only too willing to sag even without permission.) In this sorry posture, gaze into the mirror until tears of self-pity actually begin to well up in your eyes. Some women will be reminded of those last troubled weeks before the twins were born. I myself think of a horrendously overendowed Samoan woman whose picture appeared in an early issue of the *National Geographic.* Remember when you were a size twelve, and everyone said you looked just like Loretta Young? (Oh, time, go backward in your flight!)

But never mind the past. You are here eyeball to eyeball with reality. And there is no use recriminating. You've got to change the menu. Of course it is easier and cheaper to feed the kids what they really like, which is spaghetti and macaroni and chili and lasagna and large leaden cheeseburgers brought in from a roadside stand. But your path lies elsewhere. Are you a woman or are you a mouse? Are you a molehill or are you a mountain? All right, we're not going to cry and we're not going to panic. We're going to take steps and not be like those women who, as my husband says, watch their weight constantly. They don't do anything about it, they just watch it.

8. *Exercise to Restore Lost Nerve. Time: add up all previous times and subtract them from the basic 21 minutes; if you find*

that you are already over 21 minutes, so do I. Remove that ghastly
bathing suit and put on a garment that is a lot too big for you.
Any old maternity dress is good for the purpose. And if you can't
find one, put on your husband's bathrobe. If his bathrobe *isn't* a
lot too big for you, I am afraid you are in deep trouble and I
don't think I can help you. I don't think even Miss Craig can
help you. You get a little of that weight off and come back to see
us then.

Tales Out of School:
The Sandwich Crisis

I hear the most disquieting rumors that our school system is going from pot to worse and that all over America there are twelve-year-old boys who write seperate and Filladelphia and think an hypotenuse is a baby hippo. I gather it's a scandal, an absolute scandal. And if I don't seem properly irate about the whole matter, it's because I'm so grateful to schools.

I mean, think of those teachers keeping forty or fifty small children interested and occupied for five hours a day. Well, maybe they're not interested and maybe they're not occupied, but the point is they're *there*. They're not in the kitchen making flour paste or in the living room carefully writing their initials on the coffee table.

It's considerations like these that make me perfectly willing to find out what an hypotenuse is and tell them. I can do that all right, and I can do homework—up to but not including long division. What I can't seem to do is pack a school lunch.

To begin with, I always pack lunches the night before, because in the early morning I can't remember how many children I have and naturally go wildly wrong on the number of sandwiches. At one o'clock in the morning I am in full possession of my faculties.

What I am not in possession of is something to make a sand-

wich with, unless you count that jar of what I *think* is apple butter and which I know we brought with us when we moved from
New Rochelle.

I lean on the refrigerator door for twenty minutes and stare at
the unlovely interior as though it were *Upstairs, Downstairs.*
Meanwhile all of the events of the past six months swim before
me. There is not an item on the crowded shelves that isn't rich
with bittersweet memories. There are five quart jars of mayonnaise that evidently were on sale sometime or other. There are
no fewer than six plastic "space savers" (now empty), and no
wonder there's no space in that icebox. There are two half bottles of club soda, improperly capped, and a sinister-looking turkey carcass that must have been there since Christmas (it *can't*
have been there since Thanksgiving). There are also a couple of
cans of evaporated milk which they say you can keep in the
cupboard, but I don't know that I believe that. After all, it's
milk, isn't it?

Another woman could make a tasty sandwich spread by mixing evaporated milk and mayonnaise with some curry powder.
But I lack the dash for this kind of experimentation. For that
matter I lack the curry powder, and—what is more to the point—
I lack qualities of leadership. Yes, I do. I'm an unfit mother and a
rotten housekeeper, as shiftless and improvident as a character
out of *God's Little Acre.*

What lends particular poignance to this moment is the fact
that I was in a large chain store that very afternoon and could
easily have bought some spiced ham. Of course I didn't actually
see any spiced ham when I bought those nylon stockings, a
philodendron plant, and two long-playing records, but surely
they had some tucked away someplace. I know what I'm going
to do for lunches next week, and there's no use talking me out of
it. I'm going to go to a delicatessen on Monday afternoon and
buy five quarts of lobster salad and some baked Virginia ham. Of
course it will be expensive and we will have to economize on
dinner all week by having canned chili and baked beans, but it
will be worth it.

But to get back to this moment. Let's say, just for the sake of
argument, that I find something to put in the sandwiches.
(There's always that can of plovers' eggs somebody gave us as a

joke last Easter.) The next problem is to find something to put
the sandwiches in. I know you can buy sandwich bags, but I
never feel right about that when, after all, they give you all those
nice little brown bags free with lettuce and bananas. But try and
find a little brown bag at one o'clock in the morning. I usually
wind up packing a sandwich, an apple, and two cookies in a bag
that formerly held a twenty-six-pound turkey. Even after I tear
off the top half of the bag and fold it down, it still looks as if it
contained a painter's overalls.

Now there's the little item of milk money. In the school our
children attend milk costs eight cents. Four children times four
bottles of milk should give you a figure of thirty-two cents, or
one quarter, one nickel, and two pennies. Break it down that
way and one could just possibly locate thirty-two cents. In
theory, the oldest boy could take the money and pay for the four
bottles of milk when all assemble in the lunchroom. In practice, I
have only to mention this eminently sensible plan to uncork such
tears and lamentations from the other three as haven't been
heard since the time I gave that large empty crate to the trash-
man, not knowing it was a clubhouse.

I don't know whether the others are ashamed to be seen with
Chris in the lunchroom because his shirttail is always out, or
whether they are afraid that he will skip town with the thirty-
two cents. All I know is that I have to find four nickels and
twelve pennies, which means rifling through all my summer
purses, which are now in the attic. This is further complicated on
days when Col needs fifteen cents for a box of crayons and Gilbert needs thirty-five cents for a new speller. I'll be glad when
they raise the price of milk to ten cents. After all, they're entitled
to a profit like everybody else, and dimes—you can find dimes.

Another item that will have to be prepared while the children
sleep (along with the lunches) is a note to Johnny's teacher
explaining just precisely what ailed him when he was absent
from school last Tuesday, Wednesday, and Thursday. This will
be complicated by the fact that I don't remember his teacher's
name (Sister Mary Arthur was his teacher last year, but that's no
help) and I will have to address the note "Dear Teacher," which
reveals not only that I am woefully out of touch with my son but
clearly without even the most rudimentary interest in the fine

young woman who is molding his character. The next thing is that I haven't the least idea what ailed him last Tuesday. His eyes were glassy and he was burning up, just burning up, but I couldn't call the doctor because he didn't have a rash.

If the children are going to be sick anyway, I am always relieved to see spots. Anybody knows that you are within your rights to call a doctor if there's a rash. If, however, you are heedless enough to call the doctor just because your child has a temperature of 104 and you're frantic about him, you face the possibility that by the time the doctor arrives, a day after he's been called, the invalid will have a perfectly normal temperature and will be calmly engaged in making a tepee out of the bedclothes. The doctor may be perfectly polite (just keep him in bed for forty-eight hours) but he knows, and you know, that you're an idiot and a hysteric who thinks nothing of taking up a doctor's valuable time while all over the community genuine cases of chicken pox wait unattended.

But I am still left with that note to the teacher. And since I honestly don't know what blight was upon that boy, I will have to select an illness more or less out of the blue. This involves a nice balance of tone. Anything too casual suggests that I kept him home on a mere idle whim, perhaps to polish the silver. On the other hand I don't want to raise alarums by pretending that he was at death's door with diphtheria, which he is even now prepared to spread through the whole fourth grade. I usually settle for "stomach virus." That seems decently incapacitating without being too worrisome. I mean, anything in the stomach seems private and contained and wouldn't appear to invite the scrutiny of the Public Health Department.

Once I have the note and the milk money and lunches, I have only to locate hats, jackets, rubbers, schoolbooks, and underpants. Now, I buy underpants the way some people buy gin—recklessly, extravagantly—and I secrete them at various key points throughout the house. As a result, I can always find eleven clean pairs of underpants in size eight. Of course there won't be a single pair in size four or size twelve, which means that I will have to go wash out three pairs, just exactly like those feckless, unthinking mothers who never buy underpants.

I know it's an admission of failure to say that I have to set out the boys' clothes for them. I understand that in well-regulated households the children perform these little services for themselves. Indeed, I have heard, though I won't say that I believe it, that in various parts of this country there are nine-month-old infants who rinse out their own diapers.

What remarkable mothers these wee ones must have! I stand behind them every inch of the way. The only reason I don't make our boys get everything ready for the morning is that I have sensitive eardrums and, in the morning, a nervous stomach, and I find that I tend to become unhinged by the sobs of the doomed as they race up and down the stairs at a quarter to nine, hunting for left shoes and right mittens while announcing to the empty air, "I'm gonna be late and Sister'll *kill* me!"

To avoid this kind of thing and start the day sane, I do the amount of planning and co-ordinating that would be involved in landing two battalions in North Africa. So what happens? All four fly out the door, blessed silence descends—and then I look up to see Colin, who is inexplicably back and shouting frantically, "Quick, quick, the bus is waiting! I have to have an empty tomato can, eighteen inches of silver foil, and some Scotch tape. I'm making a lamp!"

One solution would be to tutor them all at home, but I think that's illegal. In any case, it's impossible. If Colin didn't go to school, *I'd* have to show him how to make a lamp.

Operation Operation

Obviously this is not the moment to be talking about operations when here we all are—in the very bloom of health. But these are troubled times, and there are people in St. Vincent's Hospital today who, as recently as yesterday, didn't know they *had* a spinal disk. The thing to do, I say, is be prepared, bone up, get the facts so that your stay in the hospital will be the jolly, satisfying interlude it ought to be.

I don't know whether or not I am speaking for convalescents everywhere, but I can tell you that *my* big mistake when I go to the hospital is being too cheerful. I arrive the day before the operation and, while it would be stretching things to suggest that on this occasion I feel fit, I at least feel human. So I try to be agreeable. Agreeable nothing; I'm adorable to a point just short of nausea. With my gay sayings and my air of quiet self-deprecation, I creep into the heart of one and all.

"Yes," I murmur to the night nurse, "I did ring for you an hour ago, but that's *perfectly* all right." And I reassure the orderly who forgot to bring my dinner tray with a blithe "Don't worry about it, I'm not the least bit hungry and besides I have these delicious cherry cough drops."

But then the morrow comes, and with it my operation. As I'm wheeled back from the recovery room it becomes absolutely clear that, while the operation was a great success, I am a total failure. I feel completely, utterly, unspeakably miserable, and I see no reason why any member of the staff should be kept in ignorance of this sorry state of affairs. I ring bells, buzz buzzers, snap at nurses, and generally behave in a manner that can best be described as loathsome.

Of course, the nurses have seen postoperative cases before, but clearly they expected more of *me*. It's as though June Allyson had been transformed into the Bride of Frankenstein right before their eyes. And they feel, not unreasonably, that they have been betrayed. As a result, the whole staff gives me approximately the same brisk, gingerly attention they would bestow on an old bandage. Even at the end of the fourth day—when I'm once again feeling prosocial and want to kiss and make up—they will have none of me.

The best solution to this problem, short of being a good little soldier all the time, is to be a teensy bit curt when you first arrive. Don't pose as an Eva Marie Saint. Show your true colors. Keep your tone brisk. Then there will be no unpleasant shocks later.

And there are other steps you can take. Actually, to cope with ordinary hospital routine you really ought to be in good physical condition. Since this is hardly practical—you wouldn't be in the hospital if you were in good physical condition—you can do the next best thing: be mentally alert, be systematic. Remember: if they have rules, *you* have rules.

Rule One: *Refuse to be bullied.* It is the custom in most hospitals for the night nurse to wake all her patients before she goes off duty at six o'clock in the morning and present each of them with a basin of lukewarm water and a bar of soap. Then, a few seconds later, the incoming day nurse rushes in and takes everybody's temperature. This is a very sensible procedure because most people say they notice a very definite rise in temperature (together with a tendency to break down and sob) merely at being required to *look* at a basin of water at six o'clock in the morning, and the day nurse now has something concrete to put on her chart. She doesn't have to feel a failure.

How do you eliminate this dawn patrol? It's no use complaining to the nurse; she's met your type before. Any piteous explanations on your part like "Nurse, please, I haven't been to sleep at all, they just gave me a sedative half an hour ago and besides I'm clean, look, *clean!*" will only confirm her growing suspicion that you have no team spirit and, what's worse, no regard at all for personal daintiness.

After much trial and error I have worked out a rather neat little system for beating this game. I simply explain to the nurse that I am undergoing psychoanalysis for an old guilt trauma which dates back to the time when I was three years old and shoved my little sister into a golf bag. Ever since, I tell her, I've shown manifestations of the Lady Macbeth complex, an aberration in which the victim has a continuous and compulsive desire to wash her hands. Consequently, as a part of my therapy I am forbidden by my analyst to wash more than three times a day.

I am also working on a plan—it's unfortunately still in the blueprint stage—that would limit the number of times a nurse took your temperature to something reasonable, say eight or nine times in a single afternoon. At that, it's not really the frequency that's so maddening, it's the duration. What do you suppose there is in the Nightingale code that impels a nurse to put a thermometer in somebody's mouth just before she goes off to assist at an appendectomy? There you are, left like a beached submarine with this little periscope poking from your mouth while all about you life goes on, children are born, and you who have so much to contribute can do nothing but nibble on that damn little glass tube.

I just take it out the minute her back is turned and carefully replace it about five minutes before she returns. There's no real risk of detection, because a truly conscientious nurse will always stop at the linen closet on her way back and her approach will be heralded by the snatches of fascinating dialogue that float down the corridors:

"Listen, fourteen needs a top sheet."

"Nonsense, I gave fourteen two sheets yesterday."

"Okay, you tell that to fourteen."

The system is practically foolproof.

Rule Two: *Act your age.* One of the most difficult things to contend with in a hospital is the assumption on the part of the staff that because you have lost your gall bladder you have also lost your mind. Personally, I find it rather piquant to be treated like a four-year-old. ("Are we feeling any better? Shall we sit up and eat our nice lunch?") The only objectionable aspect of this constant use of the plural is that it leaves me with the feeling that I'm *two* four-year-olds. And speaking of food. In many hospitals you are given a menu the night before and allowed to check off your choices. Then the menu, with your signature on it, is delivered along with your dinner tray. This puzzled me at first. But actually it is a splendid idea. At least you know what you're eating. I mean you could get very depressed, and the food could get even colder, if you had to spend ten minutes trying to figure out just what that grayish-white thing lying on your plate could possibly be. What it looks like is a child's attempt to make a relief map of Florida. However, a quick glance at the menu clears up everything. It *is* broiled flounder.

Don't you think it's curious that all hospital food, not just fish and potatoes and boiled onions, but even hamburgers, looks grayish-white? And it all has a tantalizing aroma that suggests someone has added a pinch, just a touch, of Lysol. My guess is that they wash the food by throwing it in with the sheets. In any case everything is white but the canned pears, which are brown. But there is this to be said about the canned pears. They have more body and crunch than the pork chops.

To get back to the hospital staff. You do have to say one thing for these cuddly, nursey-knows-best disciplinarians: they're loyal, they complete the task assigned. Neither storm nor sleet nor gloom of night will stay them from the swift completion of their appointed rounds. This was brought home to me in a very real way during my last sojourn in the hospital when a dear little night nurse woke me from a sound sleep to give me a sleeping pill. Sometimes this business of hewing to the narrow line of duty produces results bordering on the miraculous. A writer I once heard about flew to Evanston to visit his eighty-year-old mother, who had just had an operation. Arriving, he met a nurse in the corridor, asked for a report on the patient, and was told that she had made all the routine objections to being put on her feet five days after the operation but that the staff had been firm, quite firm, and now the old lady was trotting around like everybody else. The writer was deeply impressed. "Good Lord," he said, "she hasn't walked in five years."

You see the point, don't you? If the lady in question had stood on her rights as an eighty-year-old, she'd still be sitting pretty in that rocking chair, where she wanted to be.

Rule Three: *Get the facts.* It seems to me that too many people accept hospital routine with cowlike apathy, whereas a little intellectual curiosity would be broadening to the patient and stimulating to the staff. Let's say that two interns approach you with a cartful of sinister-looking tubes and announce casually, "We're going to give you a Harris Flush."

Don't just lie there. Get the whole story. Who was Harris? What is this flush? When did Harris get the idea in the first place? Whatever happened to Harris?

Why shouldn't you ask a question from time to time? It's only quid pro quo. From the moment you get into that hospital coat and they lock away your shoes, there is a constant parade of cheery interns, all of them popping with more questions than Mike Wallace on a hot story. What was your mother's maiden name? Did you ever have any broken limbs? How old were you when you had chicken pox? If there is anything more striking than their fascination with that attack of measles you had in 1947, it's their total disinterest in that ruptured appendix which explains your presence here at this moment.

My father spent some time in a hospital a couple of years ago, and he began by being very patient and co-operative about answering all the routine questions. At the end of an hour's inquisition the intern asked him how old *his* father was when he died. Dad explained, with pardonable pride, that his father had died at the age of ninety-five. The intern looked up from his notes and inquired, with the air of one about to make a significant discovery, "What did he die of?" Whereupon my father exploded. "My God, man, he died because he was *ninety-five!*"

While interns may be lacking in other qualities, I want no one to tell me that they don't have a sense of humor. At first glance, this sense of humor may seem to be a trifle macabre. Actually, it fits perfectly into the cold, brilliant tradition of Ben Jonson, Dean Swift, and Charles Addams. Why else would an intern deposit a patient due for an eight-o'clock operation outside the operating-room door at seven-thirty, where she will be in a position to overhear the highlights of the preceding operation?

You can picture the scene, can't you? There is the patient, strapped to a cart, partially sedated, and feeling a good deal less than hearty. And through the transom comes a rough male voice saying, "Boy, I never thought it would spurt like *that*." Oh, there's no end to the possibilities for good, clean, sinister mirth.

Rule Four: *Look the part*. Let's not pretend that all the mistakes made in hospitals are made by the staff. I've known patients who have made beauts. As far as I'm concerned, there is nothing more idiotic than the spectacle of a woman just coming out of ether who immediately struggles into a fluffy pink bed jacket and ties a tender blue ribbon into her limp curls. Though scarcely able to lift an arm, she somehow succeeds in applying two layers of make-up before the stroke of visiting hour.

What happens? Cheery husband arrives, bearing an azalea, and announces, "Boy, honey, *you* look great, but let me tell you about the day I had!"

My own theory, which owes something—at least in spirit—to T. S. Eliot's principle of the "objective correlative," can be stated simply: if you feel terrible, look terrible. Save that blue ribbon until the happy moment arrives when you notice that you can comb even the back of your hair without becoming so faint that you have to lie down for half an hour afterward. In addition to the fact that by simulating recovery you get none of the sympathy which psychologists tell us is so necessary in convalescence, you run the further risk of being brought home from the hospital prematurely. There you'll be, back in the kitchen frying chicken, when everybody knows you need rest, rest, rest. So I say: no lipstick, forget about the cold cream, *let* those fine lines appear. Make it very difficult for your friends to tell you that they never saw you looking better in your life. With any luck, you may even startle an acquaintance into making an intelligent remark, like "Helen, you poor darling, you look ghastly—I bet you feel rotten, don't you?"

Rule Five: I'm sorry, but Rule Five seems to have gone out of my head. I have this sharp pain. Well, it's more like a twinge than a pain—but a *deep* twinge. Excuse me while I call my doctor.

How to Be a Collector's Item

I was reading another volume of collected letters last night, and it sent me right back to worrying about that old problem. On what basis do you decide that your friends are going to be famous, and that you ought to be saving their letters? Naturally, you save everything you get from Henry Kissinger and Simone De Beauvoir. But think of the smart boys who were saving Edna Millay's penciled notes when she was just a slip of a thing at Vassar. What gets me is how they *knew*.

As sure as you're born, I'm tossing stuff into the wastebasket this minute that Viking would give their eyeteeth for twenty years from now. But you can't save *everybody's* letters, not in that five-room apartment. When I was young and naïve, last year, I used to file away mail if it seemed interesting or amusing. But that was a trap. For instance, I have a marvelous letter from my cleaning man explaining how he happened to break the coffee table. But clearly this is a one-shot affair. *He'll* never be collected. You have to use a little sense about these things.

No doubt the safest procedure is to confine yourself to those friends who have demonstrated a marked literary bent. Even then, I wouldn't collect anybody who didn't seem a good risk. If you have a friend who is a novelist, you might play it very close to the ground and wait until he wins a Pulitzer Prize. Of course, by that time he may not be writing to *you* anymore. His correspondence will very likely be limited to letters to the American Broadcasting System explaining why it isn't convenient for him to be interviewed in prime time by Barbara Walters.

If you have a friend who is a playwright, it's simpler. You begin collecting *him* immediately after his first failure. As letter writers, playwrights are at the top of their powers at this moment. For color, passion, and direct revelation of character you simply can't beat a letter from a playwright who has just had a four-day flop.

And sometimes you can see a talent bloom before your very eyes. I have one friend, a poet, who used to write nice little things about "the icy fingers of November" and "the strange stillness of ashtrays after a party." I admit I didn't take him very seriously. But just last week he had a long poem in the *Partisan Review* and I didn't understand one word of it. Well, let me tell you, I'm saving his letters *now*.

You've got to keep your wits about you. It would be terrible to think you were brushing with greatness and didn't even notice. Oh, I'll admit there are times when you just can't be certain whether or not a friend has talent. In that case, just ask him. He'll tell you. But here, too, some discretion is necessary. For example, I don't give any serious attention to friends who get drunk at cocktail parties and announce they could write a better book than *The Other Side of Midnight*.

On the whole, I'd say that if you have a very promising circle of acquaintances who appear regularly in the newspapers announcing that their beer is Rheingold the dry beer and on the networks pouring out their little secrets to Johnny and Merv, your path as a collector is clear. Leave town. Otherwise, they won't have any opportunity to write to you.

But who am I trying to fool with all this nonsense? Obviously, I'm not really worrying about my friends' letters. What keeps me awake nights is the question of my letters, the ones *I* write. Are they being saved? Fat chance. I know my friends—it simply wouldn't enter their scatterbrained heads that they ought to be collecting me. And poor Doubleday, how will they ever scrape together a book? Well, they won't, that's all, if I don't take steps.

So I'm taking steps. From now on I keep carbons of every

word I write, and to hell with my cavalier pen pals. I've got a very decent sampling already:

Dear Mabel,

   Johnny doesn't seem to have a pair of socks without holes so tell him he is to wear one brown sock and one green sock. If he makes a fuss—tell him he can wear his long pants and they won't show. And another thing, very important—it's Gilbert's turn to drink his milk out of the beer mug.

                                                  Mrs. K.

Joan, dear—

   Well, we finally moved into Hilltop and what a magical place it is! High, high above the slate-blue waters of the Bay. We have our very own special, sad, sighing wind. It seems enchanted, and, we fancy, it is full of ghosts of Heathcliff and his Catherine. Promise you'll come and see us. We're always here.

                                                  Love,
                                                  Jean

The All-Season Window Corp.
Mount Vernon, N.Y.

Dear Sirs,

   Listen, are you going to come and put in those storm windows before we are blown out into the damn Sound? You said Monday and here it is Wednesday. We keep the thermostat up to eighty-five and still the toast is flying off the plates. And I had to put mittens on to type this.

   I hope to hear from you soon or never,

                                                  Jean Kerr

Dear Phyllis,

   Thank you, thank you, thank you—for an evening of pure bliss. Your book arrived yesterday morning and

it hasn't been out of my hands since. Much have I trav-
eled in realms of gold—but truly, Phyllis, this is a coup.
It *needed* to be said. As Sainte-Beuve once remarked,
"Je ne sois quois pour dire."

> Gratefully,
>
> J.

Mother darling,

I'm sorry I didn't write to you for the last three
weeks but we were picking out our Christmas card. I
think your slogan for the Runyon Cancer Fund is excellent. I would by all means mail it in to the contest. Not
much news here except that for some reason Joan
dropped in yesterday with her four horrible children—
three of whom had harmonicas. Oh, and did you read
Phyllis's book? Yap, yap, yap over the same material.
She seems to think she owns the seventeenth century.
No, I haven't seen Nick Nolte in *The Deep*, but if you
say it's a "must" I'll have to catch it.

> Love and kisses, J.

Treasurer
Alvin Theatre
New York, N.Y.

Dear Sir,

What do you mean by returning my check and saying there are no seats available for *Annie*? I asked for
two good seats on the first available Wednesday evening. Do you mean to suggest that down through the
echoing corridors of time there will *never* be a Wednesday night on which two seats will be available? I don't
wish to inject an empty note of pessimism but even you,
in the first flush and fever of success, must concede that
there is a possibility—at least in theory—that sometime,
say in 1982, you might be willing, even anxious, to sell
two seats.

In the meantime, I'm going to see *Chorus Line*.

> Outraged

Honey,

I seem to have lost my car key in Schrafft's so will you please take a cab and go pick up the car, which I left in front of Bloomingdale's in New Rochelle? It's in a no-parking area but I don't think that matters because it's raining and Peggy says they never check in the rain. There are a lot of groceries on the back seat and I don't know what you're going to do with the ice cream.

Love, J.

Funnell's Market

Dear Sirs,

Enclosed you will find a check for my February bill. However, I wish to draw your attention to one item which reads "Eighty cents' worth of spiced ham @ $1.25 cents." I am aware of rising costs and the resultant strain on independent grocers, but nevertheless when I order eighty cents' worth of spiced ham I expect to get it @ .80.

Yours cordially,
Jean Kerr

Dear Chris,

Daddy and I are going out to supper and I want you to pay attention to this list:

1. No "Disneyland" until your homework is done.
2. Get your bicycle and all those guns out of the bathroom.
3. Take a bath and be sure to put one cup of Tide in the water.
4. Don't wear your underwear or your socks to bed.
5. Col says you swallowed his whistle. If you didn't, give it back to him.

Love, Mommy

Mr. Ken McCormick
Doubleday & Co.
New York, N.Y.

Dear Ken,

Thank you for saying the letters were interesting,
and I shall, as you suggest, try Random House.

As always,
Jean

P.S.: Will you kindly return this letter?

I Just Stepped Out of *Vogue*

One night I saw a play called *And Things That Go Bump in the Night*. I won't tell you the plot. But it was about this young man who was so disturbed that he turned up in the second act wearing a dress.

I don't know what he was disturbed about. But I know what I was disturbed about. He was wearing my dress. I mean the one I had on. There it was, the same check, the same little pique collar, the same dreary buttons down the front. Except for the fact that I wear my hair shorter and I'm getting quite gray, we could have been twins.

My first instinct was to flee the premises immediately, perhaps on the pretext that I was suffering appendicitis pains. (After all, it is not widely known that I have already parted with my appendix.) But it occurred to me that if I dashed up the center aisle looking precisely like the leading man I might be regarded as part of the entertainment. So I just slouched down into my seat and pressed my purse up under my chin in the hope of covering at least the collar of that wretched dress. Thereafter I just waited until the entire audience had dispersed before I crept out under cover of darkness.

The incident left its mark on me. But it did serve to clear up an episode that had always been something of a mystery. Two years earlier I had been standing in the lobby of a hotel in Venice. Right next to me, waiting for her key, was a woman I recognized as the celebrated couturier Valentina. I noticed that she was looking exquisite in beige linen. I also noticed that she was staring at me in some perplexity. It was as though she were mentally snapping her fingers.

Thinking I understood the situation, I said, "Madame Valentina, we've never met, but my husband reviews plays and I see you very often at opening nights." And I told her my name. She smiled, and said very quietly, "Oh, I *knew* the name."

I didn't have the wit, or perhaps I didn't have the heart, to ask the next question: "What didn't you know?" So we bowed and parted gravely. Of course, it's all clear enough to me now. I was wearing that same damn brown check dress, with—oh, my God—blue tennis shoes. And Madame Valentina was asking herself "Where did she buy it? When? Why?"

Well, that's what happens when you try to hobnob. As for that particular dress, I have already taken a garden rake and some matches and burned it in the driveway. But the question remains: Why *do* I have all these horrible golfing-type dresses when, for one thing, I don't even golf? It's true that I am tall and hard to fit, but I don't think the salesladies I get even try. At the first sight of me they smile wanly (as though greeting the recently bereaved), waggle their heads, and say, "Oh, I'm afraid I wouldn't have a thing."

Now how can they tell that when I haven't even taken off my coat? Eventually, they brighten up just enough to ask, "Has Madam tried our sportswear section?" Passing the buck is what I call it. Anyway, that's my problem. I've been trying the sportswear section for twenty years.

Other women arrange their wardrobes with such *élan*. I have read that Mrs. Michelene Lerner keeps life-sized foam-rubber models of her figure in various fashion houses in Rome, Paris, London, and New York. Then, if she sees a picture of a dress she admires, she doesn't even have to go in for a fitting. She can just call London or Paris and order it. I think this is a marvelous plan. And the reason I haven't had a dozen foam-rubber models made of my figure is not just that there isn't enough foam rubber in the world. The real reason I'm hesitant is that I don't think a life-sized foam-rubber model of me could be stashed away in a closet someplace, between fittings. It would absolutely require a proper setting. It would have to be placed like Michelangelo's David—in a rotunda, with perhaps a skylight. Now, I have never been in a fashion house but I doubt if they have rotundas. Also, I have the feeling that it would be rather depressing to have oneself duplicated all over the place. Imagine trying to eat some crème brûlée and realizing that you were getting fat in four different cities.

Mignon McLaughlin has written that a woman can remember exactly what she was wearing on every important occasion of her life. I believe that. I can remember. I just wish I could forget. Because even when I find a dress that is pretty and becoming, it turns out, in one way or another, to be a mistake. Let me give you a typical example.

Years ago, when my husband first went to work on a newspaper, we were invited to a dinner party by the man who was the managing editor. Now I didn't really suppose my husband would be fired if I should prove unsuitable (I don't think newspapers worry about their "image" the way corporations do) but I did suppose that I couldn't appear at a chic dinner party in a dress that buttoned down the front. I knew I had to take steps.

I went to Lord & Taylor and bravely marched into "Better Dresses." Then I stood in a corner for a while and studied the salesladies. What I did *not* want was an elegant saleslady. I knew, from past experience, that in the presence of a really elegant saleslady with a really elegant European accent I tend to drop my purse and my gloves and to develop coughing spells.

I finally selected one who seemed a little shy and nervous. I went over to her and took hold of her elbow. "Don't *argue* with me," I said, "I want to buy a dress. I want to buy a fancy dress. And I want to buy it this afternoon." She didn't seem startled by my outburst. She just sighed a little sigh that seemed to say "Boy, I get all the nuts!" Then she went to work and found me a pretty dress. It was made of yellow silk pongee with metallic gold thread woven through the fabric. And so I went to the party calm in my conviction that for once I was wearing something that did not look as though it had been run up by loving hands at home.

My husband and I were the first to arrive because we had
made the youthful error of arriving at precisely the time for
which we had been invited. The editor and his wife greeted us
in the foyer and were most gracious. I felt, however, that the
wife's smile was a little bit strained. I understood everything
when we walked into the living room. Three walls of the room
were covered from floor to ceiling with draperies. And the draperies were made of exactly the same material as my new dress.
What depressed me most was my feeling that I *wouldn't* die of
embarrassment.

I tried to appraise the over-all situation. It wasn't so terrible. It
just looked as though they'd had enough material left over to
make a dress. But then why, in heaven's name, would I be wearing it? Actually, it didn't matter so much to me that when I was
standing in front of a drapery I seemed to be a disembodied
head. It mattered more to the other guests, who were hard put to
analyze what they assumed must be an optical illusion. Conver-
sations with me had a way of sputtering out. In fact, one man
left my side in the middle of a sentence muttering, "I don't know
what they put in this drink." Finally, I had to devote all of my
energies to keeping near the one undraped—or safe—wall, where
the heat from the open fireplace promptly took the curl out of
my hair. Needless to say, we were not invited back.

Another reason I have so many dreary dresses is that I *know* I
am a difficult size, which means that whenever a saleslady produces a dress that actually fits me I feel a sporting obligation to
buy it. (I consider a dress fits me when it reaches to my knees
and can be zipped up by only one person.) I seem unable to
make plain statements like "I can't wear beige because I *am*
beige." I may venture a feeble question—"Don't you think it's a
little on the beige side?"—but if I do the saleslady instantly
counters with "Madam must imagine it dressed up with spanking white accessories." So naturally I buy the dress. I'm certainly
not going to confess to that girl that I don't own one single
spanking white accessory.

By contrast, my mother has great authority in these situations.
I once went shopping with her when she was looking for a dress
to wear to my brother's wedding. The saleslady brought out a
somber mauve lace with that ubiquitous rhinestone pin on the

hip. Mother waved it away. The saleslady turned frosty on the instant and asked, "Would you care to tell me what you don't like about it?" Mother smiled cheerily and said, "My dear, all my friends are being *buried* in that dress." She got results, and a very becoming gray chiffon, in ten minutes.

There is this to be said for my ill-purchased dresses. They are, almost invariably, of such stout material and such sturdy construction that it gives me a very good feeling when I pack them off to the Clothes for Korea collection. Some people are denied even this small comfort. I have a friend, a very pretty girl named Margaret Mary, who in spite of the fact that her weight fluctuates wildly (that is to say, she keeps getting fatter) continues to buy chic clothes at fashionable boutiques. Of course she can't wear them. And she tells me that when she opens her closet doors it gives her the sensation of drowning. It's as though all the sins of her past life were swimming before her eyes.

The question is: What do you do with a closet full of unused velvet Capri pants or sequined bikinis? These cannot be dispatched to the deserving poor. Indeed, they don't even make good dusters. They just hang there, a reminder of the folly of human aspirations and the futility of nine-day diets.

Greenwich, Anyone?

The thing that worries me is that I am so different from other writers. Connecticut is just another state to me. And nature—well, nature is just nature. When I see a tree whose leafy mouth is pressed against the Earth's sweet flowing breast, I think, "Well, *that's* a nice-looking oak," but it doesn't change my way of life.

Now I'm not going to stand here and run down trees and flowers. Personally, I have three snake plants of my own, and in a tearoom I'm the first one to notice the geraniums. But the point is, I keep my head.

However, I've been reading a lot lately, and it's clear that I'm out of step. Most serious writers of stature (I consider a writer serious when he makes more than twenty thousand a year) are giving up their psychiatrists and going back to the land. You can't pick up a book these days without getting all involved with the inspirational saga of some poor, harried writer who was making sixty thousand a year and taking the five fifty-one back to Pelham, but it was all ashes—ashes.

Then he found this old abandoned sawmill in Connecticut that was three hours from the station and twenty minutes from the bathroom, and there he found contentment.

Right from the beginning the golden days were flowing to the brim with the real stuff of life and living. No matter that the maid quit because she wasn't used to cooking over an open hearth. As soon as the wife opened a can of Heinz's spaghetti, sprinkled it with marjoram, chervil, anise, and some dry vermouth, she once again felt the sweet fulfillment of being a mate and a mother. The children were no problem, because they had to walk eight miles back and forth to school and were scarcely ever around.

And Truth itself came knocking one morning, along about ten-fifteen. It was a pretty spring day, the buttercups were twinkling on the grass, and the only sound was the song of the whippoorwill until the chimney broke off and fell down through the dining-room ceiling, scattering beams, bricks, and mortar here and there and quite demolishing the French Provincial table.

Our writer came upon the wreckage on his way back from the well. Although he was dismayed at first, he took hold of himself and did what anyone else would have done in the situation. He went out and sat on the back stoop. Pretty soon a chicken came strolling by. He picked it up, and suddenly he became aware that it was warm and that it was making little cheeping sounds and that it was *his* chicken. He held it against his last clean shirt. Now he was lost, lost in the miracle of the warmth and the scratching and cheeping—even though, as I understand it, cheeping is not at all unusual in chickens. Forgotten was the hole in the roof, forgotten the dining-room table. He realized that nothing else really mattered: from now on it was going to be him and this chicken.

Well, you see how different we all are. I simply can't think of a household disaster that would be in any way mitigated by the presence of a chicken in the back yard. And on the day the roof fell in, a smart chicken would keep out of my way. At a time like that, it would be nothing for me to go out and kick one in the tail feathers. But then I hate chickens, with their blank beady eyes and the silly way they keep shaking their scrawny little heads.

Formerly, when our writer lived in the sinful city, five o'clock was a nightmare of cocktail parties at which he could never get a martini that was dry enough (his own method with martinis seems to have consisted in keeping the gin locked away in a separate closet and walking past it once a week carrying a bottle of vermouth). Now five o'clock finds him up to his elbows in cows. "The Boy and I finished the milking, and there, in sight of the cows, we sat down with a pail of the rich, warm brew and refreshed ourselves." Of course, he may only mean that they washed themselves in it, but doesn't it sound like they *drank* it?

Then he adds, "My, how The Boy is shooting up. He is already an inch taller than The Girl." I don't know what gets into writers when they move to the country. They can't remember the names of their children. Two weeks in the dew-soaked fields, and the best they can do is The Boy and The Girl. Notice, though, the way they keep tabs on the livestock. You're always reading how "Lord Peter Wimsey got a nail in his hoof today," or "Thank heaven, Edith Sitwell finally had her kittens."

All is not work, work, work in Utopia. Oftentimes, in the evening after they have finished spreading the fertilizer, the writer and his wife sit on the fence—with a wonderful sense of "togetherness"—and listen to the magic symphony of the crickets. I can understand that. Around our house we're pretty busy, and of course we're not the least bit integrated, but nevertheless my husband and I often sit together in the deepening twilight and listen to the sweet, gentle slosh-click, slosh-click of the dishwasher. He smiles and I smile. Oh, it's a golden moment.

But to get back to the writer. Even from his standpoint, there is one tiny flaw in all this bucolic bliss. What with setting the winter potatoes and keeping the cows freshened, he hasn't done a lick of writing since he got there. Of course, he *has* kept a diary—and this becomes our only means of studying the effects of contentment on a writer's style. The effects are awesome.

Here was our boy, writing lovely, depressing stories for the more advanced magazines. (I remember a typical one about a stout woman of fifty with an Italian haircut, who got very drunk in a club car and proceeded to tell a lot of perfect strangers why she wouldn't give Harry a divorce.) *Now* listen to him:

"Up at five-thirty to help with the lambing.

"Saw a yellow-bellied snipwhistle.

"Oh, such excitement as there was today. The corn shucker arrived."

Help with a lambing at five-thirty? That settles it. I won't *be* a writer.

What to Do When Your Husband Gives Up Smoking

The best thing to do when your husband gives up smoking is to leave him—just temporarily, of course. He will most surely follow his final cigarette with what appears to be a nervous breakdown, and you may not be able to keep your own cool when all about you this madman is stuffing his face with chocolate-covered peanuts, chewing on the horn rims of his glasses, and otherwise behaving like a panther with four sore paws.

Simple efforts to help the victim ("Why don't you calm down, honey?") will go unappreciated. And tempers are prone to rise as the new nonsmoker, in a voice rigid with martyrdom, replies, "Boy, that's rich—you sit there puffing away and tell *me* to calm down!" This way lies madness and the marriage that can*not* be saved.

Sneaking your cigarettes in the garage the way the children do is not the real solution. No, the only safe thing to do is clear out of the area for the first week of The Great Experiment. It would be ideal if you could afford to go to Elizabeth Arden's Main Chance Farm from whence you might return so rejuvenated (if not downright catnip) that your husband would be reminded that there was a time in his life when you meant more to him than a cigarette could. If you cannot afford Arden's, remember that your mother in Scranton is always saying how she would enjoy a little visit with you alone sometime.

The reason *I* didn't leave town for that first week is because I was given no advance warning. It was another one of those cases where the wife is the last to know. On a perfectly ordinary day in February my husband's part-time secretary called and asked me to give him what I considered a rather cryptic message. When he came home, I passed it on. "Marguerite phoned," I told him, "and she said to tell you *not* to sit at the table after dinner. And do you know what I think? I think you're overworking that nice girl."

"Oh," he explained, "she must mean that's when you want one worst." I may have paled as I inquired, "That's when you want one *what* worst?"

Then he made a full confession. He was going to stop smoking beginning tomorrow, and he'd been asking Marguerite for advice because she'd kicked the habit a year earlier. He seemed entirely cheerful about the prospect. In fact, his face was wreathed in smiles. Of course, his face was also wreathed in smoke from one cigarette in his fingers and another lighted cigarette in the ashtray. But he sounded game as an astronaut ("This voyage to the moon is procedurally routine"). Secretly, all I could think of was Kipling's lament: "Oh, they're hangin' Danny Deever in the mornin'."

The condemned man arose the next day later than usual, because, as he subsequently explained, he couldn't think of any *other* reason to get up. Perhaps I should mention at this point that my husband has always been a serene man. He taught all six children how to tie their shoelaces without once losing his patience. He has been known to go off to his desk humming snatches of "Swanee." And, what is more to the point, he hasn't been sick one day in twenty years. When he does complain, it's never about his health, but about something important, like "Chicken again? Why don't we ever have anything good, like chili or baked macaroni and cheese?"

Anyway, when I came upon him around noon his desk was a sea of cellophane candy wrappers. Naturally, I asked him how he was managing without cigarettes. He replied that there was no problem about the cigarettes, he was hardly giving them a thought, but his swollen cheeks were bothering him. Furthermore the roof of his mouth felt funny, and what about these strange red marks on the palms of his hands?

I assured him that his face was not swollen and explained that his palms looked exactly as they always did. He just never happened to notice them before. As for the roof of his mouth, I suggested that his consumption of one pound of sour balls in two hours might have something to do with it.

I thought he'd be delighted to learn that all his fears were foolish fancies. On the contrary, he looked forlorn, actually morose. In fact, he hadn't looked so distressed since he finished reading Rachel Carson's *Silent Spring*. I thereupon resolved to treat new symptoms with new respect.

The following day he reported once again that the absence of cigarettes was no problem at all. He didn't even *want* a cigarette. His problem was his eyes. He was very definitely suffering from double vision. I immediately called an oculist, whose nurse explained that it would be six weeks before he could be given an appointment. I begged to speak to the oculist himself and, when he came on, asked if he could possibly see my husband today after office hours. "My dear Madam," he began very impatiently. "But Doctor," I said, "this is an emergency." He asked me to describe the emergency, and I said, "My husband has given up smoking." His whole tone changed. "Of course," he said, "in that case we'll make room for him this afternoon." A humane man— and one who, it developed, had given up smoking five times. There was, of course, nothing the matter with my husband's vision.

Two days later he had a new complaint. His jaws ached and his teeth felt loose, definitely loose. The dentist he consulted could find no sign of any deterioration in the alignment of gum and molar. This surprised me. He had been chewing gum eleven hours a day (two or three sticks at a time) with maniacal fervor, tossing his head from side to side like the M-G-M lion. I thought it likely that he had loosened not only his teeth but his collarbone. It seems that he had never learned to chew gum as a child, and while I know a woman who learned Greek at ninety there are nevertheless some skills, like ballet dancing and gum chewing, which can only be mastered by the very young.

Different people attack the problem of withdrawal symptoms

in different ways. I met a professor of economics who told me that after giving up smoking he always kept a child's coiled-wire toy—a Slinky, I believe it's called—on his desk to play with. My husband thought this was an idiotic idea, but I don't know that it's any more idiotic than unbending a bowl full of paper clips and twisting them into tiny nooses, which is what he was doing.

In any case, during this ghastly period I was the perfect portrait of patience, as warm and wise in my answers as Marmee in *Little Women*. In fact, the whole family was treading as softly as pilgrims in an unfamiliar shrine. Our faithful housekeeper, Mabel, was heard to admonish eight-year-old Gregory, "Don't you throw that ball at the window! Don't you know your father has given up smoking?" When I accepted an invitation to a party, I felt it necessary to add, "We'd love to come, but I think you should know that Walter has given up smoking." It wasn't that he was disagreeable or snappish. But he did wear an air of autumnal suffering, like King Lear having just divested himself of his kingdom. And he also gobbled canapés in a manner that six-year-old children would have been rebuked for. Furthermore, it was a problem just to *get* to the party. He would part from his bag of potato chips just long enough to button his dress shirt, the while muttering "Now that I've given up cigarettes, nothing fits me." It was uncanny the way he connected everything that happened to him with the absence of cigarettes in his life. If he passed a red light it was "Now that I'm not smoking, my reflexes are off." I honest to God think that he believes there was some connection between his giving up smoking and the crisis in the Middle East.

As I've tried to make clear, throughout all of this I remained as vibrantly cheerful as those addled females I see on television who apparently find all happiness here below in a new lemon-flavored furniture polish. Then the day came when I snapped. I found him at his desk looking even more forlorn than was becoming quite usual. Studying his dachshund expression, I was moved to invoke Shakespeare, quoting aloud, "Oh, bare, ruined choir, where late the sweet birds sang."

"It's *not* funny," he said.

"I never said it was funny," I said.

He went on to elaborate. "I haven't mentioned this before, because I didn't want to complain (ho, ho, ho, ho), but I can't work, I can't write, I can't think. And I can't think because my mind is so furry and fuzzy." It turned out that he had had to look up the spelling of the word "neighborhood" because when he'd typed it, it looked peculiar. It wasn't misspelled, it just looked peculiar.

I allowed myself to sound sarcastic. "And I suppose you think it's all because you've given up smoking." "Absolutely," he replied. "Now, honey," I began, "this is ridiculous and you know it's ridiculous—how could not smoking make your head fuzzy?" He looked me straight in the eye and said, absolutely seriously, "I think I'm getting too much oxygen."

That did it. My brusque remarks and clarion tones would have been appropriate coming from a responsible person announcing a fire at sea. But I ask you. A middle-aged man, respected in his field, seriously announcing that his brain is being damaged by breathing in too much unpolluted air!

We have decided to remain together for the sake of the children. And then, too, I have been told that one of these days, when all those noxious tars and resins have finally disappeared from his system, he will be a new man, with new exuberance and new wind. Except that to really appreciate that new wind he will have to lose the eighteen pounds he has gained while giving up cigarettes. And if he gives up eating—no, no, it's too grisly to contemplate.

I Was a Sand Crab

I do crazy things; I'll be the second to admit it. For instance, I will buy anything—*anything*—that has been reduced to one third of its original price. I now own, among other things, a wonderful emergency repair kit for patching up plastic swimming pools, which was an absolute steal at ninety-eight cents and which will doubtless prove invaluable when and if we get a plastic swimming pool. And just last week I bought a brown shantung dress at Saks Fifth Avenue for twenty-eight dollars (a fraction of its former price) which, on closer inspection, seems to give me the distinction and the interesting contours of a large bran muffin. Of course the dress is not a total loss, because for the first time in my life I have something that's fit to wear shopping in Saks Fifth Avenue.

But there's one mistake I've never made. I have never taken our children on an extended vacation. I understand that other people do it all the time. They pack up the whole brood (and Nutsy the dog) and go camping in the Canadian Rockies, or, with Daddy at the helm, they sail around Cape Horn on an old sand barge. Not only that, but they have enough energy left over to write a book about it. It all sounds so jolly. I find myself speechless with admiration as I read: "Oh, what a breakfast that was! Skipper and Dad came home with their catch, a brace of gleaming sunfish, and noted with approval that the four-year-old twins had already built a roaring fire in the grate. Susie made several loaves of her special Indian-meal bread, and Little Joe, our toddler, crept around the rough-hewn table, spreading the large ferns that were to serve as table mats." Now there's an integrated little group—and talk about teamwork! Of course, that mother doesn't seem to have lifted a finger. But then, she wrote the book, and that takes it out of you.

Up to now the farthest we've ever taken all six children is to the mailbox on the corner. We do, however, take them to the beach—which is closer than the mailbox, being directly across the road. And I have discovered that those long, hot afternoons on the sand can be fun for young and old, provided you keep your wits about you.

The first time I took our boys to the beach I was so naïve that I actually brought along a copy of Sheed's *Theology and Sanity*. It was my plan to loll in the deck chair and improve my mind while the happy children gamboled and frolicked on the sand. That was my plan. *Their* plan was to show me two dead crabs, five clam shells, one rusty pail they found under two rocks, the two rocks, two hundred and seventy-two Good Humor sticks, one small boy who had taken off his bathing suit, one enormous hole they dug (and wasn't it lucky the life guard fell in it, and not the old gentleman in braces), fourteen cigarette butts, and a tear in Gilbert's new bathing trunks.

I don't mean that it's impossible to read, but you do have to select the reading material with some care. *Theology and Sanity* is out, and so is any book in which the author writes an introduction acknowledging his indebtedness to more than thirty-eight sources. The ideal thing would be a mail-order catalogue, or, if you insist on narrative, there is a wonderful little Golden Book about a boy named Timmy who wanted to be a choo-choo.

Speaking about dead crabs, I have found it advisable when presented with any species of marine life, no matter how advanced in decay, to assume that it is still alive. In this way you can appeal to the children's nobler nature. I have stood, as close as my nose would allow, over the ghastly carcass of some unlovely denizen of the deep (now clearly past the reach of all wonder drugs) and muttered sagely, "The thing is, darling, he seems dead because he's scared. [*He's* scared?] He's just lonesome, so why don't you put him back in the water and let him swim with his brothers and sisters?" It's better this way, really. Otherwise they will take him home to bury him, which would be all right if they buried him. But they don't bury him—they leave him in the garage or in a wastebasket in the bathroom. I know one little boy—in fact, he's related to me—who once put an enormous dead horseshoe crab in the Bendix. As a matter of fact, it couldn't have been that enormous or I'd have noticed it before I put in all those sheets.

It's a simple enough matter to sit back and admire the constant stream of salvage that the little ones dump in your lap. You need only the vivacity of Arlene Francis, the unfailing cheer of Merv Griffin, and the natural instinct for hyperbole of an ad man working on a new toothpaste account. You must be careful, though, not to shoot your bolt on sea shells. Save a little enthusiasm for when you have to watch them "swim." You don't want to break down completely, like one harassed father I heard bellowing at his four-year-old, "I don't call that swimming, Ralphie —I call that *walking!*"

For the record, Ralphie was certainly walking, but he had a magnificent overhand splash, and around here we give points for that. If you are given a choice, it is much less taxing to watch them swim under water than over water, because you don't have to shout encouragements while they are actually submerged. In fact you can more or less think your own thoughts until they reappear. The demonstrations, however, had better take place in very shallow water—otherwise, if they're one second late in reappearing, your own thoughts may give you a heart attack.

We come now to the subject of discipline at the beach. Personally, I marvel at how calm other mothers stay (I'm told it has something to do with the presence of B_1 vitamins in the diet). Recently I heard one tranquil lady gently admonishing her son, "Brucie, I don't think you should pour water on that lady until she changes into her bathing suit." And when Brucie continued to pour, his mother played what was clearly her trump card and said firmly, "Very well—you go right on doing that and you'll see!" This worried me. That large, fully clothed, damp lady was carrying a purse, and she might, just possibly, have had a gun.

When I see my boys dropping wet seaweed on somebody's

sound-asleep face or spilling sand into an open jar of cold cream, I simply shout, "Little boy! Stop that immediately or I will ask your father to spank you!" This stops him without exactly revealing my true identity as the parent of the delinquent.

It's nice when the whole family goes to the beach together and you can occasionally turn the kids over to their co-host, Daddy. Otherwise you may go the whole summer burned only on one side. There is just one difficulty: fathers are even more trouble at the shore than small children. For one thing, fathers are nervous. There are fathers who can detect menacing possibilities in the spectacle of a four-month-old infant lying flat in the exact middle of a perfectly clean, perfectly bare nine-by-twelve rug.

Take such a man to the beach and you have a really classic bundle of nerves, sensitive as a piece of gold leaf, alert to every danger, suspicious of the hostile elements of sea and air, ready always to defend the nest. He demonstrates his vigilance by asking a series of hoarse, rhetorical questions: "Should Col be out that far? Do you let John climb up on those rocks, come *down* off there, you idiot! Don't you think Gilbert should go home, he's blue. Doesn't that kid have a bathing suit that fits him? Good Lord, did we pay forty bucks to teach him to swim like *that?*"

Another thing. If you want stability in a marriage, it is obviously wiser to work out any policy involving the children in advance. For instance, I think you should know before you leave the house just how many times you are prepared to replace ice-cream cones that topple off into the sand. Twice, three times—it doesn't matter, so long as both parents are agreed. If you haven't taken this precaution there are apt to be painful little scenes, with Daddy saying, "Sooner or later that kid has got to learn how to hold onto it," and Mommy muttering, "Poor little lamb— they just don't push them *down* far enough."

I don't know whether children actually do make more loud, embarrassing statements at the beach than in other public places or whether it merely seems that way because the acoustics are better. Once, in a crowded subway where he couldn't be heard anyway, our four-year-old pointed to a highly painted lady who was clearly no lady and said, rather winningly I thought, "Oh, Mommy, see her pink cheeks—she must eat a lot of carrots!" But at the beach all chivalry vanishes. The same child will stare at the kindly gentleman who has just smiled at him and ask in precise, pear-shaped tones, "Why has he got black hair on his head and white hair on his chest?" Which is one reason why I wear very dark glasses and very large sun hats even on overcast days.

Sometimes I can sense an unfortunate remark in the making (for instance, when the woman walking toward us looks pretty peculiar to me too) and I can forestall it by the simple device of saying, "Here, I bet you can't get this whole banana into your mouth at once." But the day comes when, in spite of all your precautions, one of them will spot the oldest and most venerable member of the community and sing out at concert pitch, "Mommy, is that man a lady?"

What you do then is just pack up everything and go home. And that's no hardship, really. After all, what does a day at the beach do for you? It just brings out all your freckles and ruins a perfectly good five-dollar hair set.

Letters of Protest
I Never Sent

It seems to me that I used to sleep better before we had all these conveniences. Lately I find that just as I am sinking into that first sweet slumber of the night I suddenly remember I forgot to take a leg of lamb out of the freezer. At this point I have two clear alternatives. I can pad down to the garage and get the lamb, or I can lie there and figure out what else we could have for dinner tomorrow night (hamburger or what our five-year-old calls "creamed chipped beast").

Either way I'm fully awake now, bright-eyed, alert. Indeed there seems to be a penetrating sharpness to my mind, a quickness that I never notice in the daytime. At this moment I feel that I could be profitably reading Toynbee's *A Study of History* or the directions on the Waring Blendor.

The problem is, of course, to channel this alarming mental energy before I lapse back into that old, and disastrous, habit of reviewing the low points of my life (the night I swallowed an inlay in the Oak Room at the Plaza, the day I dropped—and smashed—a large bottle of mineral oil in the elevator of the Time-Life Building, the Sunday that Honey, our cocker spaniel, ate my mother-in-law's wrist watch).

It was only recently that I discovered that one could put this otherwise lost time to work and make it pay off in terms of mental health, which, I am sure we are all agreed, becomes more elusive all the time. Now I just make a list of all the tiny irritations that have been nibbling away at my subconscious, and I compose dignified letters of protest. (Major irritations, like plumbers who come and make extensive repairs on the wrong bathtub and dry cleaners who press boys' jackets without removing the chocolate kisses from the pockets, I omit on the theory that these really require a stern phone call.) I find that after I have written one of these letters mentally I forget the whole matter and the next day my mind is clear to grapple with real problems, like where on earth I put all those Halloween costumes last November.

And, actually, these nocturnal doodlings hurt nobody. I never do type them up in the morning because I'm too sluggish and, on the various occasions when I suggested that I might really mail one of them, my husband has always stopped me by asking a simple question: "Are you out of your mind?"

I am putting down a few sample letters here in case there is another insomniac somewhere who would like to be as disagreeable as possible (without repercussions) but hasn't quite got the hang of it.

The Ever-Krisp Curtain Co.

Dear Sirs:

In what mad burst of whimsy did you adopt the slogan "These curtains laugh at soap and water"? Now, I begrudge no man his flights of fancy. We are all poets at heart. And when I purchased my Ever-Krisp curtains I did not really expect them to burst into wild guffaws or even ladylike giggles the first time I put them in the sink. (As a matter of fact, with five small boys and one loud Siamese cat I don't want to hear *one word* from those curtains.) But, in my incurable naïveté, I did take your claim to imply that these curtains actually *survived* contact with soap and water. I don't mean I expect them to remain ever-krisp. I'm quite accustomed to ever-limp curtains. I did, however, expect them to remain ever-red with ever-white ruffles. As it happens, they are now a sort of off-pink strawberry ripple, which of course doesn't go with my kitchen.

Ever-Disgusted

Acme Novelty Co.

Dear Sirs:

I am writing to you about your water guns. They leak. And not out of the muzzle, which would be logical, but out of the top because the little stopper doesn't fit. And if you put the gun under your pillow (naturally, I don't put it under *my* pillow) the water seeps out and wets the whole mattress.

I really can't imagine why you discontinued the plastic model you featured last year. This was an admirable, indeed an ideal, water gun. It worked perfectly for fifteen minutes and then broke into two equal halves. It was worth twenty-five cents. I wish I could say the same for this year's model.

Distressed Consumer

The Pilgrim Laundry

Dear Sirs:

For years I've rather admired the crisp little messages that appear on that paper strip that is wrapped around the shirts when they come back from your laundry. The sentiments expressed may not have been very original or very imaginative ("Merry Christmas," "Have a safe Fourth of July") but one felt there was a nice spirit there, and if the tone was sometimes a shade dogmatic it was never carping.

Well, gentlemen, you must try to imagine my shock when, last week, I discovered the new message, which read "Have you kissed your wife this morning?" I don't know what you call this, but I call it prying. Furthermore, my husband never sees these wrappers because I tear them off before I pile the shirts in the drawer. And since I don't have a wife, I feel like an impostor and a perfect idiot.

Because I have a sincere interest in consumer research, and kisses, I decided to show one of these strips to my husband and test his reaction. What he said was (and these are exact quotes), "You tell that laundry that if I had a wife who ironed my shirts I'd kiss her."

Now, Pilgrims, *think!* Surely you never meant to stir up that little kettle of fish. Not only does it lead to apartness, or whatever is the opposite of togetherness, but one sees how easily it could boomerang on the whole laundry business. You were just trying to help, I know that. But let me suggest that you concentrate on those shirts. Would you sew the buttons back on and try not to press the wrinkles *into* the collars, please?

Thanks

To a Columnist

Dear Sir:

In a recent column you ran the item "What titled English actor is serious about a current aquatic star (initials L.D.) now hitting the bottle?" Well, this was a real puzzler. I was able to figure out the English actor part easily enough by getting hold of a copy of Burke's Peerage. But that current aquatic star (initials L.D.) has me stumped. I admit I just don't keep up on things (it was July Fourth before I discovered that June was National Dairy Month) but even so, I feel I would have noticed the emergence of a new swimmer named Lorna Doone (Lola Duprez? Lana Durner?). I used to know a girl in Wilkes-Barre named Lorraine Dickson who was a marvelous swimmer, but she uses her married name now, which is Ruffo. Anyway, she wouldn't be hitting the bottle because she has only one kidney and she doesn't drink at all. I will be anxiously watching your column for further details.

Baffled Reader (initials J.K.)

Bergdorf Goodman

Dear Sirs:

In Sunday's paper you had an advertisement for "a casual little go-everywhere frock @ $225." Now what I want to know is, just exactly how casual is this dress? I mean, it isn't *too* casual, is it? Would it really give one a feeling of social security and a sense of "belonging" in the A&P? If you wore it to Parents' Night and had to talk to the principal, would it perhaps seem just a trifle slapdash?

Bergdorf's, oh Bergdorf's, can you hear me? You must come down off that mountaintop. I'm afraid you've been overprotected. People you trusted have been keeping things from you. Promise you won't get mad if I tell you something: you're on the wrong track. I know women who spend that kind of money on clothes. (Well, I don't exactly know them, I overhear them talking during the intermissions at First Nights.) But I feel myself to be on solid ground when I say that, @ $225, they're not looking for a frock, they're looking for a dress and one that would make Oscar de la Renta think twice.

Are we still friends?

Little Cinema Movie Theater

Dear Sirs:

I called your theater yesterday afternoon and I said to the woman who answered the phone, "Young lady"—from her voice I judged her to be at least sixty-five but I wanted to get on her good side—"young lady," I said, "will you please tell me at what time this evening you are showing *Cousin, Cousine.* Also, please tell me at what time you are showing *Kentucky Fried Movie.* I was very calm. I didn't prejudice the case. Nor did I reveal by any hint of hysteria which picture I was trying to avoid. Anyway she told me that *Cousin, Cousine* began at 8:10 and *Kentucky Fried* began at 10:16. Not satisfied with this (I am unnaturally cautious ever since I saw, as a result of circumstances beyond my control, a picture called *Herbie Goes to Monte Carlo*), I called back in five minutes and, in an assumed southern accent (which I do rather well, having once played an end man in a minstrel show), I asked the same question and got the same answer. It was, then, with complete confidence that my husband and I arrived at the theater at 8:10 to discover the opening credits of *Kentucky Fried Movie* rolling onto the screen. Now this may seem a very trifling mistake to you, but I assure you that my husband is a very nervous man (of course, he wasn't this nervous before *Kentucky Fried Movie*) and his condition has worsened noticeably. Little things, like the children banging the basketball against the plate-glass doors, that he used to be able to pass off with a joke and a smile now reduce him to screaming and shouting. This you must put on your conscience, Little Cinema. You may ask why we didn't leave and come back for *Cousin, Cousine.* Well, for one thing we had already parked the car, and my husband didn't feel that at his age he could walk up and down in front of the theater with that big bag of popcorn—and he wouldn't throw it away.

Aggrieved Moviegoer

Dear Sister Saint Joseph:

Colin tells me that he is playing the part of the Steering Wheel in the Safety play. He feels, as do I, that he could bring a lot more to the part of the Stop Sign. I know Stop Sign is a speaking part, and while I realize that Colin is not ready for "leads," still he did memorize all three stanzas of "America, the Beautiful," and I myself would have absolute confidence in his ability to handle the line "I am the Stop Sign, and I am here to help you," which I understand constitutes the whole part. Also, Colin is very tall for seven and I'm sure we're agreed that height is very important for this role. Finally, let me mention (although I do not expect it to influence your decision in any way) that I just happen to have a Stop Sign costume which I made for his brother three years ago.

Cordially,
Colin's Mother

Dear Doctor Lipman:

Those new sleeping pills that you said would "fell an ox" don't work either. Now what will I do?

Desperately,
Jean

The Poet and the Peasants

We have made mistakes with our children, which will undoubtedly become clearer as they get old enough to write their own books. But here I would like to be serious for a few minutes about the one thing we did that was right. We taught them not to be afraid of poetry.

For a number of years, or until the older boys went away to school, we gathered the protesting brood in the living room every Sunday evening, right after dinner, for what the children scornfully referred to as "Culture Hour." Each boy would recite a poem he had memorized during the week, after which we would play some classical music on the hi-fi for twenty minutes or so. This will sound simple and easy only to those who refuse to grasp that if there is an irresistible force there are most definitely immovable objects.

Actually the program came about by accident. One night I went into the den and turned on a light which promptly burned out. Then when I turned on a second light the same thing happened. Cursing the darkness, I muttered "When I consider how my light is spent . . ."

My husband surprised me by asking, "What's that from?" I recoiled as though he had just announced that he couldn't remember the colors of the American flag. "It's not possible," I said, "that you don't know what that's from. Everybody knows what that's from."

His look was short-suffering. "You don't have to sound so superior," he said. "The first present I ever gave you was a book of poetry." (I was eighteen and it was *The Collected Poems of Stephen Crane*.) "I know that's a poem. I just don't know *which* poem."

"Well," I continued, fatuous as before, "that is Milton's *Sonnet on His Blindness* and it's inconceivable to me that a man who used to be a teacher wouldn't remember." But he had left to get two new light bulbs and out of the range of my voice.

That started me mulling, which is one of the things I do best. Were our five boys going to grow up knowing all about such folk heroes as Joe Namath and Vince Lombardi and nothing whatsoever about Milton or Keats or Yeats or even Ogden Nash? Steps, I felt, had to be taken.

When I first proposed the idea to my husband his enthusiasm was less contagious than I might have hoped. "I don't suppose it will kill them" is what he said. "Them" at that point were Chris, aged fourteen, the twins, Colin and John, aged ten, and Gilbert, aged seven. There was also Gregory, aged two, who could recite "I love Bosco, that's the drink for me," but I didn't suppose his talents could be pushed further at that juncture.

I did suppose that we could plunge ahead with the four older boys. But if their father felt it wouldn't kill them, they had no such confidence. As I unfolded The Plan they couldn't have been more horrified if I had suddenly suggested that all of them wear hair ribbons to football practice. Nevertheless, I was adamant, and, as it turned out, rather obtuse. At that stage of my life I was still in good voice and bigger than they were. And I was used to giving commands. "Go," I would say to one, and he would goeth, "Come," I would say to another and he would cometh. (Or most of the time he would cometh. Occasionally he would runneth out the back door.)

I always tried (and still do try) to be very specific. To say to a ten-year-old boy "If you don't start keeping that room tidy, I am going to go absolutely crazy" is a waste of time and breath. To begin with, he doesn't know what the word "tidy" means and he won't find out until he marries the right girl. And since he considers that you are already crazy, he will not believe that his actions are likely to worsen the situation. It may not be infallible, but it surely is more practical to say "You don't leave this room until I say it is *perfect* and I do mean all those Good Humor sticks under the bed."

Anyway, it was with this sense of being totally explicit that I told the boys one Monday morning, "I want you to find a poem that you like and I want you to learn it so you can say it out loud next Sunday night. Is that clear?" The sighs and the groaning reassured me. I had been perfectly clear. During the week I nudged them from time to time: "How is that poem coming, do you know it yet?"

On Sunday evening there was the usual hassle over whose turn it was to dry the silver and whose turn it was to line the kitchen wastebasket, etc. My own mother used to solve this problem by saying "Just don't bother, I'll do it myself," but I am too judicious for that and also too lazy. So getting the dishes put away is always a long-drawn-out process. Tonight it was a longer-drawn-out process. But eventually the victims presented themselves in the living room, and the recital began. Three of the boys had selected limericks and poor limericks at that (imagine anybody rhyming "breakfast" with "steadfast") while the fourth recited a lengthy and truly dreadful verse about a Cookie Jar Elf. My husband, more than most men of his generation, has seen some pretty horrendous performances, but this was in a class by itself. He polished his glasses, presumably to make sure that these *were* his children. As for me, I had intended to make a few illuminating comments. Instead I was left as slack-jawed and as speechless as those television commentators who were picked up by the camera minutes after President Johnson announced he would *not* run again.

In the vacuum I put a record, "The Nutcracker Suite," on the hi-fi and warned the boys they were not to talk, they were to listen. They were not to whisper, they were to listen. The boys kept to the letter, if not the spirit, of the instructions, with the result that I was the one who talked and talked all through the music: "Stop kicking him in the ankle, take that ashtray off the top of your head, I know you can hear the music from there but get out from under the coffee table."

The whole thing was a disaster but, while I was definitely daunted, I was not yet ready to give up. (Remember that *Hello,*

Dolly! looked like a failure when it opened in Detroit.) Eventually I was able to identify Mistake Number One. Asking the boys to find a poem they "liked" made about as much sense as asking me to select a rock group that I liked. Of course they didn't like poems, any poems. How could they, why should they? When I was the age of our oldest and was required at school to learn whole passages of *The Lady of the Lake,* I thought "The stag at eve had drunk his fill/Where danced the moon on Monan's rill" was pretty ghastly stuff. (To tell the truth, I still think it's pretty ghastly.) Once, as a senior in high school, I got sixty on an English exam because of the way I answered a forty-point question which read: "Discuss Wordsworth's *The World Is Too Much with Us* and explain what it means to you." You will not have to remember the poem to grasp that I was not only saucy but asking for trouble when I wrote that, whatever Wordsworth was looking for as he stood on that pleasant lea, the *last* thing I wanted was to see Proteus rising from the sea or, for that matter, hear old Triton blow his wreathed horn. I mention this only to make it clear that I was not among those prodigies who are reading Shakespeare's sonnets for pleasure at the age of five. Poetry struck me as an arbitrary and capricious method of avoiding clarity, and where my betters heard lyricism I kept hearing foolishness. If the poem said "Go, lovely rose!" I found myself thinking "Scram, rose. On the double. Take a powder, rose."

What happened to open my eyes and shut my mouth was quite simple. I was a freshman in college when a Jesuit poet named Alfred Barrett came to lecture. I attended with the same enthusiasm that characterized my presence in Advanced Algebra, sitting way at the back of the hall behind a pillar on the theory that I could live through it if I could sleep through it.

It's hard for me to remember, all these years later, what Father Barrett said about poetry, if indeed he said anything. What he did was to read poetry—some of his own, a great deal of Gerard Manley Hopkins (whose existence I was unaware of), Yeats, Shelley, Donne, and Housman. He read with such clarity, such melody, and, above all, such directness that even I—sixteen-year-old skeptic—was converted on the spot. It wasn't so much that I cried "Eureka—I see!" I felt like a woman I know who swears she didn't get her first kiss until she was twenty-three and who exclaimed, on that occasion, "Hey, why didn't they *tell* me?" Later in my life I was to meet a teacher and a director, Josephine Callan, who read poetry even better than Father Barrett did but by that time I was already a believer.

Okay, that was *my* story. To get back to the indoctrination of our boys, it was clear that their taste was decidedly peccable and that we would have to select the poems for them, keeping in mind the difference in the boys' ages. (My husband was quick to point out that fortunately there was no difference in the ages of the twins.) We went through the bookshelves, leafed and leafed, and gave each of the boys a book with the poem he was to learn. This was another error because by the end of the week our good books were dog-eared or rat-eared, depending upon the age and irresponsibility of the boy. For a while after that we typed out copies of the poems, but that was a chore and a nuisance (why is poetry harder to type than *anything?*) so eventually we did in the last place what we should have done in the first place, which was to go out and buy a pile of cheap paperback anthologies (these are widely available and often surprisingly good).

The second, or return, engagement of "Culture" night was hardly an improvement on the first. The fact that the poems were of better quality and somewhat longer made the recitations even more agonizing, if that were possible. The younger boys stared at the rug and mumbled like altar boys answering their first Mass in Latin, while Chris stared at the ceiling and chanted in a loud, dum-de-dum see-saw-Margery-Daw rhythm (banging on every end rhyme until I could definitely feel my inlays ache).

As I see it now, the surprising thing is that I should have been surprised. Even granting that I was much younger then (I was, you will be able to surmise, over twenty-one), there was no excuse for my being so dim-witted. Did I really believe that we were harboring a gaggle of Laurence Oliviers? (Ellen Terry heard Olivier in a school play when he was eleven and instantly announced, "That young man is already an actor.") Not, heaven forbid, that we were trying to develop actors. In my opinion, young people who wish to become actors have an addiction only a little less dangerous than heroin. No, we didn't want them to qualify for a Tony or an Emmy, we just wanted them to feel at home with language that was different from and better than the

colloquial speech they heard every day. We wanted them to accept poetry without embarrassment and perhaps finally to realize
that a good poem is an emotional short cut and not just the long
way around.

My husband gave a deep sigh as he faced up to the obvious.
"We're just going to have to work on them," he said. And so we
did. One week he'd work on two of them while I worked on the
other two (the following week we alternated so that the hostility
engendered would be evenly divided). Getting a boy and his
poem together (a not inconsiderable feat), we read the poem
aloud to him, slowly. Ignoring giggles and glassy-eyed boredom,
we read it again at the proper speed and then asked questions:
What do you think this poem means, is it happy or sad, and so
on? Even a piece of verse as simple as *Little Boy Blue* holds
mysteries for a seven-year-old. He may not know what the word
"staunch" means, or even "musket." Perhaps he may not get the
point at all and will be as perplexed as the little toy soldier and
the little dog as to "what has become of our Little Boy Blue
since he kissed them and put them there."

Once we determined that the child actually understood the
whole poem, we got *him* to read it aloud, correcting him when
he mispronounced words, correcting him when he misread
phrases, persuading him not to say the rhyming word louder
than any other word in the line. Two of the boys were very
quick to grasp inflections; the other two were so slow that rehearsing them was like the Chinese Water Torture and I found
myself wondering if there was some way to withdraw from the
whole plan—with honor. What kept me resolute was the conviction I read in all those clear blue eyes that I would soon come to
my senses, that this madness too would pass.

On the third Sunday night the boys were not exactly ready to
cut a tape for Angel Records but they were definitely improved.
In fact, the session was almost endurable, and we had some general discussion afterward about what the four poems meant, with
even Gilbert making a contribution: "When the angel waked
him up with a song it means he was dead, stupid."

Thereafter the Sunday hour became just another fact of life
around this house and the boys seemed to accept it with hardly
more resentment than they accepted baths or sweaters or my no-

tion that a present that came in the mail required a thank-you
letter. And, of course, they did get better. The day finally came
when they were really able to tackle a poem without our having
to tell them "What Tennyson is trying to say here is . . ." They
knew. And if they made mistakes, these were fewer and fewer.
Sometimes they came up with an unusual interpretation that
was, we had to concede, quite possibly valid.

But this didn't happen until we'd been through years of poetry, yards of poetry, volumes of poetry. We made a number of
discoveries along the way. Christopher in his mid-teens and already a little world-weary had a particular affinity for the cynical
or sardonic, whether it was in a simple lyric form like Housman's

> When I was one and twenty
>   I heard a wise man say,
> 'Give crowns and pounds and guineas
>   But not your heart away;
>
> . . . .
> 'Tis paid with sighs a-plenty
>   And sold for endless rue.'
> And I am two and twenty
>   And oh, 'tis true, 'tis true.

or in the rich resonance of Arnold's *Dover Beach:*

> Ah, love, let us be true
> To one another! for the world, which seems
> To lie before us like a land of dreams,
> So various, so beautiful, so new,
> Hath really neither joy, nor love, nor light,
> Nor certitude, nor peace, nor help for pain;
> And we are here as on a darkling plain
> Swept with confused alarms of struggle and flight,
> Where ignorant armies clash by night.

I can still see him—he must have been fifteen, messy and
mussed with dirty sneakers and a deplorable shirt—reciting
Browning with all the hauteur and severity of George Sanders:

> That's my last Duchess painted on the wall,
> Looking as if she were alive. . . .
>   She had
> A heart . . . how shall I say? . . . too soon made glad,
> Too easily impressed; she liked whate'er
> She looked on, and her looks went everywhere.

George Sanders chilled into George C. Scott as he came to the lines

> . . . This grew; I gave commands;
> Then all smiles stopped together.

Colin was a very serious ten-year-old and it seemed to us that he did better with the dark and the dire. "Out of the night that covers me, black as pitch from pole to pole," he would say in a voice that was at once sweet and piercing, "I thank whatever gods may be for my unconquerable soul." He was downright threatening as he recited John Donne's

> Death, be not proud, though some have called thee
> Mighty and dreadful, for thou art not so:
> For those whom thou think'st thou dost overthrow
> Die not, poor Death; nor yet canst thou kill me.

John had a good voice, a trace of ham, and a total lack of inhibition that made him a natural for the more flamboyant ballads. His early *pièce de résistance* was *The Highwayman* by Alfred Noyes. I'm sure he couldn't do it as well today as he could when he was twelve. But then I don't honestly think *anybody* can do *The Highwayman* the way John could when he was twelve. John began the opening lines with a sense of excitement that never flagged:

> The wind was a torrent of darkness among the gusty trees.
> The moon was a ghostly galleon tossed upon cloudy seas.
> The road was a ribbon of moonlight over the purple moor,
> And the highwayman came riding—
>   Riding—riding—
> The highwayman came riding, up to the old inn door.

And he handled the love story of the highwayman and the inn-keeper's daughter with great tenderness. Describing how she loosened her hair in the casement window, he would pause before saying, ever so gently, "Oh, sweet black waves in the moonlight!" and then flash with the fire of a prosecuting attorney as the highwayman went

> Down like a dog on the highway
> And he lay in his blood on the highway, with a bunch
>   of lace at his throat.

With John's passion, one felt that the body was there on the living-room floor. Another of his early hits was *Barbara Frietchie*, and if you think that one is just another chestnut ("Who touches a hair of yon grey head dies like a dog! March on! he said.") you haven't heard it read by someone who doesn't *know* it's a chestnut and who believes he was there and is giving you an eyewitness account. John was always awfully good with people who died, or were about to die, like dogs.

Having tried the tried and true, John gradually moved on to the intricacies of Hopkins, where he could be majestic:

> The world is charged with the grandeur of God.
> It will flame out, like shining from shook foil. . . .

Or filled with righteous indignation:

> Thou art indeed just, Lord, if I contend
> With thee; but, sir, to what I plead is just.
> Why do sinners' ways prosper? And why must
> Disappointment all I endeavor end?

Or rueful, as in *Spring and Fall*, which he recited often because it's a particular favorite of mine:

> Margaret, are you grieving
> Over Goldengrove unleaving?
> Leaves, like the things of man, you
> With your fresh thoughts care for, can you?

Ah! As the heart grows older
It will come to such sights colder
By and by, nor spare a sigh
Though worlds of wanwood leafmeal lie;
And yet you will weep and know why.
Now no matter, child, the name:
Sorrow's springs are the same.
Nor mouth had, no nor mind, expressed
What heart heard of, ghost guessed:
It is the blight man was born for,
It is Margaret you mourn for.

Gilbert, being much younger, was limited to what we thought
was "easy," which meant that he got relatively cheerful poems
and we got some relief. As I remember it, in his poems he was
always planning to go someplace. He was going to see the cherry
hung with snow, he was going to go down to the lonely sea
again, he was going to arise and go to Innisfree. He was also
going to leave Lucasta and go to war, but that was later.

During these evenings we continued to play twenty minutes of
music. This became more bearable after I stopped trying to
make the boys *look* attentive; it had occurred to me, after many
a grinding play and many a dull sermon, that no matter how
hard you try *not* to listen, something sticks to you anyway. And
some nights we broke the pattern by running the films Leonard
Bernstein had made for "Omnibus." My husband had worked for
"Omnibus" and was able to borrow kinescopes of the Bernstein
talks on Modern Music, Jazz, The Beethoven Manuscripts, The
Art of Conducting, and so on. I think these programs are as ex-
hilarating as anything ever done on television. What the children
thought was harder to fathom, since they remained totally non-
committal. Clearly, though, Bernstein made some impression on
them. I know this because, months after we had played the last
of the series, I discovered that Colin had built a new fort in the
back yard. It was a crude affair made from two old card tables,
an abandoned playpen, and some tar paper. However, insubstan-
tial as it was, the fort appeared to have a name. A tattered
banner floating over the entrance bore the legend *Fort Issimo*.

We also began to get evidence that gallons of nineteenth-cen-

tury poetry hadn't washed over them in vain. I recall one night—
the twins were twelve—when John was made an Eagle Scout.
Driving home from this awe-inspiring ceremony (oh, the Nobel
people could take lessons!), I started to tease John. "Well," I
said, "you've reached the top. Now what are you going to do?"
The answer came from Colin in the back seat. "Oh," he announced briskly, "I expect he will go down to the vile dust from
whence he sprung, unwept, unhonored, and unsung."

Sometimes, I must confess, this readiness with the apt quota-
tion could be quite maddening. I think of another night when
the two smaller boys were supposed to have gone to bed but
had, against all orders, slipped outside to bat a few balls directly
under the living-room window. Suddenly there was a splatter of
broken glass and a baseball on the rug. Chris grinned cheerfully
as he said, "Come to the window, sweet is the night air."

During all the years we continued our program I never at any
time was given any hint that the boys approved. Not ever, not
once. So I was thunderstruck one summer, after they'd all returned from school, when the boys themselves suggested that we
resume "Culture Hour" for the weeks they were to be at home. I
couldn't have been more startled if they had suddenly volun-
teered to clean out the attic. In fact, it occurred to me that they
were making an elaborate joke (irony is frequently wasted on
me), so I pressed for an explanation. It turned out that they
thought it was time for Gregory to have "his turn." This might
have been taken as further evidence that the older children felt
they had been made the guinea pigs of the system while their
younger siblings got off scot-free, but here they were volunteering
to suffer right along with him. Now I believed them capable of al-
truism, particularly where Gregory was concerned, but not hero-
ism. It had to be, it just had to be that they enjoyed it.

So we started over with Gregory, who, at seven, was already
as complex as John Kenneth Galbraith. Not necessarily smart,
you understand, just complex. Some days he'd come bursting in
the back door with the air of one who'd just been rescued from a
burning building and call out for his father, "Where's Mr. Kerr?
I need him." (No, no, no, none of the other boys ever called their
father Mister.) The next day he'd drift in as slowly as smoke, like
a character out of Chekhov who has just lost his country estates.

Certainly *we* didn't understand him, but he did seem to have certain intimations about himself. Let me explain. On the opening night of the cultural revival, Gregory—with much prompting —struggled and stammered his way through no more than six lines of *The Gingham Dog and the Calico Cat*. It wasn't just that he was confused about gingham and calico. I began to wonder if he knew what dog and cat meant.

I don't remember what the other boys recited that evening, but Chris recited a long section of T. S. Eliot's *Prufrock*. The next morning I was passing through the garage and came upon Gregory building a birdhouse. He was also muttering something to himself. What with the noise of the saw, he wasn't aware that I had come up behind him, so I was able to overhear him. What he was saying, thoughtfully and precisely, was "I am not Prince Hamlet, nor was meant to be."

Soon the summer was over, school began, the Captains and the Kings departed, and the program was dropped. It was never to resume again because the following summer the older boys all had jobs away from home. It was never to resume and something special, I realized, had gone out of our lives. You lose not only your own youth but the youth of your children. Sweet things vanish and brightness falls from the air.

Now all those Sunday nights blur in memory like the ghost of birthdays past. But if there is one night that remains more vivid than the others it is because of my own strange behavior. Colin was just finishing *John Anderson My Jo*. Do you remember it all?

> John Anderson my jo, John,
>   When we were first acquent,
> Your locks were like the raven,
>   Your bonnie brow was brent;
> But now your brow is beld, John,
>   Your locks are like the snaw;
> But blessings on your frosty pow,
>   John Anderson, my jo.
>
> John Anderson my jo, John,
>   We clamb the hill thegither;
> And monie a canty day, John,
>   We've had wi'ane anither:

> Now we maun totter down, John,
> And hand in hand we'll go,
> And sleep thegither at the foot,
> John Anderson, my jo.

I already knew the poem by heart, so how it happened that I heard new meanings in it I cannot exactly explain. All I can say is that after Colin had finished, to the horror of the boys and to my own acute embarrassment, I burst into tears. An uneasy silence prevailed until John said, very quietly, "Mom, it is Margaret you mourn for."

And he was right, you know. He was absolutely right.

Out of Town with a Show

Or What to Do Until the Psychiatrist Comes

I used to love to go out of town with a show—you miss so much at home. Oh, the exhilaration of being in Philadelphia just as the air is turning nippy, and knowing that somebody else back in Larchmont will have to find the storm windows. Indeed when I was younger and still in love with room service, I felt, like any other red-blooded American housewife, that a whole day spent rewriting the first act was a small price to pay for the privilege of having somebody else make my breakfast and bring it up to me on a tray. I don't know just when the truth caught up with me. But I have noticed recently that the mere thought of going to Boston with a musical causes me to tremble and drop small objects.

Many people have asked me—well, my father has asked me several times—why playwrights have to take a show out of town to try it out. Can't they tell anything from rehearsals?

The truth is that the playwright learns a great deal from rehearsals. He learns that the play is brave, haunting, luminous, tender, and hilarious, and that a cardboard container of coffee sent in from the delicatessen costs thirty cents. Everybody tells him how great the play is—the producer's secretary, the press agent's wife, the leading lady's mother. In fact, after spending only twenty minutes peering at a rehearsal from the back of an empty theater, they are so choked up with the magic of it all that they can barely vocalize. They squeeze the author's trembling hand and mutter hoarsely, "This is it, Sam—it can't miss." Not wishing to dispel the universal euphoria, Sam dismisses as unlikely his own secret theory that the play was badly cast, is being badly directed, and may have been badly written. Soon he is making discreet inquiries as to when the balloting closes for the Pulitzer Prize, and finally he comes home to tell his wife, "Honey, I don't see how it can miss."

And that's why he goes to Philadelphia: so he can see how it can miss.

Out of town the first thing he is up against is Murphy's Law. In Abe Burrows' definition, Murphy's Law states simply: if something *can* go wrong, it will. Now you wouldn't think it to look at me, but I just happen to be the world's expert on the things that can go wrong out of town. That's why I've taken up finger painting. The doctor says it will help me to forget. But while I can still remember, I would like to point out a few of the simpler rules for survival, for those of you who may be thinking of writing a play. And it's no use pretending that you have no intention of writing a play. There are distraught playwrights locked away in the Touraine Hotel this minute who, as recently as last year, were decently and profitably employed by Young and Rubicam or the Chock Full o' Nuts Company.

Learn to Cope with Room Service

We will start with the idea that the play will have to be entirely rewritten (there is no other possibility). This means that you will have to spend twenty-two hours out of every day closeted in a small hotel room with a rented typewriter and a very bad reproduction of a Utrillo.

Entombed as he is, the playwright usually makes the foolish mistake of supposing that he can count on room service to sustain the slender thread of life. This is patently ridiculous, as anyone who has ever waited three hours for two pots of black coffee will know. The thing to do is to bring along a couple of Care packages, or even a tin of biscuits. This will eliminate that air of panic which brings out the beast in room service, and will allow you to order with the proper air of detachment. With any luck, you may stun the girl on the other end of the wire into instant action. A good method is to begin by asking her what day it is. Greet the news that it is Thursday with real appreciation. Then say, in an offhand, casual way, "Thursday, eh? Well, look, sometime over the weekend send me up a chicken sandwich, but there's no rush, I won't be checking out until the end of the month." Sometimes you'll get it in ten minutes.

The worst possible thing you can do, however, is to throw yourself on her mercy and suggest that you are dying of starvation. I know one playwright who swears he could have fixed that play if he hadn't spent all his time calling to inquire what had happened to his breakfast. And a pitiful sight he was, too—a large man of fifty-four shrieking into the telephone, "Yeah, yeah, yeah—I'm the scrambled eggs in 412!" Many writers of comedies exhaust their best energies composing humorous insults to hurl at room service (one I know went so far as to send a large funeral wreath to the kitchen "in memory of all those who have passed away in the last twenty-four hours"). I've never been up to anything so daring or original. I'm not the rugged type, and in the total absence of food, sleep, and clean laundry I tend to sink into childish incoherence. I take the phone in faltering hand and say, with what I assume in my enfeebled state to be dignity, "Hello, Room Service, is this Room Service—well, you're the *worst Room Service I ever met!*"

I know one hotel in Philadelphia (name supplied on request) in which there is only one possible way to get room service. If you take off your clothes, climb into the shower, and begin to lather, the boy will start banging on the door with your tray. You will go through a great many bath towels in this way, which will lead to further quarreling with the maid, but at least you'll get something to eat.

Stay Out of the Lobby

Most authors waste a great deal of valuable energy slinking about the lobby during intermissions in a foolish effort to overhear the comments of the paying customers. They do this, mind you, even on those occasions when the audience has coughed and muttered throughout the entire first act with an animosity that has caused the actors to fear for their safety and the producer to leave town. Even in these circumstances the playwright somehow imagines that he will overhear a tall, distinguished man (clearly a United States senator) say to his companion, "Egad, Helen, it's plays like this that make theatergoing worth while."

Alas, this never happens. The people who attend the theater in tryout towns do not seem to recognize their obligation to discuss what they have just seen. Indeed, there is something downright perverse in the way they persist in believing that they are free to chat about their own affairs. Should you rub shoulders with a vivacious group out on the sidewalk, all you'll hear is a lady saying, "That's Jim for you, he *will* drink manhattans when he knows how I hate to drive the station wagon."

When I was in Philadelphia some years ago with a comedy called *King of Hearts,* I brushed so close to so many strangers that it's a wonder I wasn't arrested for soliciting. However, in two weeks of eavesdropping I heard only one remark that was in any way relevant to the show. This happened when a lady got up after the first act with dismay written all over her perplexed face. She turned to her husband and said plaintively, "George, this *can't* be *Dial M for Murder!*"

Even this wasn't as devastating as the experience a friend of mine had in Wilmington. It was opening night of his new melodrama, and after the second act he flew to his lookout in the lobby, where he was rewarded by hearing two couples actually discussing the play. "Well, Bill," asked the first man, "how do you like it?" My friend held his breath. Bill's answer was not long in coming. "You'd better ask Grace," he said, "she stayed awake."

Another reason authors should stay out of the lobby is that they look so terrible. Our playwright friend Sam, who is normally so natty that he has actually posed for a vodka advertisement, will turn up in the Shubert lobby in Philadelphia looking as unshaven, unkempt, and unstrung as the end man in a police lineup. In this condition he will strike terror into the hearts of the visiting investors, who will conclude that he is not likely to live long enough to finish the rewrite. He will also come under the inspection of some acquaintance who will take the trouble to write to his poor old mother and announce, "Sam is hitting the bottle again, or else he's got hepatitis."

One season I spent three weeks in Boston with a musical, and of course went rapidly to seed. Now, a certain random, helter-skelter look is absolutely native to me. But on this occasion I sank into a really spectacular state of disrepair. I looked like a wire-service photo that would go nicely under the caption "She Survived Death March." Dear friends would take me aside and say, "I know all about the second act, but you do have a comb, don't you?" In any case it was clear that in my derelict condition I couldn't be seen moping about the lobby, so I used to stand behind a pillar that was additionally sheltered by a large palm. It was in this retreat that I was accosted one night by a young man I had never seen before but who was evidently a classmate of my brother's. "Well, hel-lo!" he said, all sunny smiles of recognition, "aren't you Frankie's sister, Jean Kerr?" I was quite naturally outraged. "Nonsense," I said, summoning all the dignity I could muster, "she's a much younger person."

Insist That All Midnight Conferences Be Held in Somebody Else's Hotel Room

Each night after the performance it is customary for all members of the production staff to meet with the author to discuss the somber past, the doubtful future, and the plain fact that the new comedy scene which just went into the show is falling rather flatter than the old one. This session, coming as it does at the end of a perfect day, may loosen your last grip on sanity. It is nevertheless obligatory. The producer insists upon it because he is still trying to persuade you to cut that God-awful scene at the end of the first act and because he is reluctant to go down to the bar and join his friends who have come from New York to see the show. (The friends will say, "I'm gonna level with you, Lou—close it," which is why, in the theater, auld acquaintances are oft forgot and never brought to mind.) And most playwrights accept the inevitable nightly post-mortem because they have learned that it is one tenth of one per cent less taxing to talk about the rewrite than to do the rewrite.

However, all of this talking should definitely be done in the producer's suite. Should the merry little band assemble in your room, not only will you have to sign the tab for all those chicken sandwiches and all that scotch, but, what is more to the point, you will have cut off your escape hatch.

Sooner or later as soft voices die and tempers rise, the director (or maybe the producer) will see fit to add to the many true remarks spoken in jest. "Look, Sam," he will say, still smiling, "we all know the first act is lousy—what you don't seem to realize is that the *second* act stinks." At this moment you should be free to arise and go without a backward glance. It might take twenty minutes if you have to throw them all out of your room.

These nuggets of advice I am dispensing so freely are all, as you can see, concerned with protecting the sanity of the playwright. Playwrights are an unstable crew at best, and they tend to become unglued in the face of the most trivial mishaps. I remember one who was carted right back to Menninger's because, at the climactic moment of his play, the bit player who had to call for the police cried out loudly and clearly, "Help! There's been a murder—call the poloose!"

But if the author, standing at the back of the house gnashing his teeth, is painfully aware that the leading man has just answered the telephone before it rang, the audience tends to remain blissfully unconscious of technical mishaps, unless, of course, the leading lady actually tumbles off the stage into the first row of the orchestra. In this connection I recall an experience I had while tending an ailing musical in Philadelphia. For complicated reasons of the plot there was a big snowstorm effect at the finale of the show. One night the ropes that controlled the snow bags (enormous canvas bags filled with tiny pellets of white paper) somehow became intertwined with the ropes that pulled up the main curtain, so that from the beginning of the second act it snowed—gently, evenly, peacefully, down through the crystal chandeliers of the ballroom, all over the sunny farm scene, without pause during the nightclub scene, it snowed on the just and unjust alike. Indeed, the prodigal flurries continued right up to the moment, at the very end of the show, when the leading lady had to say, "It's snowing, Max." She said the line looking up to the empty heavens, because by that time, naturally, we were fresh out of snow—and I sat there with my face buried in my hands, praying for guidance. When I dashed outside, still feeling murderous, I stumbled into a friend who was seeing the show for the first time. "Oh, Lord," I said, "you would have to catch this performance. Of course things go wrong every night, but this—this is the worst, the absolute worst!" He surprised me by being entirely philosophical about the whole matter. "You worry too much," he said, patting my shoulder. "Sure I noticed she was flat on that first song, but I don't think anybody else did."

By the way, many of the problems that cause faintness and loss of appetite out of town begin with simple mistakes in casting. Some performers that should never, in any circumstances, be cast are:

1. Known alcoholics. You will have trouble enough with the unknown ones.

2. Small children. It's not just that, unless, happily, they are orphans, you will have to cope with their mothers. Much worse is the fact that children, being quicker, brighter, and in a better state of preservation than their elders, can and do memorize the entire script in three days. Thereafter they conceive it to be their civic duty to prompt the star any time and every time he seems to be groping for a word. This unwise practice not only exposes the child to unsuitable language but, in general, lowers the morale and defeats the efforts of the director to create a tight ship with a happy crew.

3. Dogs. Dogs, of course, don't have mothers, which makes them a little easier to deal with, though not much. I was once connected with a production that required the services of a large English sheepdog. We began rehearsals with a beast that was supposed to be so highly trained that I imagined he would be able to do the rewrite. As it turned out, he was not trained even in the conventional sense. The circumstances over which he had no control eventually elicited howls of outrage from the manager of the theater in which we were rehearsing and resulted in our being urged—in the most intemperate language imaginable—to "go hire another hall." Furthermore, this same unfortunate animal had a tendency to bite the actors during performance, which not only lost him audience sympathy but lost us several actors.

He was replaced out of town by an enchanting dog who, unlike her predecessor, was well adjusted and secure, and limited her nibbling to the bits of liver we deposited at various key points on the set. However, she commanded a salary that was well in excess of that paid to most of the company, a circumstance which did not endear her to the other performers, several of whom claimed that, in any case, she had a habit of scratching her ears on their best lines. (I don't think she did this deliberately, but then you never know; and so far as these actors were concerned, they were already unhinged from having to compete with two very cute child actors who crept into any hearts conceivably left vacant by that dog.)

In addition to talking about the pitfalls that must be sidestepped, I might say a word about the really bad moments that may be inevitable. Many playwrights have recorded their despair at being required to attend the premature closing in New York. And this is a very grim occasion for the playwright. Since objectivity doesn't begin to set in for about six months, he still doesn't grasp what happened. The play may be a poor thing, alas, but it's his own, and around the dear ruin each wish of his heart is entwined verdantly still.

To me, however, there is a worse moment. This occurs during one of the final performances out of town, after all of the changes have been made. You stand at the back of the house and observe the results of all the work, all the sleepless nights, the conferences, the rehearsals, the arguments. And the show is better, oh, definitely better, and the audience seems to be enjoying it. You should be happy—and then, suddenly, you experience a brief but exquisitely painful moment of clarity in which you realize that what you are seeing is not really the show you had in mind at all.

This always reminds me of a story about a friend of mine. One Easter she had to prepare dinner for fifteen people, counting children and relatives. For reasons of economy she decided to make a ham loaf instead of the traditional baked ham. Obviously it was going to be four times the trouble, since the recipe for the ham loaf was extremely elaborate: there were a dozen different ingredients and the whole thing had to be made in advance and allowed to "set" overnight in pineapple juice. But she went gamely ahead, convinced that she was going to produce something tastier than baked ham, if not indeed a gourmet's dish. As she took the square pink loaf out of the oven, a sinister thought crossed her mind. She cut off a little slice and tasted it, her worst suspicions confirmed. In tears she flew out of the kitchen to find her husband. "Oh, Frank," she said, "do you know what I've *got?* I've got Spam!"

All I can say is God love you, honey, if you're in Philadelphia and you've got Spam.

The Secret of Coping
with Bad Notices

I don't know what doctors do in the summertime, or lawyers. But I know what writers do. They worry.

A television writer who has just completed a new pilot film worries because CBS won't give him a time slot until General Mills picks up the tab for the first thirteen weeks and General Mills won't pick up the tab until CBS gives him a time slot. A novelist worries because his new book, due in November, hasn't been sold to the book clubs, the *Reader's Digest*, or to the movies, and—if he grasps the situation correctly—that book is going to be sold from door to door by him. The playwright worries because it seems increasingly unlikely that he will get (a) a director, (b) Katharine Hepburn, (c) the Morosco Theatre, (d) a second act. Actually there's a certain amount of waste worry here. He could easily telescope his problems and simply worry about whether he'll get Katharine Hepburn. In that event he *will* get a director and the Morosco Theatre, and even that second act won't matter so much.

It occurs to me that since the writer is going to worry all summer anyway, he might give a moment's attention to what he will do if he gets bad notices. Now, when the problem is only theoretical, is the time to bone up on those techniques of self-preservation which, if properly applied, will save him expensive psychiatric bills later. Next October, when no man sleeps until the *Times* comes out, is much too late.

Let me make it clear that I am not talking about outright pans. There is really a kind of mercy about completely, completely disastrous notices. For one thing, they eliminate alternatives. You goofed, that's all. Even your own mother can see that you goofed. And, in the sense that one worries only while there is still hope, there is now nothing to worry about. The television series *will* disappear, the show *will* fold, the book *will* be remaindered. When the worst that *can* happen happens, it is even possible to be jaunty in the ashes. I remember when John Osborne's musical, *The World of Paul Slickey,* opened in London to reviews that ranged in invective from "dull and revolting" to "dull and abominable." Two days later Mr. Osborne announced, with what seemed to me astonishing aplomb, that he had received "the worst notices since Judas Iscariot."

However, it's rare that you get notices so bad you can brag about them. Most of the time the notices are "mixed," a euphemism which, in the words of George S. Kaufman, simply means that they were "good and rotten." Trouble begins for a novelist when he reads in *Time* that his latest effort is "a tender book, a beautiful book, yes, a *great* book" and in *Newsweek* that it is "curiously disappointing." Or vice versa. The perplexed author does not always leap to the conclusion, as is so often captiously suggested, that the negative reviewer is wrong. Deep down inside he may sense a certain justice in the blast. What really hurts is his conviction that this same reviewer has been wrong all season and there seems to be no reason why he had to be correct on this particular occasion.

Nevertheless the papers are on the street, and the future must be faced. A businessman who has had reverses just goes back to the office. But a writer with a set of mixed notices can't turn around and go right back to writing. In the first place he is in shock, and even trivial things—like accidentally coming upon one page of the second carbon of the third revision under the desk blotter—cause him to break down and sob. In the second place he would have to have the persistence of a salmon and the hide of a buffalo to be unaffected by the knowlege that there is a whole body of opinion which maintains he was never able to write in the first place. (The range of the fallout can be judged when even a Dear One says, "George, do you remember how happy we used to be when you were with Equitable Life?") Since in most cases religion and family obligations preclude suicide, a writer simply has to live through the grisly six weeks during which it will become clear whether he is going to swim with the good notices or sink with the bad ones.

During this trying period, one must keep busy. A long ocean voyage, which would be ideal, is impractical since there is as yet no money to pay for it. Of course five minutes out of every day can be consumed by calling Good Old Bill in the sales department, ostensibly to inquire for his wife's bronchitis and actually to see if he has "heard anything."

But this still leaves a large part of the day unaccounted for. One might learn to speak Chinese, or perhaps do some volunteer hospital work. I am told that at a time like this a small physical impairment often proves a blessing in disguise. A television writer assured me with tears in his eyes that, but for an ailing thumb last winter, he would have "ended up in the loony bin." It seems that on the very morning he read in John J. O'Connor's column that his new series was a "soporific, easily the equal of Nembutal," he developed a case of blood poisoning in his left thumb. (N.B. He doesn't relate this in any way to the notice.) For the next six days, on the advice of his doctor, he had to soak his hand for a whole hour, every other hour. And what with experimenting with different size basins, trying to keep the water hot, and changing his wet shirts, he was never able to give O'Connor his full attention. Clearly this was an ideal substitute for what he really wanted to do, which was soak his head.

Confronted by an absolutely infuriating review, it is sometimes helpful for the victim to do a little personal research on the critic. Is there any truth to the rumor that he had no formal education beyond the age of eleven? In any event is he able to construct a simple English sentence? Are his modifiers misplaced? Do his participles dangle? When moved to lyricism does he write "I had a fun time"? Was he ever arrested for burglary? I don't know that you will prove anything this way, but it is perfectly harmless and quite soothing.

I myself find it therapeutic to take the very worst review and heavily underline the most offending phrases, such as "heavy-handed and lumbering" or perhaps "witless and tasteless." The next step is to paste the notice on the mirror in the bathroom, where you will be able to glance at it at odd hours. In the beginning this may cause vertigo and faintness, but in no time at all you will make the cheering discovery that the words have lost their power to maim. They have even lost their power to communicate. Recuperation is complete when the phrase "witless and tasteless" seems as quaint and meaningless as "smoking in the outer lobby only," "no U turn," or "twenty-three skiddoo," as gloriously incomprehensible as "a thinking man's filter."

If he has the heart to leave the house during this period, the writer will be forced to assume an air of hearty optimism, if only because he doesn't want to contribute to his own bad word of mouth. At the same time he must be warned that any acquaintance who says "Sam, I didn't read the notices, how were they?" has in fact read everything, including that one-line reference in Rex Reed. The way to deal with this character is to mystify him. Say "Frankly, I was pretty relieved." Let *him* figure out what you're so relieved about. Or, better still, say "Well, Bob and Roger [the producers] are pretty happy." Just why they should be happy is unfathomable, but it sounds good, and if—later on—someone gets the reputation of being a little addled, it won't be you. Never, under any circumstances, indicate how far you had to go for a good notice by saying "Listen, did you happen to read *The New Statesman and Leader?*"

A slightly different situation presents itself when a close friend says "I just read that pan you got from Kerr; I don't know what he was talking about." In this instance you must fight the temptation to snap back with "Of course not—the man is an idiot." An outburst like this would not only indicate that you are a poor sport but, worse, would end the conversation then and there. The shrewd move is to adopt an air of thoughtful consideration and say "I don't know that I agree with you, Henry—after all, Kerr is a pretty sound man and I thought many of his points were well taken." Your friend, if he is any friend at all, will be outraged at this display of sweet reason and will forthwith launch into a delightful twenty-minute tirade against Kerr.

Sometimes, in a foolish effort to get publicity and stimulate sales, a writer will agree to appear on an early morning interview show. The idea may be appalling to him, but he has been persuaded by the press agent that, like an expensive funeral, this is the last thing he can do for the beloved. Needless to say, it's a mistake. For one thing, he will lose his sleep, which the doctor has told him is so essential right now. He will also lose sales. The interviewer, who is nothing if not plucky, will rush into the fray and show whose side she's on by stating flatly "I loved your book, Sam—I can't think why Christopher Lehmann-Haupt said it was stupefying." Now, alas, even those sixteen people who were as yet unacquainted with Mr. Lehmann-Haupt's judgment (having been mysteriously entombed in an old mine shaft on the day the review appeared) will be brought up to date.

In conclusion, it's all right to be discouraged by adverse criticism, but you don't have to be derailed. I give you the sad example of a friend of mine who read in a review of his first novel that he was "no Scott Fitzgerald" and went completely to pieces. The fact of the matter is that the poor soul never had any intention of being Scott Fitzgerald. In his secret dreams he was hot upon the Connecticut trail of Peter de Vries. Well, that's all changed now. The last time I met him he was drinking straight gin, teaching a girl columnist to read Schopenhauer, and claimed to be in the middle of a long novel called *The Gold Roller Coaster to Nowhere*.

There is, of course, one other possibility—if you are strong enough to face it. You might get all rave notices. In this event you will spend your days in suicidal gloom brought on by the feeling that you've hit your peak and have nowhere to go but down. As a result of this destructive thinking, you will acquire an ulcer and have to give up smoking and drinking. Having given up smoking and drinking, you will get fat.

Well, it's something to worry about.

A Child's Garden of Manners

Have you noticed a strange thing about etiquette books? They are all written for grownups. *Us.*

I really don't understand it. Most adults have lovely manners; it's a pleasure to have them around. Ask an adult to hand you your glasses and he says "Here they are, dear." He doesn't put them behind his back and say "Guess which hand?" And when you give him a birthday present he doesn't burst into tears and say "I already *have* Chinese checkers!" What I wish is that Emily and Amy and the others would get to work on the real trouble area—people under twelve.

I know that small children have a certain animal magnetism. People kiss them a lot. But are they really in demand, socially? Are they sought after? Does anybody ever call them on the telephone and invite them to spend the weekend on Long Island? Do their very own grandmothers want them to spend the *whole* summer in Scranton? No. For one thing they bite, and then they keep trying to make forts with mashed potatoes. It holds them back, socially. If you have any doubts about the matter, ask yourself one question. When, by some accident, you find yourself at a large party with children present, do you just naturally gravitate over to that corner of the room where the little ones are playing Indian Spy under the card table? See what I mean? These kids need help—and direction.

Now, I'm the last one to be talking about manners. Just this week at a dinner party I let myself get rattled by the innocent question of a young man who was the son of my hostess and a freshman at Lehigh. All he wanted to know was whether I voted for Al Smith or Hoover in 1928. In the deep, troubled reverie produced by this line of questioning, I lost my head completely and consumed not only the entire salad of the man on my right but also one of his Parker House rolls. As I say, I'm not the one to write that book, *Tips for Tots*. But in the total absence of any definitive work on the subject, and inspired as I am by a passion for public service, I would like to make a few random suggestions:

Table Manners for Children

The first point to be established is that one does not sit on the table. One sits on the chair, and in such a way that all four legs touch the floor at the same time. (I am of course speaking of the four legs of the chair; children only *seem* to have four legs.) For children who will rock and tilt anyway, I suggest (a) built-in benches, (b) the practice of instilling in such children a sense of noblesse oblige, so that when they go crashing back onto their heads they go bravely and gallantly and without pulling the tablecloth, the dinner, and a full set of dishes with them. This last may sound severe, but it will be excellent training if they should ever enter the Marines, or even Schrafft's.

We don't have to bother about little niceties such as which fork is the shrimp fork (at these prices, who is giving them shrimp?). We will suppose, and safely, that the child has only one fork. If this child is interested in good manners and/or the sanity of his parents, he will not use the fork to (a) comb his hair, (b) punch holes in the tablecloth, or (c) remove buttons from his jacket. Nor will he ever, under any circumstances, place the tines of the fork under a full glass of milk and beat on the handle with a spoon.

So far as the food itself is concerned, it would be well for the child to adopt a philosophical attitude about that dreary procession of well-balanced meals by reminding himself that in eighteen years or less he will be free to have frozen pizza pies and fig bars every single night. And he should remember, too, that there is a right way and a wrong way to talk about broccoli. Instead of the gloomy mutter "Oh, broccoli again—ugh!" how much better the cheery "I guess I'll eat this broccoli first and get it over with."

Finally, children should be made to understand that no matter how repellent they find a given vegetable, they may not stuff large handfuls of it into their pockets, particularly if the vegetable is creamed. This sorry but unfortunately common practice not only deprives the child of necessary vitamins but frequently exposes him to intemperate criticism and even physical violence.

Behavior at the Theater or Movies

Children should not bring guns or slingshots or cats to the theater. And for other reasons they shouldn't bring hats or gloves or rubbers—unless you have the time to go back to the theater and pick them all up afterward.

It is always worth while to give them exact change, especially if the movie is going to be *The Creature from the Black Lagoon.* Suspense has the curious effect on many children of causing them to swallow nickels.

The mannerly child will decide once and for all whether he wishes to sit on the seat pulled down (like old people) or whether he wants to sit high on the edge in the "up" position. Once he has made up his mind, he will not vacillate between the two positions, or he will very likely be thrown out onto the street by the ushers.

If children are going to eat at the movies, and they are, they should be encouraged to buy candy that doesn't roll. Sour balls roll. And the fallout from a thirty-five-cent box of sour balls is considerably greater than from a fifteen-cent box. If you have any interest in making a host of new acquaintances all at once, there is no better way than to escort a pair of five-year-old twins to the movies and present each of them with a large box of sour balls. With the sense of timing that is innate in even the youngest children, they wait until the main feature starts before dropping both boxes on the floor. And then they're *off,* scrambling on hands and knees, down under the seats through a forest of legs, foraging, retrieving, sobbing. And for six rows in every direction wild-eyed patrons are leaping to their feet and splitting the air with questions: "In heaven's name, what are you *doing* down there? Will you get out? Where do you belong? Where is your mother?" etc. For this reason I suggest chocolate bars. It will ruin their clothes and spoil their dinner but that can't be helped.

Rules of Peaceful Coexistence with Other Children

Children should eschew violence, by which I mean that they should not hit each other on the head with ice skates or telephones or geography books. It ought to go without saying that polite children never push each other down the stairs, but I'm not sure that it does. Karen, my four-year-old niece, recently pushed her baby sister down the back stairs. After her mother had rescued the victim, she flew at the oppressor and shouted, "What's the matter with you? You can't push Joanie down the stairs!" Karen listened carefully, all innocence and interest, and finally said, "I can't? How come?"

Parenthetical note to parents: in trying to keep older children from doing permanent physical damage to their juniors, it is probably not advisable to adopt the tit-for-tat type of punishment ("If you pull Billy's hair again, I'm going to pull *your* hair!"). This method would appear to have a certain Old Testament rightness about it, but the danger is that you may put yourself into a position where you will be forced into massive retaliation. And, when it comes right down to it, you can't really punch that kid straight in the eye or spit in his milk. Personally, I'm in favor of generalized threats like "If you make that baby cry once more I swear I'll clip you." In this instance the word "clip" is open to a variety of interpretations and leaves you more or less free to inflict such punishment as you are up to at the moment.

Respect for the Feelings of Others

One of the reasons children are such duds socially is that they say things like "When do you think you're going to be dead, Grandma?" We're all going to be dead, of course, but nobody wants to be put on the spot like that.

It is not to be expected that a small child can be taught never to make a personal remark. But there is a time and a place. For instance, the moment Mommy is all dressed up in her new blue chiffon and doesn't look a day older than twenty-five, well, twenty-eight, is *not* the time for Gilbert to ask, "Why do you have all those stripes on your forehead, Mommy?"

Children should realize that parents are emotionally insecure, and that there are times when they need loving kindness. Unfortunately, a relationship with a child, like any love affair, is complicated by the fact that the two parties almost never feel the same amount of ardor at the same time. One blows hot while the other blows cold, and vice versa. On the day you're flying to Athens (for two whole weeks) and you're already frantic with concern and full of terrible forebodings that you will never see the little lambs again, you can hardly round them up to say good-bye. And when you do locate one of them, he scarcely looks up from his work. "Darling," you say, "aren't you going to say good-bye and give me a *good* kiss? I'm going to be gone for two whole weeks." "Sure," he says, "'bye, Mom, can I have a Coke?"

Of course he too has moments when affection swells—the wrong moments. First he reduces you to babbling incoherence by (a) climbing in the kitchen window and smashing three geraniums, (b) taking the mail from the mailman and dropping half of it in a puddle, (c) spilling a bottle of navy-blue suede dressing on the cat. Then, as you are pouring Merthiolate on your scratches—incurred while cleaning up the cat—he returns covered with mud, having just buried a squirrel. You are deep in philosophical speculation centering around the miraculous fact that this child was not adopted (at least you don't have to fight the temptation to send him back). And naturally it's right at this moment that he takes it into his head to give you one of his Jack the Ripper hugs, curling muddy cowboy boots around your knees and plastering you with sandy kisses.

Respect for the Property of Others

Children should bear in mind that, no matter how foolish it seems, adults become attached to material objects, like typewriters, wrist watches, and car keys. I admit that I am once again working without statistics, but I do have the feeling we wouldn't have so many disturbed parents in this country if children could be made aware of the unwisdom of using their fathers' best fountain pens to punch holes in evaporated milk cans.

(If you're interested, there is one foolproof way of holding onto pens and pencils: you hire a man with a gun to sit by the desk all day, and then you or your husband or some other responsible adult takes the night shift.)

Just as there are animals that kill prey they have no intention of eating, so are there children who take things they have no way of using. It may be reprehensible, but it is at least understandable that a child should take a sterling-silver gravy ladle to the beach; it's almost as good to dig with as a sand shovel. But why do they take the little knobs off the tops of lamp shades, or meat thermometers, or the dialing wheels off the television set? Sometimes when you investigate what seems to be meaningless mayhem, you find that there is a certain idiotic logic behind the whole thing: when I found one of the smaller boys unfurling a roll of toilet paper out of the attic window, it turned out that he was merely trying to discover how long a roll of toilet paper really was. I can understand that, sort of. But I never did understand why he cut the bows off my blue suede shoes.

Children have such a lively sense of the inviolability of what belongs to them (as you've noticed if you ever tried to throw out an old coloring book) that it should be easy for them to remember that adults, too, have little fetishes about their personal possessions ("You don't like anybody to play with your tractor, do you? Well, Daddy doesn't like anybody to play with his tape recorder.").

Sometimes it's hard to know just what to say. One winter I found on the breakfast table a letter addressed to Mommy Kerr. It was on my very best stationery, and there were ten brand-new four-cent stamps plastered all over the envelope. When I pulled out the letter, the message read:

> Dear Mommy,
>   John is mad at you becuase you won't let us put our snowballs in the freeser but I am not made at you becuase I love you
>
>   Your Frend, Colin

Well, there you are. When you get right down to it, it was worth forty cents.

I Don't Want to See
the Uncut Version of *Anything*

Recently I was heard to murmur against the endless frustrations connected with getting a play produced. I mean I was exploding in all directions and pounding on the table with the handle of a broom. My husband finally quieted me by saying, "How can you complain so much—do you know that Euripides was *exiled?*" Actually, I didn't. But now that I know, it makes all the difference. In the future when shadows gather and vexations mount, I shall take solace from the fact that, in any event, I was never exiled.

But I don't mean to talk about playwriting. My experience as a playwright is so limited that I think it would be hasty for me to theorize about it. On the other hand, because of my husband's sorry occupation, my experience as a member of the audience is enormous. It occurs to me that in the last twenty years I have become the most experienced audience in America.

We are agreed that a critic is not, and never will be, a member of the audience. Not only is he paid to attend, he is paid to listen; and this sobering circumstance colors his whole attitude toward the material on stage. The critic says: This is an extremely bad play—why is that? The audience says: This is an extremely bad play—why was I born? There is a real difference.

Anyway, on those melancholy opening nights when one sees that the jig is up and the closing notice soon will be, I make little notes to myself. I list some of them here in the wistful hope that

somewhere there is a beginning playwright who will believe that
my prejudices are shared by some other people. I think they are.
I think I am pretty close to being the square root of the *ordinary*
audience. I notice that I perk up when other people perk up. I
slump when they slump. And I most certainly do not keep my
head when all about me are losing theirs. I think paradise will be
regained on Forty-fourth Street when young playwrights understand that they must try not to write plays that will cause nice,
ordinary people from Riverdale to wish they were dead.

Little Notes to Myself:

I believe that plays that are successful are almost invariably
more entertaining than plays that fail. This will come as a revo-
lutionary idea only to those who have spent their lives avoiding
beautiful girls because they are rumored to be dumb.

It is perfectly all right with me when a character in an avant-
garde play points to a realistic iron bed and says "That is a
piano." It is still all right with me when another character sits
down in front of the bed and plays "The Blue Danube Waltz"
on the mattress. But thereafter I expect that nobody will lie
down on the piano.

I think that if there are only three characters in a play, one of
them ought to be a girl.

I do not wish to see musical comedies performed entirely on
bleachers in which the leading man wears clown-white make-up
(the only man in the world who can put on clown-white make-
up and be Marcel Marceau is Marcel Marceau).

It strikes me as less than hilarious when an actor, imper-
sonating a foreigner, is required to struggle with our quaint
American colloquialisms. ("How ess eet you put it? I shovel you.
Ah, no. I deeg you.")

I do not like to hear the most explicit four-letter words spoken
from the stage because I number among my acquaintance persons of such candor and quick temper that, for me, the thrill is
gone.

I have noticed that in plays where the characters on stage
laugh a great deal, the people out front laugh very little. This is
notoriously true of productions of Shakespeare's comedies.
"Well, sirrah," says one buffoon, "he did go heigh-ho upon a
bird-bolt." This gem is followed by such guffaws and general

merriment as would leave Victor Borge wondering how he failed.

I'm now too familiar with regional plays in which the characters address each other by their full names in every line of dialogue. The names take up half the line, the other half is taken up by repeating what has already been said.

"Ah know what yer thinkin', Mary Lou Beth Olson."

"Ah know you know what ahm thinkin', Billy Joe Beauregard."

"Yer thinkin' ahm plum strange, Mary Joe Beth."

"Billy Joe, you ain't thinkin'."

And, to shift to sex comedies, the heroine always does look as cute as all get out when, for reasons of the plot, she has to wear the hero's bathrobe. On the other hand (and this is happening more and more), when the hero is required to wear her brunch coat, he looks just plain terrible.

I have noticed that an entertainment that opens or closes with the setting up or dismantling of a circus tent always gets good notices. I don't know what to make of this.

I have seen plays performed on steps in front of a cyclorama that I enjoyed—but not many.

I am wary of plays in which God or the devil appear as characters. We will waive any discussion of theology and I don't mean to be irreverent when I say that, for all practical purposes in the theater, God is a lousy part. (A play I really loved, *The Tenth Man,* had to do with a girl who was being exorcised of the devil, but it may be relevant to note that we never saw the devil.)

I don't want to see productions that run four and one-half hours. (I don't want to see the "uncut version" of *anything.*) In a recent production of *King Lear,* the first act ran for two and one-half hours. By that time I considered that I had given up smoking, and I spent the entire intermission wondering if I should begin again. And I was once more made aware—during that interminable first act—that the most serious materials eventually seem comic if they are allowed to go on too long. For instance, during the protracted scene in which Lear (now mad) is talking to poor, blinded Gloucester, all I could think was: first they put his eyes out, now they're going to talk his ears off.

One thing, though. Whatever their losses on other fronts, actors have got to keep their teeth in. I would have thought this went without saying until I saw two plays by Joe Orton. In one a slatternly landlady, who was competing with her brother for the affections of a male lodger, lost her dentures under the sofa. In another, a young man plundered the corpse of his recently dead mother, removing her false teeth so that he could use them as castanets. If this sounds funny, I'm not telling it right.

When *The Little Foxes* was revived recently, there were those who said it was too well constructed. To me, that's like saying a Pan Am pilot is too conscientious. What I like about Lillian Hellman's play is that you couldn't play the second act first. I know all about improvisation and the free form that mirrors the chaos of our time, but I do like to feel that the playwright has done *some* work before I got there.

I dislike seeing actors perform in the nude. Not that, at my age, I am shocked, but I become exceedingly uncomfortable as the naked performers begin to perspire under the hot lights and develop a tendency to stick to the furniture, or, worse, to each other. In the aura of silliness which prevails on such occasions, I find myself distracted from the plot (which seems merely to be against the audience) into practical considerations. Do they still call them dressing rooms? If an actor develops a boil in an unsuitable area, is a Band-Aid used, or the understudy? Is it possible to say to an actor "I saw you in *Oh, Calcutta*" without laughing?

At plays like *A Man for All Seasons, The Matchmaker, The Lady's Not for Burning, A Streetcar Named Desire, The Odd Couple, The Great White Hope, Summer and Smoke,* and *The Front Page,* I don't make any notes at all. I just sit there and bask and bask and bask and then, when the glow begins to wear off, I go back again.

As I Was Saying to a Geranium

I had to put a philodendron to death last week, and I still feel terrible about it. Actually, it was a perfectly nice little plant when I bought it two years ago for seventy-five cents. And in the beginning it seemed to thrive on the coffee table, where it put out shiny, fat leaves in a responsible fashion.

But, like so many of us, that plant didn't know when to stop, and it grew and it grew until it spread out all over the table and down the sides. When you picked it up to dust the table, you had to hold the pot in one hand and throw a great train of greenery over your shoulder. Now I would have put up with that. The real problem was that the leaves had become smaller and smaller and limper and limper and had moved so far away from their source that, in effect, what you were looking at was a pot full of dirt with a few brownish-looking legs sticking out of it. I am told that if I had "cut it back" at the proper moment this would never have happened. But I never know when to cut back. When the proper moment comes, we seem to be out to dinner or something.

In any case, it was clear that that plant had to go. But how? Where? I have known terrible people who disposed of unwanted cats by letting them out of the car in a strange neighborhood. But you couldn't do that with a plant and, in any case, in this vicinity there is a fifty-dollar fine for littering. I thought of drowning it, but that seemed impractical, and of course it wouldn't burn. Finally, I gathered it up in my arms and, feeling like a Herod loosed upon the innocents, I walked out into the driveway and dumped it into the trash can. After the deed was done I made myself a stiff drink, but I felt shaky for several hours.

I suppose I did neglect that plant. On the other hand, it would appear that some plants, like some children, require a little neglect. Two years ago a friend sent us a magnificent orange tree that was planted in a handsome Italian ceramic crock. It took two men to deliver it, and they were so patently exhausted by the time they got it from the truck to the door that I told them just to leave it there in the front hallway. As it turned out, that was the perfect place for it—against the bare brick archway. I watered it whenever it crossed my mind and, as the weeks passed, it grew even more beautiful and the tiny oranges turned golden. I would say that I found true happiness with that orange tree. I never went through the hall without stopping to admire it.

Months later, another friend who is widely consulted as an amateur gardener came to dinner. Roger took one look at my orange tree and recoiled in horror. "Good heavens!" he said. "You can't leave this tree here!" "Why not?" I asked. "Well, for one thing, it's too cold here. And every time that door opens the tree is in a draft. Furthermore, the light's wrong. That's a north light. And *feel* that dirt. It's too dry!"

He couldn't have sounded more accusing if he had discovered one of the children starving and chained to a bedpost. I agreed, naturally, that the tree must be rescued at once. Thereupon three of us hauled it, huffing and puffing, into a safe, sunny spot in the living room.

That tree never had another well day. Almost immediately it developed that clammy look that children get just before they come down with the sniffles. Then the leaves started to curl. Pretty soon you couldn't read in the living room for the plop, plop, plop of oranges as they dropped like Ping-Pong balls to the floor. We called in our friendly florist for advice. We gave it special plant food. We gave it more water, less water. Nothing availed. Too late we thought of returning it to the hallway. It had slipped away.

For this reason I pay no attention to Roger on the subject of my tulips. I planted them in the back yard ten years ago and they've been there ever since. According to my friend Roger, this is a sorry state of affairs. Every fall he keeps telling me that those tulips should not be out there in that border, they should be in the house "resting." (Presumably upstairs in the twin beds. And resting from *what*?)

I don't feel that way at all. Next year I don't want to have to hunt all over the house for those tulips. I want to know exactly where they are. And anyway, even if you were going to give them a winter vacation, *when* would you dig them up? Certainly not while they're blooming. And after they've stopped blooming you can't find them.

For the record, I will confess that our tulips are no longer the proud, pristine chalices that once they were. Indeed, they have a faintly tipsy air about them. But they are still bright and cheery and they come back faithfully, which is all I ask of a tulip—or of anybody else, for that matter.

You have no idea what foolish theories some people have about plants. My next-door neighbor believes in an afterlife for poinsettias. According to her, when the blossoms have wilted you must pinch them off. Next you place the pot containing the remains in a warm, dark place in the attic, where you water it every five days. Then in May you take it out and plant it in the garden. In September, you dig up the shoots and move them to a sunny window indoors. Eventually, if you have been constant in your ministrations, the plant should bloom again.

Listen, I would do all that for a friend but not for a five-dollar poinsettia. Furthermore, if you kept *all* the poinsettias you get, you wouldn't have room in that attic for the trunks. Actually, what I like best about a big, healthy poinsettia is that it lasts about two and a half weeks, which is enough, and then it goes out when the Christmas ornaments come down. Anything else upsets the natural order of things. For instance, two years ago we received a beautiful white poinsettia, and it bloomed on, not losing a leaf, after all of the red ones were gone. We were charmed when it was still there on St. Valentine's Day. It was even amusing that it survived until Easter. But by July first there was something downright sinister about the whole thing, and

people visiting us would say "That *can't* be a poinsettia, can it?"
I think they were bracing themselves to find a trimmed Christmas tree in the next room and learn that we were celebrating
early because we didn't expect to live until the Feast proper.
And when that plant died (a natural death) in August, there was
much relief. It boils down to this: if you're going to live to be a
hundred and ten, you're going to be in the way.

There was a time when I supposed that I knew, at least in
theory, how plants grew. However, it now appears that plants
need more than sunlight and water. They need conversation.
Librettist Alan Jay Lerner, who had been doing some research
on extrasensory perception, explained the matter in the *Times*
awhile back. "Anybody can make flowers grow by talking to
them," he said. "It's a fact. Take two flower pots with the same
soil, the same seeds, the same amount of water, and talk to one
of the pots. You'll see for yourself."

I don't doubt this for a minute. But it does present certain
problems. To begin with, what do you *say* to the pot? Okay, you
can start off with something simple like "Hello, Ivy, how's every
little thing? What kind of a night did you have?" But it seems to
me that after that the conversation would sort of bog down. The
truth is, I'm not any good at small talk. And how could talk get
smaller? The next thing: if you were conducting a controlled experiment with two different plants, would you have to keep the
plant you weren't speaking to in a separate room? I mean, you
wouldn't want it overhearing you. Maybe it would be enough if
you simply made yourself clear on the subject. After a brief chat
with the ivy, you could say out loud, "As for the fern on the
piano, I have *nothing* to say to you."

No, no. It's too complicated. I have enough trouble talking to
the children.

Happy Motoring

We still have the first car we ever bought, shortly after the abdication of Edward VII. And, since it still goes frontward and backward, we weren't even thinking of buying a new one. Actually, we felt that our car had aged like a fine old wine. Perhaps it does tremble all over when the wheels hit a seam in the pavement, but no more than a high-spirited horse. And talk about *faithful!* Why I could tell you stories about that little car. . . .

But why do I torment myself, now that everything has changed? Last week we went to the movies and left the car in a parking lot. I gave the man thirty-five cents and was waiting for a stub when he said quietly, "Lady, you don't need a ticket—I can remember this one." At first I thought he was referring to the sand pails and the bathing suits which could be seen through the snow on the back window ledge. But it came to me later (a great many things came to me later on account of the movie, which was about this teen-ager who was misunderstood by everybody, especially me) that our venerable, trusty sedan was a source of merriment to the entire staff of Maple Street Parking. That young man was implying—implying nothing, he as much as said—that it was an antique, an eyesore, and a menace to the orderly progress of traffic on the Post Road. Isn't it strange that so often an outsider will be the first to notice that a loved one *is* failing?

So, we're in the market for a new car. We've looked at some, and they certainly are beautiful—longer, lower, faster, richer, milder. But where, I ask you, are those little features one looks for in a family car? I know they've been working day and night in Detroit achieving such wonders as power steering, which will enable you to get out of a tight parking place without so much as bending your elbows—in the unlikely event that you are able to find a tight parking place. I applaud push-button driving and air conditioning and I say hail, Henry Ford, cheers, General Motors, but what I want is a towel rack in the back seat. And if the children are going to insist on *chocolate* frozen custard it might be safer to have two towel racks.

Also, I'd like to have galvanized fencing installed from floor to ceiling just behind the front seat. This might just possibly keep small children in the back seat, and, what is more to the point, it should discourage their efforts to drop all the change from their lunch money down the back of your neck while you're driving.

I'm dreaming wildly now, but wouldn't it be nice for families with more than two children to have a car without any windows at all in the back? Not only would this eliminate all arguments about whose turn it is to sit next to the window, it would keep the children who are old enough to read from constantly informing you that you are now six mi., four mi., and one mi., away from a restaurant that features more than twenty different flavors of ice cream. Of course without back windows you wouldn't have a rear view, but do you anyway—with the ice skates, cowboy hats, and one pair of skis piled in the back?

By the way, do you know that it is possible to get a twenty-six-inch bicycle into the back seat of an average car? What isn't possible is to get it out. What also isn't possible is to find a parking place in front of the bicycle repair shop, so that you have to double-park in the roaring traffic's boom while you try frantically to claw the bike free now that the handlebars are entangled with the door handle. I find that the simplest and most efficient thing to do is just to lay your head on the hood of the car and moan. Sooner or later you will attract a crowd and it won't be too difficult for three men, working as a team, to get that bike out of there. Of course, they will tear the upholstery, but then it's never been the same since the baby was carsick. What would be a help is not, heaven forbid, a larger back seat area (then we'd be carting sailboats uptown to have them varnished) but two large hooks on the roof of the car from which you could hang the bicycle. Or a teeter-totter, to mention another item that I know positively will not fit inside a car.

Nobody else seems to have this next problem, so what I am going to suggest might not prove a popular feature. But, speaking for myself, I'd like the floor of the car lined with nails so nobody could stretch out down there. I find that I can drive through heavy traffic with one boy lying on the floor in his good clothes drinking a Coke. What unhinges me completely and leads to so many insults from passing male drivers is when three of them try to lie on the floor shouting, "We've got our eyes shut, say when we're passing the post office! Are we near Futterman's? Did we turn onto Beach?" Someday one of them is going to open his eyes and ask, "And why did you drive into this deep water, Mommy?" And Mommy will tell them.

But these are all trifles, the icing on the cake. What I really want, and what would contribute most to the joyous sense of family togetherness on those Sunday trips to Playland would be a little bathroom in the back seat. Don't ask me how, I'm not an engineer. This is something that will have to be worked out at the factory.

When I Was Queen of the May

Our eight-year-old Gregory was looking for a bottle of cherry soda one day and, after a brief, despairing survey of the bottles in the refrigerator, he slammed the door shut and asked me, quite seriously, "Mom, were you ever Miss Rheingold?"

I tried to explain to him that consumption of the product, however enthusiastic, was not the real basis for this singular honor. Eventually he grasped the picture, but I could see that it reopened avenues of uncomfortable speculation. Just last winter he had discovered that I couldn't do long division or make divinity fudge. And now this. In a wan effort to regain my lost glamour I told him about the time I was Queen of the May.

I was, at that time, a tall, gangly, giggly thirteen, and a freshman in a seminary for girls. The first hint of the celebrity that was to be mine came when I read on the bulletin board that I must report to the principal's office. I was struck numb with terror, because the only other time I had been thus summoned was after it became known that I was the girl who dared Bunny Ryan to peek over the heavy curtain that separated Sister Mary Olive's bed from all the other beds in the dormitory. (Bunny reported that she had hair all right, but it was very short.) But today I could sense, as soon as I stepped into the office, that I wasn't in serious trouble. For one thing, Mother Claire didn't fix on her pince-nez, a thing she always did when displeased. I don't know whether she thought it made her look more severe, or whether she simply wanted to get a better look at the offender.

Mother Claire was a saintly old lady of great sweetness and strange sibilance due, I now suppose, to ill-fitting false teeth. She never spoke above a whisper and one could follow her progress down the narrow corridors by the gentle tapping of a cane and a trail of hissing s's. Her standard method of greeting, wherever she encountered us and whatever the occasion, was to raise a powdery white hand and whisper, "S-s-s-softly, young ladies, s-s-softly." Mother was so far from being self-conscious about this impediment that it seemed almost as if she chose her phrases for the difficulties they presented. "Stick-to-it-tiveness is necessary for success" she said umpteen times a day, regally unaware of the small storm of whistling consonants that broke about our ears. But such was her air of gentle authority that not one of us would have dreamed of smiling. Nor did we ever mimic her at recess the way we did Sister Stanislaus, who used to clear her throat three times before she spoke and then say, in hushed, melancholy tones, "A girl who would chew gum will smoke, and a girl who would smoke will drink, and a girl who would drink [sinister pause] well, I think you know what that kind of a girl will do." We did, too, or thought we did, and we shuddered deliciously at the fearful prospect.

But Mother was a little island quite removed from our girlish jocularity. On that afternoon, when she said to me, "My dear, I see that you are growing in nature and in grace," I blushed with pleasure quite as if I didn't know that, at one time or another, she had said the same thing to every girl in the school. "Thank you, Mother," I said, curtsying so low that, to my horror, an old yellow comb in a rather forlorn condition fell out of my uniform pocket and clattered to the floor. Mother ignored the comb and my furtive efforts to reclaim it and said, "You will be gratified to learn that your good teachers have chosen you to crown the statue of Our Lady in the grove." I was more than gratified, I was stunned.

In the ordinary course of things there would have been nothing noteworthy about a crowning. Every year on the first of May each class had a private ceremony in which the statues of Our

Lady (and there were sometimes two or three in a single class-
room) were banked with flowers and crowned with wreaths. Indeed, such was our reputation for zeal in this matter that the
girls in a neighboring public school spread the entirely false
rumor that we seminarians, in our anxiety to lay laurel on every
available plaster head, had inadvertently crowned the bust of
Chopin in the music room.

What made this year's crowning a special event was the fact
that, for the first time, we were going to crown the massive stone
statue that stood in the grove midway between the school and
the old folks' home. The statue had been there from time imme-
morial. (Bunny Ryan said her grandmother remembered it from
the time she was a little girl, and since her grandmother had
once written to Abraham Lincoln one sensed that we were in direct contact with antiquity.) What was new, brand new, was the
concrete path that wound its way through the rocks and bram-
bles which had hitherto made formal processions out of the
question and limited visitors to the shrine to those solitary pilgrims who used to dash out to the grove for an eleventh-hour
"Hail Mary" just before a Latin exam.

Now, with the way paved in concrete, all things were possible,
and Mother Claire had decreed that this May there would be a
formal procession of the entire school, including even the babies
in kindergarten who only came half a day. All of us were to wear
white—pure, stainless white—right down to our toes, and that
meant white cotton stockings. This last was a great blow to the
seniors (who were by this time wearing silk stockings) and great
clusters of them sat on the window sills before class and muttered darkly about certain persons who were "positively *prehis-
toric*, forcryingoutloud."

Anyway, we knew the great day was nigh and we had all been
supposing that Denise Macy would be chosen to do the crowning. She had two aunts in the convent, and it was known that she
had obtained a doctor's certificate excusing her from gym only
because it was such an affront to her modesty to appear publicly
in those blue serge bloomers. Furthermore, and this was very
much to the point, her uncle had donated the eleven hundred
dollars for the paving of the path.

But Denise had been passed over and I had been chosen.

Why? I simply couldn't understand it. If the selection had been made on the basis of brains, why not Rosemary Schuette, who was so smart that she used to correct the pronunciation of the French teacher and, according to her roommate, frequently wrote torrid love letters to her boy friend in Latin? Alas, I would never have been chosen for my beauty, even though I had been secretly using Stillman's Freckle Cream for two months and felt that my complexion, though temporarily scaly, was much improved. Actually I had a rather realistic view of my physical charms because, as a small child, I had once overheard my mother announce to a friend on the telephone, "Jean's a plain little thing, but we think she's going to be intelligent."

No, it couldn't be brains and it wouldn't be beauty, so what was it then—goodness? I honestly didn't feel that I was very good, but, falling into the trap of even saints and mystics, I decided that the very fact that I didn't think I was good meant that I was humble. Taking logic a step further, it had to be granted that a humble person was a good person. It seemed clear enough when you put it that way.

I went home and told my family, but their enthusiasm was a little dampened by the fact that this honor involved the purchase of a white dress. To tell the truth, my mother was still feeling put out because she had had to pay a dressmaker four dollars to make me a sateen Herod costume last Christmas when my entire part consisted of saying fiercely, "Find the Babe, find Him and *kill* Him!"

The day we went dress hunting my mother swished her way through a whole rack of rather mournful-looking crepe-silk dresses before she called out to the salesgirl, "Surely you have something in size sixteen besides these funeral robes?" Eventually the salesgirl produced a white organdy sprinkled all over with red dots. Mother dismissed my anguished cries that it had to be *white*, all white, by saying reasonably, "In the name of God, girl, you want to get another *turn* out of it, don't you?" Quite apart from the red dots, the dress had a little capelet instead of the long sleeves that had been officially prescribed. But my protests were unavailing. Mother's mind was made up—clearly this investment was not going to be the total loss she had supposed—

and she said to the salesgirl, "Wrap it up," and to me, "This won't be the first pair of elbows they've seen up there."

On the morning of the great day I crept quaking into the auditorium full of girls in their pristine white dresses, looking and feeling like a bad case of measles. In my heart I fully expected that I would be replaced as crowner. However, when Mother Claire finally caught sight of me and my dots, she merely shut her eyes. A brief look of pain washed over her face. It was the expression you might expect if the chef at Lutèce were asked to contemplate a frozen TV dinner. But she said nothing, and clearly I was to crown as planned.

We assembled out in the driveway, where the nun who taught gym and was thought to have a feeling for organization pulled and pushed us into an orderly file. I was first, accompanied by a tiny girl from the kindergarten who carried the wreath on a silver tray. Then there were four music students with flutes, who were to provide the accompaniment for the hymns. Next came six first-grade girls with baskets of flowers. These were followed by the rest of the school, paired off in twos according to height. There was a slight feeling of uneasiness in the ranks because, owing to the rain yesterday, the dress rehearsal had been held in the gym and now, with the vast difference in terrain, we felt all turned around. Still, there were no mishaps as the procession wound its slow, solemn way to the shrine.

On arrival, the wreath bearer and I stepped forward while all the other girls fanned out until they had formed three large circles around the shrine. Then, after a warning tweet from the flutes, we sang "'Tis May." I was beginning to feel nervous: the crowning hymn came next.

"'Tis May" proved to be very effective because the five girls who always flatted on the final high C did remember to drop out before the end, as instructed. At last the crowning hymn began. I listened very carefully, for there was a definite place in the lyric indicating the moment when the crowner was to step forward.

It came. The voices rang out high and sweet in the open air: "Oh, Gray-shus Queen of Hea-von, we haste to-oo crown thee-ee now." Then a silence fell—the song was to be continued after the actual crowning—as I picked up the wreath and walked slowly up to the statue.

It was then that I realized, and with a stab to the heart, why I had been chosen. I had been chosen because I was the tallest girl in the school. It was equally clear, as I peered at the massive stone figure looming four or five feet above me, that, tall as I was, I wasn't tall enough. Hoping for further instructions, I shot a look of desperation and panic over to the right, where the nuns were standing in a little clump. But their heads were bowed in benediction and they seemed totally unaware of the crisis.

Finally, Alice McClain, who was class president and a girl of some resourcefulness, signaled the flutes to start up again. Once more the voices sang out, though not, of course, with the same dash: "Oh, Gray-shus Queen of Hea-von, we haste to-oo crown thee-ee now." This time the word "now" seemed a reproach. Was it possible, I wondered, that we would all have to stand here until I grew another six inches?

Just as it seemed fearfully likely that the singing was going to begin for a third time, I remembered Mother Claire's oft-repeated adage: "Desperate diseases require desperate remedies." I took the wreath firmly in my two hands, grasping it like a basketball, and hurled it up onto the head of the statue. For a brief moment it looked as though I had succeeded, for the wreath seemed to be resting firmly on the prongs of the stone crown. But then, slowly and majestically, it slid down until it settled rakishly over one large stone eye. The effect was decidedly disreputable, and there was a hiss of horror from the nuns as well as a gasp from the girls that quickly degenerated into muffled laughter. The first to be affected were the flautists, who, in an effort to suppress their giggles, had blown spit into their flutes and rendered them useless. The singers, without a flute to guide them, fell silent. The little girl who had borne the wreath burst into tears, and a first-grade flower girl was heard to inquire loudly, "Is it over?"

This was all too much for Mother Claire, who wheeled slowly in her tracks and marched back to the school, followed by the other nuns. Only the gym teacher remained to see that the retreat didn't turn into a rout.

I stood there, bleary with grief, feeling like the captain of a ship that was going down with all aboard. In my own mind I was the innocent victim of fate, but I knew perfectly well that in the minds of the departing nuns I was now an irresponsible defiler of sacred objects. Suddenly, I broke out of line and ran down the path until I caught up with Mother Claire. "Oh, Mother," I said, the tears splattering down my cheeks. "I am sorry." Mother put on her pince-nez and looked at me. "Dots," she said sadly, "and now this." "But Mother—" I explained in what may be the most poignant statement ever made by a thirteen-year-old, "I'm *only* five feet nine."

Even great disasters have a way of being forgotten (who today talks about the Chicago fire?) and pretty soon everybody stopped discussing the crowning and my unworthy part in it. Nevertheless it was instrumental in changing my life, because two days later I was invited to join the Seven-Uppers. This was a club formed by the seven most popular girls in the school, girls of such incomparable chic and elegance that I had aspired to be one of them only in the dim, helpless way that a copyboy aspires to be managing editor. They had evidently decided that my errors on crowning day were all part of a calculated plan and that, however rough hewn my appearance, I was to be regarded as a cutup and a card. Under these decidedly false pretenses, I joined the Seven-Uppers (there was some talk of changing the name to the Eight-Teens, but that died out). Now I, too, rode in raffish splendor in Dottie Long's maroon roadster after school. And with the others I huddled under the porch at recess and puffed away at an Old Gold. I had come a long way.

The Conversation Gap

Of course, I have no statistics, and nobody ever tells me anything. But I suspect one reason marriages break up is that some wives, after spending a full hour in rich, deeply shared silence with the beloved, are apt to remark, "In heaven's name, *say* something, will you?"

The problem stems quite naturally from the fact that women speak because they wish to speak, whereas a man speaks only when driven to speech by something outside himself—like, for instance, he can't find any clean socks, or he has just read in a headline that Con Edison is asking for a new rate increase. A wife who really feels cheerful and chatty early in the morning (a circumstance that can be explained only by a faulty metabolism) can always inveigle her husband into conversation by using a little imagination and by learning to snap up cues. She might say, "Speaking of clean socks reminds me, did you read Anatole Broyard's review of *Humboldt's Gift?*" Now he's on the spot. He has to say something, even if it is only to comment on the total absence of any connection between his socks and *Humboldt's Gift*.

I have a rather engaging little trick for stirring my own husband into statement. I just quote a few lines from the balcony scene of *Romeo and Juliet*.

"He speaks," I say in mock lyrical tones, "but he says nothing.

What of that? His eye discourses. I will answer *it*." Thus prodded, he is apt to say things he will have to retract later, but there
are risks to everything.

Actually, if you had wanted a husband who would be a stimulating conversationalist, you should have married a mechanic or
even a gardener—certainly not an author or a professional man
or, last of all, a lecturer. When we got married, my husband was
a lecturer and professor of drama and I used to imagine the
stimulating, intellectual conversation we were going to have at
breakfast. Like this:

Me: That play last night was interesting, didn't you think?
Him: Very. Of course, the author is still heavily in debt to
      Chekhov—the despairing protagonist, the shackling en-
      vironment, the complete stasis in the third act, and, of
      course, the total absence of climax.
Me: Yes, he has an almost kinetic sense of atmosphere, but
      he never licked the story line.
Him: Licked it? He should have joined it.
                 (Appreciative chuckles all around)

This, however, is a transcript of the actual conversation:

Him: (Despairingly) I'll bet this is diet bread.
Me: What's the matter with diet bread?
Him: (After a pause) Everything. Why don't we eat things
      other people eat?
Me: Such as—
Him: (Passionately) Those flat sticky things with jam inside
      them. Or muffins. Why don't we ever have muffins?
Me: (Evenly) Very well, dear, we'll have muffins.
Him: (Suspiciously) Oh, I know you. You'll get diet muffins.

We really should have our own radio show.

It's interesting to observe the phenomenon that will cause a
husband who hasn't opened his yap in weeks suddenly to find
the gift of speech. Just order a new coat that differs in any way
at all from the last five coats you have owned and watch Big

Chief Still Waters blossom into Alistair Cooke, a veritable fount of articulation. "Yes, I know it's the new style, but we haven't got a space ship yet. Oh, I see, all the fullness in the back is *supposed* to make you look as if you're standing in a head wind! Well, never mind. It'll be economical, anyway—in the summer you can take it to the beach and use it as a cabana." Etc.

There is a cure for this. Just take him with you when you go to Bonwit Teller's. Once you deposit him on that chaste Empire sofa in Misses' Suits, his whole attitude will change—not to mention his pulse, temperature, and rate of breathing. Precisely what causes men to go into shock in Bonwit's I can't imagine. My husband keeps looking from right to left in a state of ashen panic, as though he feared at any moment one of those elegant salesladies was going to snatch him and set his hair. But at any rate he brings a more judicious attitude to the subject of high style. "Yeah, yeah," he mutters at my first appearance from the depths of the dressing room, "it looks great, let's get out of here."

Some men do most of their talking at the movies ("Good Lord, I knew I was in for *Moby Dick,* but you didn't say there was going to be forty minutes of cartoons!") My father is a man like that. The most he has spoken in thirty years was on a certain unfortunate occasion when my mother (who can't remember the titles of movies) took him for the second time in three weeks to see Bob Hope in *Son of Paleface.*

But let's get down to cases:

How to Talk to a Man When He's Snoring

When I speak of snoring I do not refer to the simple, rhythmic snorp-bleet, snorp-bleet to which every loyal, understanding wife should adjust. I am here talking of snoring which has the range and crescendo of a musical composition—where you can actually detect a verse, two choruses, and a release. I used to give my husband a gentle shove and whisper, "Honey, turn over—you're snoring." The result was that he turned over and in two minutes was snoring louder than before, while I lay awake for hours planning a separation and wondering what we were going to do about the children and all those monogrammed towels.

Then I learned the trick, which is to get the snorer interested. Don't make statements. Ask questions. Shake him and say, "Dar-

ling, what are you trying to say?" Eventually, after a few inco-
herent "huh, huhs" and "what, whats," he'll ask, "What do you
mean, what am I trying to say?" After a few more equally point-
less questions and answers he will be so cross that it will be at
least fourteen minutes before he'll be able to snore again, giving
you ample time to get to sleep first.

How to Talk to a Man in a Fashionable Restaurant

I once read an interview with the Duchess of Windsor in
which she said that she and the Duke hated to eat in public restaurants because they had to converse so animatedly and affect
such feverish interest in each other—lest rumors start that they
were estranged—that she never could enjoy a bite of her dinner.
It ought to be (but somehow it isn't) helpful to tell yourself that
you're not the Duchess of Windsor and that nobody is even the
tiniest bit interested in whether you and your husband have
spoken since 1963. The point is that in a restaurant (like Sardi's,
for instance) where you are surrounded by the tinkling laughter
of beautiful models engaged in vivacious conversation with
movie actors, you do feel somehow that you can't just sit there,
specters at the feast, looking like two people who have just
learned that their 1976 income tax return is being investigated.
Of course there are lots of things on your mind that you could
say ("Well, you saw that Chris got D in Health Habits again,"
or, "The exterminator says our new bugs are silverfish") but this
doesn't seem to be the time or the place.

A couple I know have solved the problem beautifully. She just
tells him the story of "The Three Bears," a narrative which is admirable for the purpose because of its many rising inflections.
And he helps her out by occasionally interjecting a remark like
"By George, you mean she ate every last bite of the baby bear's
porridge?" Do try it some time. Anybody overhearing you will
conclude that you are discussing a new television spectacular—
either that, or you're both a little bit dotty. If you should be concerned about this aspect of the matter, or if you should happen
to intercept a stunned glance from the waiter, you can always
drop in a covering remark like "Woody Allen—*there's* your Baby
Bear!"

How to Talk to a Man When He's Taking a Shower

Here you have a captive audience and an ideal opportunity to tell a husband a number of things that you don't want him to hear. (Later on you can say, "Of course I told you, you just don't listen!") There is no limit to the amount of unwelcome information you can get off your chest at one clip in these circumstances: "The man from Macy's was here and I took thirty dollars out of your wallet," and "Betty called, she and George are going to drop in," and "This is our weekend to take care of the school rabbit."

How to Talk to a Man on the Telephone, Long Distance

When a man calls you from Tulsa, he invariably makes the mistake of calling either from a public bar or from his mother's living room. Neither setting is exactly conducive to a free exchange of ideas. There, within earshot of his fellow revelers or his mother, he can hardly say the one thing you want to hear, which is that he misses you terribly, it's been a nightmare, a nightmare! and he's never going to make a trip alone again. For that matter, you can't tell him you miss him either, because the children are there with you and they become downright alarmed at any hint that their parents have preserved this degrading adolescent attachment so far into senility. So, if you're not careful, it's going to be a total loss of five dollars and eighty-five cents.

Don't, whatever you do, launch into that foolish litany of last-minute health bulletins: "Yes, I'm fine, yes, Chris is fine, yes, Gilbert is fine, etc." Let it be understood in advance that if one of the children should be rushed to the hospital for an emergency appendectomy, you'll mention it.

Use the time to clear up some matter that has really been troubling you. Explain that you finally saw *The Bridge on the River Kwai* on television and that it was marvelous, marvelous, but you didn't understand the ending. Get him to explain it. Did Alec Guinness mean to set off that dynamite or didn't he? What about William Holden? Who really killed him? This is important. When William Holden gets shot, a woman wants to know the facts. Later, when you hang up, you may discover that you've forgotten to ask what time his plane arrives at La Guardia, but the call won't have been a total loss.

How to Talk to a Man Before a Party

There are two occasions when a wife absolutely expects that a
loyal husband will cleave to her side: when she's having a baby
and when she's having a party. (It's interesting to note that the
announcements on both occasions always seem to imply that
these are joint projects, but, when it comes right down to it, who
has that baby and who has that party? You do.) No one expects
a husband to go out in the kitchen and stuff eggs, but he might
try being a moral support during that horrible, hollow half hour
before the first guest arrives. There you are, wandering aimlessly
about from ashtray to ashtray, suddenly feeling as strange and as
lost as if you had just checked into a motel in downtown Pitts-
burgh. And one of the reasons you can't rely on your husband
for a comforting remark is that this is precisely the moment he
chooses to lay a few asphalt tiles on the floor of the rumpus
room.

If you should stand on your rights and say "Don't you disappear anywhere at all, just stay right here!" he will eventually
lighten the tension by muttering "Great Scott, you forgot limes!"
What he should say, of course, is something soothing like "Darling, you look charming in that dress. It reminds me of the night
we met, do you remember? You were dancing with Hugh, and I
came in with Connie and Leo . . ."

The last time we had a party I suggested this constructive line
of conversation to my husband. He claimed that he'd once said
something very similar, and what I said was "In heaven's name,
stop chattering about the night we met and go get some ice."

*How to Talk to a Man After You've Told Him That if He
Doesn't Stop Fiddling with That Old Toaster He Is Going to
Blow a Fuse, and He Does.*

There is no way. Just light a candle and count ten or your
blessings, whichever is greater.

How to Get Unhooked
from a Soap Opera

I'll tell you the exact moment I knew I had to give up my soap opera. One of my best friends called me on the telephone recently and I said, "Hey, Peggy, can I call you back? My other phone is ringing." There was a silence, and then she said, rather plaintively, "Jean, you don't *have* another phone." And of course I don't. It was all a tissue of lies, part of a cover-up that wasn't really fooling anybody. But there it was. Even to Peggy, who has been a solace for twenty-eight years, I couldn't blurt out the truth, which was that I was watching "One Life to Live."

Furthermore, the day she called wasn't just an ordinary day in Landview. You see, the Craigs were having this wedding reception for Larry and Karen and, right smack in the middle of things, Mrs. Magruder arrived with Vickie and Joe's baby, which had been kidnaped—oh, months ago—by Cathie Craig, who was disturbed by the loss of *her* baby, which was also Joe's baby. And everything would have been marvelous except that while Vickie was hugging her now recovered baby, Kevin, Joe was drunk in a bar punching out a stranger. Well, you can see why I had to be there.

The funny thing is that until about two years ago I had never seen even one episode of a soap opera. I had a definite idea, though, of the kind of woman who would watch them: a gin-soaked slattern in her husband's old bathrobe, dirty dishes mounting in the sink, waxy build-up piling up on the linoleum. Actually, the gin-soaked part is patently absurd. You have to be alert to follow these plots.

But in spite of all my hifalutin attitudes, I have lived, I have learned. It's not just pride. *Everything* goeth before the fall.

Like most affairs, the whole thing began so innocently. I looked at "One Life to Live" just once (ha!) to catch a glimpse of Erica Slezak, who plays Vickie Lord. I should tell you that Erica lived right across the street from us when she was a little girl (no, this part is true; in fact, one of our boys was in love with her when he was ten). Anyway, I wanted to see if Erica was still so pretty. As it turned out, she was even prettier. But I couldn't tell right away because the first time I looked she was in a coma from a car accident, which occurred while she was rushing Megan, Joe's illegitimate daughter who had a congenital heart condition, to the hospital, where she (Megan) perished. And, for that matter, it was touch and go with Vickie for about six weeks. I felt that I should keep looking until she (Erica/Vickie) was well enough to open her eyes and get her hair done. And by the time Vickie, radiant once more, was taking her first halting steps in a walker, I was hopelessly hooked.

Not just with Vickie and Joe's problems (she's a saint, and God knows he *means* well) but also with the hazards facing Timmy Siegel, who wanted to marry Jenny—who was a nun—as soon as he got out of jail. And I really became fond of Victor Lord, who was slipping into the clutches of rotten Dorian. By the way, I can't bring myself to tell you how many of these characters have since expired. That hospital in Landview is a death trap.

No matter. In those days the show ran only one half hour, which means twenty-two minutes if you take off eight minutes for commercials. Now, when they take off eight minutes for commercials, *I* take off eight minutes for commercials, leaving the area entirely. There is no need for me to stay, since I am already convinced beyond the need for further persuasion that if you wash with "ordinary detergent alone" you are a slob and your children's spotted, messy clothing will be the scandal of the entire neighborhood.

But I did feel I was entitled to my full twenty-two minutes of actual diversion. It was Thomas Aquinas, or somebody sensible, who said that "No man can exist without pleasure." And there were no calories involved, no hangovers. Look at it another way. Every single day of his life, my husband wastes twenty minutes on the *Times* crossword puzzle (he says it's more like seven minutes, but then he's not the one waiting for the paper), and he isn't looked down upon as a pariah or a second-class citizen. Of course, he is willing to take phone calls during the puzzle, but what, in fact, is he learning? I asked him that once and he said he was learning that a nef is a ship-shaped clock and an oda is a room in a harem.

But we're not talking about his conscience and his wasted life. We're talking about me and how the whole thing escalated and finally got out of hand. First "One Life to Live" extended to forty-five minutes. Then, last winter, I was confined to my bed with some kind of grippe and, feeling rather too languid to turn off the set when my show was over, I discovered what millions may already have known. "General Hospital" follows immediately after "One Life to Live," and is, in turn, followed by "The Edge of Night." Now, about "General Hospital." *There* is a perfect maelstrom of seething personalities. I myself think that Terri and Dr. Mark Dante will get together in spite of Mark's meddling wife, Mary Ellen, who has tried to kill two people (since she was released from a mental institution), including Terri, who then lapsed into the customary coma before brain surgery.

Before you say it, I'll say it. *I* was in a coma. The world was passing me by. I was giving the most bizarre explanations for why I *never* could go out in the afternoons on weekdays. I was even testy with my charming dentist, because he claimed that he saw patients on Saturday afternoons only if there was a real emergency. The whole thing was actually beginning to cost me money. With the car just sitting in the garage while I was glued to the set, I sent a taxi to the vet to pick up Frosty, our dog (he wasn't sick, he was just in for a shampoo and a set). I know that sounds awful, but I figured Frosty would understand (certainly the cab driver didn't understand) that I had to be present for Leslie's caesarean section.

Now that it's all behind me, now that I have quit forever, I am not taking a holier-than-thou attitude. Luckier-than-thou, perhaps, but not holier. Nor would I dream of suggesting that there is anything "wrong" about following a soap opera. Listen. Miss Lillian, President Carter's remarkable mother, watches one. My idol, the late, great P. G. Wodehouse, who was still working at full tilt at ninety, *never* missed an episode of "The Edge of Night." I simply address myself to those who find, for whatever reasons, that they can't handle it anymore.

Now I don't recommend just quitting cold turkey. In my experience, the only thing you can quit cold turkey is cold turkey. No, the best thing to do is to wean yourself gradually away from the soap opus, soap opera, of your choice. A good way to start is to tell your husband the plot every night at dinner. He'll have the weekends to recover. And if the children are listening, so much the better for your eventual rehabilitation. Tell them all that Terri is herniating. If your husband is supportive and wants to help you lick this thing, he will encourage you to babble on by asking provocative questions like "Herniating, *what* is herniating?" You probably should have looked that up, but it's always safe to say that in "General Hospital" if a person is unconscious and a doctor pops a tiny flashlight in her eye and says "She's herniating" that's *real* trouble. And you can go on to explain that they're going to have to suction out a haematoma, which, as anyone could guess, is a pretty iffy proposition. If the left temporal lobe is breached, the patient could suffer a speech deficit, which would certainly affect the whole plot. By the time I had finished weaving my tale one evening, I thought I could detect a certain bemused—no, wary—look in my husband's eyes. On the other hand, my son, who has just completed medical school, was so impressed he had to leave the room.

Another thing that will help in your rehabilitation is to discuss the matter at dinner parties. Should you be introduced to a celebrated surgeon, you might say "Oh, Dr. Cahan, I've always wanted to meet you because I have a question. Lee Baldwin's stepson in 'General Hospital' is suffering from Malenkov's Disease. Is that a real disease, and, if so, what is the prognosis?" This will bring all conversation to a halt, and, in the silence, you can reflect upon the gravity of your situation. Furthermore, you won't need to write a thank-you note, because you *won't* be asked back.

Finally, I find it helpful to invite somebody, preferably a house-guest (who can't exactly get out of it), to watch along with me. Make girlish, fluttery excuses: "You may not enjoy this all that much because, you know, you'll be starting in the middle." (There's no point in explaining that down through all eternity there will be no beginning and no end—just always, always the middle.) And then make note of what your friend says even if it enrages you.

My friend Charles, whom I love like a brother, and my brother, whom I love like a brother, both watched with me one afternoon. My brother, rather intemperate by nature, suddenly looked at me in some confusion and exclaimed, "I don't believe this, you've gone mad." Charles, who writes for a living (I think that makes him kind of jumpy sometimes), kept shaking his head from side to side and finally muttered, "Did I hear that line, did I really and truly hear that line?" "What line?" I asked, honestly perplexed. He was quick to clarify: "That man on the sofa just pointed his finger and said, 'Okay, Dorian, but if Vickie loses this baby she's carrying it'll be on your head.' "

He didn't really like the second program, either. In fact, he seemed to find something humorous in this perfectly straightforward statement: "I know you don't like Monica, but before you evaluate her personality please remember her skill at fibrillating Mr. Daniels." Of course, if you're going to be all that picky, you're going to miss a lot.

In due time I began to realize that I no longer enjoyed the high regard that my age and my position in the community enti-tles me to. I was an idiot, is what I was. So I swore off, which you, too, may be able to do by following my simple pre-scriptions. If, however, by any chance one of you is still back-ward enough to be watching "One Life to Live," would you please write and tell me if Joe and Vickie still have a security guard for the baby? And how *is* that marriage?

My Marshmallow Fudge
Wonder Diet

Fred Allen used to talk about a man who was so thin he could be dropped through a piccolo without striking a single note. Well, I'm glad I never met *him*; I'd hate to have to hear about *his* diet.

I can remember when I was a girl—way back in Truman's administration—and Tab was only a gleam in the eye of the Coca-Cola Bottling Company. In those days it was fun to go to parties. The conversation used to crackle with wit and intelligence because we talked about *ideas*—the aesthetic continuum in Western culture, Gary Cooper in western movies, the superiority of beer over lotion as a wave-set, and the best way to use leftover veal.

Go to a party now and the couple next to you won't say a word about the rich, chocolate texture of their compost heap or how practical it's been to buy bunk beds for the twins. They won't talk about anything whatsoever except their diets—the one they've just come off, the one they're on now, or the one they're going to have to start on Monday if they keep lapping it up like this.

I really blame science for the whole business. Years ago when a man began to notice that if he stood up on the subway and he was immediately replaced by *two* people, he figured he was getting too fat. So he went to his doctor and the doctor said, "Quit stuffing yourself, Joe." And Joe either stopped or he didn't stop, but at least he kept his big mouth shut about the whole matter. What was there to talk about?

Today, with the science of nutrition advancing so rapidly, there is plenty of food for conversation, if for nothing else. We have Dr. Stillman's "Water Diet," Dr. Frank's "No Aging Diet" in which every cell in your body becomes young as a result of your consumption of sardines and lentils, Dr. Rubin's "Save Your Life Diet" in which you duplicate the eating habits of the developing African nations (fibers, you eat more fibers), Dr. Jollife's "The Prudent Diet," Dr. Atkins' "The Super Energy Diet," and finally Dr. Linn's "The Last Chance Diet" in which you don't eat anything whatsoever except two tablespoons of a cherry-flavored potion called Prolinn. (It's called other things by people who have to swallow it.)

But where do people come across all these crazy diets, anyway? Obviously in the magazines; it's impossible to get a diet from a newspaper. For one thing, in a newspaper you can never catch the diet when it *starts*. It's always the fourth day of "Ada May's Wonder Diet" and, after a brief description of a simple slimming exercise that could be performed by anybody who has had five years' training with the ballet, Ada May gives you the menu for the day. One glass of skim milk, eight prunes, and three lamb kidneys. This settles the matter for most people, who figure, quite reasonably, that if this is the *fourth* day, heaven deliver them from the first.

However, any stoics in the group who want to know just how far Ada May's sense of whimsy will take her can have the complete diet by sending sixty-two cents in stamps to the newspaper. But there you are. Who has sixty-two cents in stamps? You're not running a branch of the post office. And if you're going to go out and get the stamps you might as well buy a magazine which will give you not only the same diet (now referred to as "*Our* Wonder Diet") but will, in addition, show you a quick and easy way to turn your husband's old socks into gay pot holders.

In a truly democratic magazine that looks at all sides of the picture you will also find a recipe for George Washington's favorite spice cake, which will replace any weight you may have haphazardly lost on that wonder diet.

If you have formed the habit of checking on every *new* diet that comes along, you will find that, mercifully, they all blur together, leaving you with only one definite piece of information: french-fried potatoes are out. But once in a great while a diet will stick in your mind. I'll never forget one I read about last summer. It urged the dieter to follow up his low-calorie meals by performing a series of calisthenics in the bathtub. No, not in the bath*room*. I read it twice and it said in the bath*tub*. What a clever plan! Clearly, after you've broken both your arms you won't be able to eat much (if at all) and the pounds will just melt away. In fact, if you don't have a co-operative husband who is willing to feed you like a two-year-old you may be limited to what you can consume through a straw, in which case let me suggest "The Last Chance Diet."

The best diet I've heard about lately is the simplest. It was perfected by the actor Walter Slezak after years of careful experimentation. Under the Slezak plan, you eat as much as you want of everything you don't like. And if you should be in a hurry for any reason (let's say you're still wearing maternity clothes and the baby is eight months old), then you should confine yourself to food that you just plain hate.

Speaking about hateful food, the experts used to be content with merely making food pallid—by eliminating butter, oil, and salt. Not anymore. Nowadays we are taught that, with a little imagination and a judicious use of herbs, anyone can turn out a no-calorie dish that's downright ghastly. Just yesterday I came across a dandy recipe for sprucing up good old boiled celery. You just simmer the chopped celery (with the tops) in a little skim milk. When it's tender, you add chopped onion, anise, chervil, marjoram, a dash of cinnamon, and you have a dish fit for the Dispose-All. And you'd better have a Dispose-All, because it's awfully messy if you have to dump it into a newspaper and carry it out to the garbage can.

And where is all this dieting getting us? No place at all. It's taken all the fun out of conversation and all the joy out of cooking. Furthermore, it leads to acts of irrational violence. A friend of mine keeps all candy and other luscious tidbits in the freezer, on the theory that by the time they thaw out enough to be eaten she will have recovered her will power. But the other night, having been driven berserk by a four-color advertisement for Instant Brownies, she rushed out to the freezer, started to gnaw on a frozen Milky Way, and broke off her front tooth.

But let's get to the heart of the matter. All these diets that appear so monotonously in the flossy magazines—who are they for? Are they aimed at men? Certainly not; most men don't read these magazines. Are they intended for fat teen-agers? Probably not; teen-agers can't afford them. Do not ask for whom the bell tolls. It tolls for you, Married Woman, Mother of Three, lumpy, dumpy, and the source of concern to practically every publication in the country. And why, why is the married woman being hounded into starvation in order to duplicate an ideal figure which is neither practical nor possible for a person her age? I'll tell you why.

First, it is presumed that when you're thinner you live longer. Those people in the Russian Ukraine who eat so much yogurt apparently live to be a hundred and thirty-four. (And when they have a cake with candles it must be something to see.) Second, it is felt that when you are skin and bones you have so much extra energy that you can climb up and shingle the roof. Third—and this is what they're really getting at—when you're thin you are so tasty and desirable that strange men will pinch you at the A & P and your husband will not only follow you around the kitchen breathing heavily but will stop and smother you with kisses as you try to put the butter back in the icebox. This—and I hope those in the back of the room are listening—is hogwash.

Think of the happy marriages you know about. How many of the ladies are still wearing size twelve? I've been giving this a lot of thought in the last twenty minutes, and I have been examining the marriages in my own troubled circle. More than that, I have taken a cross section of the divorcees. (Cross? My dear, they were irate!) What I have discovered—attention, Beauty Editors everywhere!—is that the women who are being ditched are one and all willowy, wandlike, and slim as a blade. In fact, six of them require extensive padding even to look flat-chested.

That the fourteen divorcees, or about-to-be divorcees, whom I happen to know personally are thin may be nothing more than a coincidence. Or it may just prove that men don't divorce fat wives because they feel sorry for them. Then again—and this is rather sinister—men may not divorce fat wives because they imagine that the poor, plump dears will never locate *another* husband and they'll be paying alimony to the end of their days. (I mention this possibility, but my heart's not in it.)

The real reason, I believe, that men hang onto their well-endowed spouses is because they're comfy and nice to have around the house. In a marriage there is nothing that stales so fast as physical beauty—as we readers of *Modern Screen* have observed. What actually holds a husband through thick and thick is a girl who is fun to be with. And any girl who has had nothing to eat since nine o'clock this morning but three hard-boiled eggs will be about as jolly and companionable as an income-tax inspector.

So I say, ladies, find out why women everywhere are switching from old-fashioned diets to the *modern* way: no exercise, no dangerous drugs, no weight loss. (And what do they mean "ugly fat"? It's *you*, isn't it?) For that tired run-down feeling, try eating three full meals a day with a candy bar after dinner and pizza at eleven o'clock. Don't be intimidated by pictures of Farrah Fawcett-Majors. That girl simply has more teeth than other people. Just sit there smiling on that size twenty backside and say "Guess what we're having for dinner, dear? Your favorite— stuffed breast of veal and corn fritters." All of your friends will say "Oh, Blanche is a mess, the size of a house, but he's crazy about her, just *crazy* about her!"

I Saw Mommy
Kicking Santa Claus

There's nothing like an old-fashioned Christmas—goodies on the groaning board, halls decked with holly berry, gaily wrapped presents piling up on the window sills, loved ones chiming carols. It can put you flat on your back for a month. For years I spent the whole of January in bed with what was diagnosed as "my bronchitis" but was clearly battle fatigue brought on from my days in Macy's and my nights in Bloomingdale's.

It was all my own fault. I had no sense and no system. Only staying power. I was always the last woman on the last down elevator as the store was closing. As a consequence, I was the first one out of the "play" area on Christmas Day. I used to spend the entire afternoon huddled in a chair next to the oven, ostensibly to baste the turkey, actually to put as much distance as possible between me and toys that tooted and growled and beeped and trilled and said "Hey, Doc, wanna carrot?"

It was in this retreat that my husband discovered me one typical Christmas afternoon. He studied my wan and woebegone expression and said, not unsympathetically, "You know, we have two spirits of Christmas around here. We have Santa Claus and then we have anti-Claus—you." And he was right, of course. I had spent all my energy planning and shopping for the Great Day and now that it was here I was, for all practical purposes, absent, a bump on the yule log.

It now seems to me, looking back in anguish, that I hadn't been shopping to buy things, I was shopping to shop. I mean, shop *around*. A person of any intelligence who was looking for a red and black cowboy suit in size eight would buy the first red and black cowboy suit (size eight) that turned up at a reasonable price. Not me. I felt compelled to go to five more stores and check on *their* cowboy suits. Perhaps these might be cheaper or blacker or redder. I could spend an entire afternoon selecting a rattle for a five-month-old infant even though I had already observed that this infant preferred to play with the lids of old cold-cream jars and a tin spoon.

Even so, I was all right years ago when the department stores —in their mercy—used to delay their decorating until after Thanksgiving. Then we had a breathing space, a time to be thankful before it was yet time to be joyful. Now the decorations go up any time after Labor Day, and I suspect they'll be sneaking back to Columbus Day any minute. You can be wandering down Fifth Avenue on a day of golden Indian summer, thinking your own thoughts, step inside the store to buy nothing more than a pair of nylons, and suddenly find the place a thicket of holly and a downpour of tinsel. When this happens, I panic. I get the same sinking feeling that I experience when the pilot's voice comes over the intercom saying "Fasten your seat belts, we are moving into turbulence." In the plane and in the shop I have the same sensation: *It's all over and I've done nothing.*

I don't know what these merchants have in mind. Maybe they're just trying to be helpful. But I'll tell you what I think. I think they've escalated Christmas.

In the days of my energy, not only did I shop like one demented. I made Christmas decorations *with my own hands.* I, who cannot place eighteen perfect roses in a vase without losing either six roses or the vase, used to experiment with pine cones and lemons. With every florist shop in the neighborhood filled with charming and inexpensive arrangements, I had to paint sticks and glue sequins on them. I will draw a veil over my efforts to create a castle centerpiece from a cardboard box and three thousand gumdrops. For your information, gumdrops will stick to carpets and to sweaters and to cats. They will not stick to cardboard. But I was intrepid.

By Christmas Eve I was so rattled from being intrepid that I couldn't even make a simple decision of policy like: Does Santa bring the tree or does Daddy bring the tree? For years Santa brought the tree, which is ridiculous. It's just one more burden for Santa added on to everything else in that sleigh. It's also one more burden for Daddy since, under these terms, the tree can't be purchased until after dark on Christmas Eve and it can't be trimmed until the small children go to sleep, which could be as late as ten o'clock. The obvious thing, the humane thing, is for Daddy to buy the tree to *welcome* Santa and to *show* Santa where to put the presents. This way it can be trimmed any old time, even by the small children, if you have lots of extra ornaments. But that was a solution which came to me years later.

Another thing that came to me years later was that I ought to buy an ax. Since the trees were pretty well picked over by the time we got out to buy the one that Santa was going to bring, we were invariably stuck with a tall, skinny tree which was four feet higher than the ceiling or a short, fat tree with a trunk too wide for the Christmas-tree holder. Lacking the proper tools, we used to hack at the trees with bread knives and tiny toy saws, a practice which led to wistful exchanges:

"Honey, why don't we buy an ax?"

"We *did* buy an ax."

"Then where is it?"

"We hid it so the children wouldn't find it."

"Where did we hide it?"

"We don't know. The children never found it."

Another thing you need an ax for is to uncrate the toys. Oh, wouldn't it be wonderful if some manufacturer would make a toy as tough, as staunch, as hard to crack open as the carton it comes in! I never did learn any right way to open these seamless, impenetrable fortresses. I do know some wrong ways: jumping up and down on what may or may not be the lid, kicking and clawing with bare fingernails, attacking them with ice skates.

I have often found myself wondering what model household inspired the bard who penned the immortal lines "And all through the house not a creature was stirring, not even a mouse." We used to stir until six in the morning. Once the tree had been trimmed (late), and the cartons opened (later), we began the real work of the night, which was to put together all the toys that had arrived in separate pieces. It has been explained to me that toys are packaged in shards, to be assembled by the middle-aged and butter-fingered, because this makes it easier for the shippers. It has not been explained to my satisfaction. I am sure that shippers are human. I am also sure that they are, none of them, fathers. If they had to spend hours and hours putting handlebars onto bicycles and fumbling through the wrappings to find the spring marked A that must be attached to the C sprocket of the rail marked YF, they would repent their ways and deliver something that looked like a rocking horse and not like the result of a small street accident.

Anyway, I used to get to bed at six and try to sleep very fast so that I could arise larklike at seven. Alas, I was never larklike. Once up I could do nothing more than subside gently into the softest pile of discarded wrappings, a wreck, gazing glassy-eyed at the frolicking children and moaning in a low voice, "Please save the cards. Don't throw away the cards. You won't know who to *thank* if you throw away the cards."

Even before all the presents are unwrapped, the battery crisis will have begun:

"Why is he crying?"

"Because his dinosaur won't go anymore."

"Why won't it go?"

"Because Col took the battery for his fire engine."

"Col, that fire engine has its own battery."

"No, it doesn't."

"Then use the battery from the Marx-a-Cart."

"That's too big."

"*Give him back his battery.*"

"It seems to be dead now."

Some enterprising youth should go from door to door on Christmas morning peddling batteries. He'd not only make his name and fortune, he'd be first in the hearts of his countrymen. The very worst thing about running out of batteries is that the children are now left free to play with their new games, which would be all right if they would play their new games with each other. But they don't want to play with each other, they want to play with you. Speaking for myself, I don't mind playing any

game where there is skill involved. Checkers, for instance. A
moderately intelligent adult who is playing checkers with a six-
year-old child can usually manage to lose. And in about ten minutes. On the other hand, you can play one of those games with
tiny rabbit markers that move forward inch by inch and in
which you select cards that tell you—in terrible rhyme—how
many hops you may take to the Blueberry Patch. You can play a
game like that for one whole hour and then—sweet heaven!—you
win. If a child can count, there is absolutely no way to "fix" an
Uncle Wiggily game. Soon a sad, defeated voice will be saying
to Daddy, "Mommy beat me at Uncle Wiggily." It's degrading.
Would you believe that I am the Uncle Wiggily *champ* around
here? I am unhinged by all my victories. I am also good at
Tinker Toys, probably because I have to pick them up all over
the house and it's easier to make something than go find the cyl-
inder they came in.

One thing I am definitely tired of is coloring in coloring books.
The reason for this is that children have no sense of quid pro
quo when it comes to coloring books. They always want to color
the cute little tulips which are so neatly outlined in window
boxes, while they insist that *you* color that vast, vacant shape
that represents a grizzly bear on a unicycle. And besides, grizzly
bears are brown and I hate brown.

Toys can lead to strange new problems and bring about
strange new rules ("Do not shoot arrows out of the bedroom
window. Do not try out your sled on the stairs, and Yes, I *know*
the stair carpeting won't hurt the runners"). We ran into a really
iffy situation the year when Gregory was six. He had received a
small, battery-propelled car (*with* batteries, I don't know how it
happened) which he drove all day long without respect for life,
limb, shin, or table leg. I must explain that I am one of those
mothers who prefaces most directives with the phrase "I've told
you a hundred times (not to leave Coke bottles under the bed,
not to crack walnuts with the steam iron, etc. etc.")." On that particular Christmas night we were all finally assembled at the dining-room table and I was busy burning my fingers passing the
sweet potatoes when Gregory suddenly got up, left the table
solemnly, put on his crash helmet, stepped into his car, and
sailed out of the room at the majestic speed of three miles an

hour. When I recovered from my astonishment, I called after him, "Where on earth are you going?" His tone was quite matter-of-fact. "I'm going to the bathroom," he replied. "Gregory," I began automatically, "I've told you one hundred times—" and then I stopped, noticing the expression on my husband's face, which had suddenly become deeply and genuinely contemplative. At last his brow cleared and he spoke. "I don't *think* you've ever told him he can't go to the bathroom in his Marx-a-Cart," he said.

I suppose I would have gone the rest of my life as the Mad Shopper and January Dropout if it hadn't been for a small accident. What happened was that, four years ago, just as I was getting ready to make my first field trip to Thirty-fourth Street, I slipped on a crayon and sprained my ankle. Clearly I couldn't get to Bloomingdale's when I was having trouble getting to the sink. I sulked like a ball player who's been benched in the last inning, I inveighed against the powers that be, I cursed all crayons. I knew how important executives solve the problem; but you can't mail a seven-year-old child a card telling him that a donation has been sent in his name to UNICEF. And my husband's suggestion that *he* do the shopping I ruled out entirely. I still remember the time he bought an electric letter opener for a five-year-old boy on his birthday. When I made the obvious remark, "But that kid doesn't get any mail," he cheerfully said, "That's all right, he can open ours." This might have worked out all right if this boy had confined himself to opening letters that were coming *in*.

Eventually, but only eventually, I came to my senses. Then I used my head, I used the store catalogues, I used the telephone. Did you know that the eight red Santa Mugs (@ $4.98) that you order on the telephone are exactly the same Santa Mugs that you go from the third floor to the seventh floor to the fifth floor to find?

That's all behind me now. The only thing I insist on seeing with my own eyes, touching with my own hands, is batteries. In the hardware store I pick over—and perhaps bruise—batteries the way some women handle tomatoes. Locally, I am known as the Battery Lady. But, you see, I have time for such things nowadays. I even have time to listen to the children while *they* trim the tree.

Let me tell you how hale I was all day last Christmas, and how I entered into the spirit of everything. I was playing "Rollo Revels and Romps Away," the only composition I know, on Kitty's toy piano when I received a request: "Hey, Mom, would you stop playing that for one minute so I can hear what this rabbit says?"

We had a lovely Christmas, thank you, and I hope you had the same.

Confessions of a Sea-Lubber

It's strange the number of people who take planes when they might take a ship. I don't understand it. The plane trip is so much longer.

Surely you must have noticed that a whole year goes by between that moment when you fasten the seat belt and the time when the stewardess wheels out that first highball. I've noticed, and I'm not even a serious drinker. But if there are no atheists in foxholes, there are no abstainers aloft. I've seen the most proper people lapping up that third scotch as though they thought they'd never see another—which *is* what they thought.

Now, while a forty-minute shuttle flight from New York to Washington, D.C., can seem as long as a trip to Jupiter, an eight-day sea voyage to Naples is as fleeting as love's young dream. There are those who mourn the passing of the white sperm whale; I grow melancholy as I watch the passing of the great ocean liners. Not that I am indifferent to the whale situation. I consider myself in the forefront of those who brood about the day-to-day problems of those surviving whales. It's just that I myself have never seen a white sperm whale, so their predicament is not entirely real to me. (I never even saw the movie of *Moby Dick*, though I understand that the Moby was poor, very poor, not even as spirited as Gregory Peck.) But I have seen the old *Queen Elizabeth* and *Queen Mary* and the *Liberté*, and when I consider that these liners are gone, gone, gone, I want to sob or riot or write to my congressman. I really miss those ships.

Being on a ship is something like being pregnant. You can sit there and do absolutely nothing but stare at the water and have the nicest sense that you are accomplishing something. I mean, you're getting there.

Being on a ship is also really nicer than being in a luxury hotel in a foreign country. You have all the comfort and all the fattening food without being nagged by the feeling that somehow you ought to be out broadening your cultural horizons. For instance, you don't have to think about getting up at dawn, hiring a car, and driving fifty miles into the mountains to see a rare old tapestry in a quaint old chapel.

By the way, those who cannot be deterred from their pursuit of out-of-the-way art objects should be warned that they will undoubtedly find that chapel closed because it happens to be Monday (or Tuesday or Friday or Sunday) or because the chapel is being repaired or because the Vienna Boys Choir is recording within. The custodian will explain, in the language of the country and with the charm of custodians the world over, "Don't blame me, lady, I don't make the rules, I just work here." Personally, I wouldn't go to see the Pacific Ocean without checking with three responsible people to find out whether or not the ocean is open on weekends.

Everything on shipboard seems better than life in real life— even the movies. It's not that the movies are better; actually, they're worse. But, for one thing, they're free and you're free. I mean, you can leave and go back to your cabin without having an argument with your husband. ("Oh, come on, be a sport, it's bound to pick up in the last reel.") My husband once got me to sit all the way through *The Fox* (a film about lesbians) because he was curious to see what happened to the fox (who was, I must say, a splendid animal, loaded with talent, a regular Rinty, and probably—I feel certain—sexually impeccable). In any case, being free to leave somehow keeps you sitting there. I know a neurosurgeon who walked out of *The Graduate* at the Sutton Theatre and sat all through *Swingers in Paradise* on the *Michelangelo*.

And people on shipboard are so nice and approachable. At a

cocktail party in town, the stranger sitting next to you on the love seat (in these circumstances shouldn't it be called the like-seat?) will meditate for five minutes before he finally asks, "Well, what do you think of this weather we're having?" Your fellow passengers at sea never ask you such trivial, boring questions. Invariably they sweep to the larger issues and the heart of the matter and ask, "How much do you plan to tip your cabin steward?" (Incidentally, the only conceivable virtue in undertipping is that you will be thought a seasoned traveler and/or rich.)

Speaking of cabin stewards, I still remember my horror on my first crossing (several years back) when I returned to my cabin after a moonlight stroll on deck to discover that the steward had found my ghastly pink seersucker pajamas and had lovingly spread them on the bunk. I wear seersucker pajamas because I like them, and I like them best when they are soft and old and the nap has worn off. But, as a result of this chastening experience, I always bring along a couple of satin nightgowns which I strew casually about the cabin so that the steward can take some pride in his work. This may seem extravagant, but since I never wear them, they'll never wear out. And unless we actually sink the steward will never find my seersuckers because I hide them under the life preserver in the closet.

Most people embarking on an ocean voyage bring along a book they've intended to read forever, like *Martin Chuzzlewit* or *The Education of Henry Adams*. I don't find this necessary because (a) I never intend to read *The Education of Henry Adams* and (b) I find so many interesting things to read right there in the cabin. First, there is this little booklet full of tantalizing information about the ship. You will learn that the keel was laid in Genoa in 1962 (which, I am sure, was a vintage year for keels). In addition, I find it reassuring to learn that the ship is equipped with "Denny-Brown stabilizers with four automatic fins." That sounds about right to me. Six would probably be too many. And, while I don't happen to know anything about the Denny-Brown people, I'm sure they're the best. There is, however, one instruction that always disturbs me. It reads, "Anyone seeing a man falling overboard should shout MAN OVERBOARD STARBOARD or PORT SIDE (Starboard or Port is referred to the right or left of a man facing forward to the bow). Whosoever should hear the call should repeat it loudly and attempt to pass it to the Bridge."

I can't figure that out right this minute, when I have all the time in the world. In an emergency, heaven knows what I'd say. I mean, I know the difference between right and left, but I don't always know where the bow is. As a result, I simply never go on deck unless I am sure that there are a number of responsible people about. I can always put in time in my cabin studying my bilingual dictionary, especially the section marked "Phrases Most Often Used." Others have observed that the authors of these dictionaries do not seem to have a firm grasp of colloquial English. I want to say I am more struck by the fact that they can't seem to get through a page without foreseeing disaster. An air of doom prevails. After intense study, and only a little Dramamine, I am now able to say in flawless Italian, "Conductor, I have experienced misfortunes with my luggage," "Quick, summon a physician, my husband appears to ail," and (my favorite) "Mistress, this plumbing is imperfect and I am unable to bathe."

Another bonus for readers is the Program for the Day, which is slipped under the door each morning. This not only gives you the times of the meals and the titles of the movies but goes on to reveal the wealth of other goodies that await you. "Eleven-thirty: Organ Recital in the Bamboo Lounge. Tunes from Yester-year." (Okay, but think about it: it's better than tunes from *this* year.) "Three-thirty: Complimentary Dance Lesson on the Main Deck with Florio and Janet, weather permitting." I happen to feel that this "weather permitting" merely injects an empty note of pessimism, but I suppose you can't have people frugging right over the rails.

The best thing of all, though, is the ship's daily newspaper. This is the absolutely ideal publication. It's as peaceful as a Zen garden. No screaming headlines to ruin your breakfast and make you wonder if you shouldn't take the younger children and move to New Zealand. No headlines at all. The news, if any, will be found underneath a perfume advertisement in very small type. Sometimes it's no more than two or three sentences, and, with any luck at all, you could miss it entirely.

The rest of the paper, however, will be filled with nourishing tidbits. Just last summer I came across a splendid piece that ran under the caption "Not All Beavers Industrious."

It appears that someone had spent a great deal of time in a beaver community, along with the beavers, trying to discover just how busy they really were. And he did come upon a certain number of upright, responsible beavers who got to the dam on time. On the other hand, there are beavers who loll around all day and never get to the dam at all. And, when they do, they have a couldn't-care-less attitude. They chew indifferently on the wrong kind of twigs and slap mud around carelessly, while taking frequent cat naps or beaver naps. They have no group spirit and their work is messy. They are slobs. I hate to say it, but there you are. Nowadays, when *I* loll around, I comfort myself with the thought that I'm just as busy as your average beaver.

I don't want to make it sound as though all were perfection on shipboard. Of course potential hazards lurk everywhere: storms, slippery decks, eccentric people who may sit beside you near the pool. I made one crossing with my deck chair exactly next to the chair of a woman who—all afternoon, every afternoon—read to her husband aloud from Harold Robbins' *The Carpetbaggers*. While this gave me shooting pains in the back of my neck and caused me to take brisk walks around the deck, which is what I should have been doing anyhow, it was a source of great fascination to the pool attendant, who, clearly, didn't know such things were going on in this world, even in Hollywood.

Something else you may or may not have to deal with is cocktails with the captain. You may be invited for cocktails because you are a movie star or because you happen to have the same name as the president of the Cunard Line and are mistaken for a relative. In any case, most people make the obvious mistake of trying to be interesting, whereas the captain is (quite understandably) tired of interesting people. The average captain, while being as cheery as a Santa Claus in Macy's, is hardly more articulate. He smiles and smiles and mutters things like "Oh, ho, ho." You can look him straight in the eye and recite the third stanza of "America, the Beautiful" without his perceiving anything amiss. In fact, you can say anything you please so long as you don't make the mistake of referring to his ship as "this boat." This will alert him, and you will then have to listen to a sharp disquisition on the number of significant ways in which a ship differs from a boat. (Billy's *Blue-Jay* is a boat. The *Michelangelo* is a ship. Have you got that now?)

No matter. I want to go down to the sea again. To the lonely sea and the sky. And the nice steward who brings my breakfast to the cabin and the deck steward who tucks a rug around my knees and the good food and the bad movies, and the bingo and the horse racing, and the salt spray that makes my hairdo sticky, and the cocktails in the bar as the sun goes down over the ocean, and the telephone in the cabin that never, never rings. I want to go. And I want to go this summer.

The Children's Hour
After Hour After Hour

There is this to be said about little children. They keep you feeling old.

Naturally, they don't mean to do this. And when a four-year-old boy presents you with a bouquet that he has picked himself from your neighbor's prize tulip bed, he has the best intentions in the world. When this first happens to a young mother—say, in her early twenties—she can usually keep her head even if all the tulips have lost theirs. After all, it *was* rather sweet of Billy, and surely an abject letter of apology and two dozen roses will square things with Mrs. Hayden.

If, however, nineteen years later this same woman receives the same offering of tulips from another four-year-old boy, brother of the first, she is very likely to snap ("Oh, my God, we're just going to have to move away from here, that's all!"). In the intervening years this woman has lost muscle tone and confidence. In fact she has lost everything but weight.

The problem of the large or medium large family is that the parents keep growing older and changing, while the children stay the same. One after the other they get the same knots in their shoelaces, the same ink on the sheets, the same pennies in their ears. They lose the same book bag, they get holes in the same sweaters (sometimes they *are* the same sweaters), and one and all they keep dinner from being a gracious occasion. Let me explain. Our oldest, who is now a lawyer, no longer spills milk at the dinner table. (I'm not bragging, I'm just stating a fact.) But of course his little sister still does. And all the others in between did. Now I do not cry about the spilt milk. I don't even mind cleaning it up. That's why we have plastic table mats. What I do mind (Doctor, I just feel old and tired) is that every night for almost twenty years I have felt obliged to make the banal but stunningly prophetic remark, "Don't leave that glass there, you're going to knock it over with your elbow." But what else can you do? You've got to prepare for the fact that someday one of those kids may be invited out to dinner, and he can't be sloshing milk all over Westchester County.

I'm sick of talking about milk. When do we get to the great topics, like art, music, McLuhan? And what about people like the Kennedys, who, they say, had such brilliant conversation at the dinner table, even when the children were young? How? Didn't those kids get any milk?

There are those who distinguish between bright children and slow children, between extroverts and introverts. From my point of view—twenty years after—there are only two kinds of children. There are picky eaters. And then there are the stuffers.

The picky eater holds his fork limply, resting his cheek on his left fist and staring at the best-dinner-in-the-world with such evident loathing that all appetites vanish. Now I know that pediatrician Dr. Lendon Smith says, "If the child can get up and walk around, he's eating enough," and if I'd ever been able to believe this, my whole life would have been different. But, due to my conviction that one spoonful of mashed potatoes and three cookies does not constitute a balanced diet, I have gone right on making idiotic and demonstrably unworkable rules like: "You're not going to leave this table until you eat every bite of that dinner. Not if it takes all night." I've done this year after year until I don't have to think anymore. I'm a prerecorded announcement. Once, after a prolonged stretch with a particularly picky eater, I was invited to a dinner party. I am told that I caused some astonishment when I remarked, rather crisply, to the gentleman on my right, "Why, you haven't touched one thing on that plate but your chicken!"

As for the stuffers, there are two varieties. The first, and quite harmless, sort is the great bottomless pit who can consume more food in a day than one person can carry home from the supermarket—while still remaining lean and sinewy (and bottomless). The true or troublesome stuffer, on the other hand, suffers from a low metabolism and a poor memory, both of which cause him to gain weight. He doesn't seem to realize that the eight square meals he eats a day play some part in his ever-increasing amplitude. To hear him tell it, he was betrayed by a Chiclet. Actually, the effort of consuming three helpings of a turkey dinner mysteriously causes this child to work up an appetite. Before the dinner dishes are yet washed he will require a peanut butter and jelly sandwich. And if he is not hounded into total alienation by terrorist tactics, such as having his pockets checked for extra brownies and his bureau drawer checked for Cokes (and, would you believe it, chocolate Metrecal), he will presently assume those odd contours that suggest someone removed a cork from his big toe and blew him up. True unhappiness comes when you have a picker and a stuffer at the same dinner table, so that you wind up saying, "Won't you have a little more gravy—no, no, no, not *you!*"

By this time wouldn't you think I could stop sounding like a top sergeant and become the gracious person I am? After all, the whole theory of the well-spaced family is that sooner or later there will be older siblings around to take over some of these chores, like demonstrating the fashionable use of the fork and getting knots out of shoelaces. (Where knots are concerned, my right hand has lost its cunning.) The dream goes something like this. You've been in hand-to-hand combat with a rambunctious two-year-old (and a two-year-old who is not rambunctious is coming down with something) for an entire afternoon. You have removed him from high places, you have taken foreign objects out of his mouth, you have kept him away from the stove and electrical outlets, you have answered nine hundred and seventy-three questions dishonestly. You are not yourself any longer. Enter his cheerful older brother, the Peace Corps. He says, "Hey, Mom, want me to take this kid for a walk?" It is a moment of magic which makes everything seem worth while. I know because it has happened to me as many as three times in twenty years.

If I've grown too old to dream, it's not because the bigger boys are less agreeable. They're just less present. It has been my observation that as soon as a boy has become housebroken and a pleasure to have about, he is no longer about. He's in school all the time. I consider a boy housebroken, by the way, when you can watch him going out the back door into fourteen inches of snow without feeling you ought to say, "Be sure and wear your rubbers." Another sign of maturity in a child is when he no longer asks questions like where is his Batman cape while you are in the middle of a long-distance call ("Stop pestering me. No, Mother, you're not pestering me. I'm talking to Gregory").

Clearly other women have coped better than I can. All the time I find myself ruminating about Longfellow's *The Children's Hour*. If I grasp this poem correctly, Longfellow didn't lay eyes on those kids until sometime "between the dark and the daylight when the light is beginning to lower." I take that to be about five-thirty (depending on the time of year). Wasn't that Mrs. Longfellow a marvel to keep those children out of his hair all day long? Remember, he worked at home. I can see it may have been easy enough with Grave Alice. But what about that Laughing Allegra? Can't you just hear her? I'd have been out in that den saying, "Henry Wadsworth, *you* watch Laughing Allegra for an hour!"

Why is it so hard to say *nice* things to children? We're being told all the time that little children need love. All psychiatrists understand this. I think most parents understand it. But there is a whole group that seems to have been left in the dark on this matter. Children. Surely if those kids knew they needed love, they'd be more lovable.

Let's get this thing down to strict logic. Obviously the psychiatrists aren't trying to tell us to love children when they're being adorable. Heaven knows that's easy enough. Even your true Monster Mother (who never made cookies in her life) is tempted to give hugs to a nice little boy who is drying the silver. And when a three-year-old girl looks in the mirror and says, "I'm going to be tall and pretty—just like Mommy," Mommy does not require professional guidance in order to feel loving. Even the psychiatrists, mired as they are in terminology, know this.

So they must mean something else. Apparently they mean that you should love children when they are driving you absolutely out of your mind. But I really don't know how practical that would be. Imagine this scene. Nine-year-old Billy comes home from school. You say to him, "Billy, your teacher called. She said you were late for school again. She also said you didn't bring in your homework any day this week and that you deliberately spilled water paint on Mary Dee's jacket. Furthermore, she said that you constantly disrupted the entire class with your foolish antics. I love you, Billy."

I think Billy would definitely be rattled. He may be only nine but he's heard a little something about mental illness. I think he would feel better oriented (if that's the word, and it is) if he heard you say what he expects you to say, which is "Just wait until your father hears about this. Just you wait."

It is a mark of really mature, really experienced parents that they are very repetitious. Having learned, down through the years, that small children must be told everything a number of times, they try to cut corners by saying things twice in the first place. For example: "Wash your hands. Did you hear me, I said wash your hands. And with soap. Got that? *With soap.*" The alternative is to wait fifteen minutes and then say, "Look at those hands. Just look at those hands. Do you mean to tell me you think those hands are washed?" Personally, I talk like this all the time and I hear myself. Hear myself? I hate myself. I sound dithering if not deranged. But that's how you get with a well-spaced family.

The ideal thing, the perfect solution, would be to have sextuplets when you were in your early twenties. Then, when the children were two years old, *all* of them would untie their shoelaces and remove their shoes. It would be quite a pile of shoes, but once that phase was over it would be over. Likewise when six of them were spilling milk it would be pretty damp around the house for a while—but not forever. I imagine it would be pretty rough the year *all* of them were telling you riddles. But remember. You'd be young and willing to learn which state was high in the middle and round on each end (Ohio, of course, it couldn't be New York). The point is, you wouldn't find yourself in golden middle life still shouting, "Don't run, please don't run! *Not* with that lollipop in your mouth."

My Wild Irish Mother

I'm never going to write my autobiography and it's all my mother's fault. I didn't hate her, so I have practically no material. In fact, the situation is worse than I'm pretending. We were crazy about her—and you know I'll never get a book out of that, much less a musical.

Mother was born Kitty O'Neill, in Kinsale, Ireland, with bright red hair, bright blue eyes, and the firm conviction that it was wrong to wait for an elevator if you were only going up to the fifth floor. It's not just that she won't wait for elevators, which she really feels are provided only for the convenience of the aged and infirm. I have known her to reproach herself on missing one section of a revolving door. And I well remember a time when we missed a train from New York to Washington. I fully expected her to pick up our suitcases and announce, "Well, darling, the exercise will be good for us."

When I have occasion to mutter about the financial problems involved in maintaining six children in a large house, Mother is quick to get to the root of the problem. "Remember," she says, "you take cabs a lot." In Mother's opinion, an able-bodied woman is perfectly justified in taking a taxi to the hospital if her labor pains are closer than ten minutes apart.

The youngest daughter of wealthy and indulgent parents, Mother went to finishing schools in France and to the Royal

Conservatory of Music in London. Thus, when she came to America to marry my father, her only qualifications for the role of housewife and mother were the ability to speak four languages, play three musical instruments, and make *blancmange.* I, naturally, wasn't around during those first troubled months when Mother learned to cook. But my father can still recall the day she boiled corn on the cob, a delicacy unknown in Ireland at that time, for five hours until the cobs were tender. And, with a typical beginner's zeal, Mother "put up" twenty bushels of tomatoes for that first winter before it struck her that neither she nor Dad really liked canned tomatoes.

By the time I was old enough to notice things, Mother was not only an excellent cook. She could make beer, an accomplishment that set her apart and endeared her to many in those Prohibition days. Of course, Mother didn't drink beer, so it was hard for her to judge whether she was on the right track or not. And it was always an anxious moment when my father took his first sip of each new batch and declared, "Yes, Kit, I think you're getting warmer."

But beer brewing is a very involved process, as the Budweiser people will tell you, and the crock used to stand for weeks in the pantry before it was time for the bottling. I don't know how big the crock was, but I know that it stood taller than I did. One of my earliest memories—I must have been four—is of sitting on the floor handing the bottle caps to Mother. On this particular occasion the crock was nearly empty when Mother gave a little shriek. Something, something—perhaps a mouse—was at the bottom of the crock.

She took a long fork and gingerly fished out a small, sodden object. I knew in a flash what it was, but I was too terrified to speak. Then I heard Mother say, in a very strained voice, "Jean you must *always* tell Mommy where you put your shoes."

Together we sat in silence and stared at the rows and rows of shiny bottles all ready to go into the cases down in the cellar. Then Mother jumped up. A thought had struck her. She tossed the shoe into the garbage and announced briskly, "You know what? I think it will help the aging process." And it must have, too, because everyone said it was the best batch she ever made.

Just as she made beer she never drank, Mother would cook

things she had no intention of eating. Where food is concerned, she is totally conservative. She will study the menu at an expensive restaurant with evident interest and then say, "Darling, where do you see lamb chops?" Or she will glance with real admiration at a man at a nearby table who seems actually to be consuming an order of cherrystone clams. "Aren't Americans marvelous?" she'll remark. "They will eat anything."

On the other hand she was always willing to prepare all manner of exotic dishes for Dad and the rest of us. In the old days the men who worked for my father frequently gave him gifts of game—venison, rabbit, and the like. Occasionally we children would protest. I recall becoming quite tearful over the prospect of eating deer, on the theory that it might be Bambi. But Mother was always firm. "Nonsense," she would say, "eat up, it's just like chicken."

But one night she went too far. I don't know where she got this enormous slab of meat; I don't think my father brought it home. It stood overnight in the icebox in some complicated solution of brine and herbs. The next day the four of us were told that we could each invite a friend to dinner. Mother spent most of the day lovingly preparing her roast. That night there were ten of us around the dining-room table, and if Mother seemed too busy serving all the rest of us to eat anything herself, that was not at all unusual. At this late date I have no impression of what the meat tasted like. But I know that we were all munching away when Mother beamed happily at us and asked, "Well, children, how are you enjoying the bear?"

Forks dropped and certain of the invited guests made emergency trips to the bathroom. For once, all of Mother's protestations that it was just like chicken were unavailing. Nobody would touch another bite. She was really dismayed. I heard her tell Dad, "It's really strange, Tom—I thought all Americans liked bear."

Mother's education, as I have indicated, was rather one-sided. While she knew a great deal about such "useless" things as music and art and literature, she knew nothing whatever, we were quick to discover, about isosceles triangles or watts and volts or the Smoot-Hawley Tariff. As we were growing up, we made haste to repair these gaps.

One of the most charming things about Mother was the extraordinary patience with which she would allow us youngsters to "instruct" her. I remember my brother Hugh, when he was about eight, sitting on the foot of Mother's bed and giving her a half-hour lecture which began with the portentous question, "Mom, how much do you know about the habits of the common housefly?"

At that, it's remarkable how much of this unrelated information stayed with her. Just recently I was driving her to a train and she noticed, high up in the air, a squirrel that was poised on a wire that ran between two five-story buildings. "Look at that little squirrel 'way up on that wire," she said. "You know, if he gets one foot on the ground, he'll be electrocuted."

But if her knowledge of positive and negative electricity is a little sketchy, there is nothing sketchy about her knowledge of any subject in which she develops an interest. Mother always adored the theater and was a passionate playgoer from the time she was five years old. However, during the years when she was sobbing gently over *The Lily of Killarney* in Cork City, she was blissfully unaware of the menacing existence of American drama critics or the fact that their printed opinions had a certain measurable effect on the box office. Even when she came to America, she still had the feeling that five nights was probably an impressive run for a Broadway show.

Time passed, and my husband and I became involved in the theater. Mother began to get the facts. When, quite a few years ago, we were living in Washington and came up to New York for the opening of a revue we had written, I promised Mother that I would send her all the reviews, special delivery, as soon as they appeared. In those days, before the demise of *The Sun*, there were eight metropolitan dailies. Eventually we got hold of all the papers and I was able to assess the evidence. All but one of the morning papers were fine, and while there were certain quibbles in the afternoon papers, the only seriously negative notice appeared in *The Sun*. Ward Morehouse was then the critic on *The Sun* but happened to be out of town at the moment, and the review was written by his assistant, or, as I was willing to suppose, his office boy. So, with that special brand of feminine logic that has already made my husband prematurely gray, I decided to omit this particular notice in the batch I was sending to my mother, on the theory that (a) it wasn't written by the *real* critic, and (b) nobody in Scranton, Pennsylvania, knew there was a paper called *The Sun* anyway. This was a serious miscalculation on my part, as I realized later in the day when I got Mother's two-word telegram. It read, "Where's Morehouse?"

Let me say that her interest in the more technical aspects of the theater continues unabated. Not long ago we were in Philadelphia, deep in the unrefined bedlam that surrounds any musical in its tryout stage. The phone rang. It was Mother. Without any preliminary word of greeting, she asked in hushed, conspiratorial tones, "Darling, have you pointed and sharpened?"

"Good Lord, Mother," I said, "what are you talking about?"

"I'm talking about the show, dear," she said, sounding like a small investor, which she was. "*Variety* says it needs pointing and sharpening, and I think we should listen to them."

To the four low-metabolism types she inexplicably produced, Mother's energy has always seemed awesome. "What do you think," she's prone to say, "do I have time to cut the grass before I stuff the turkey?" But her whirlwind activity is potentially less dangerous than her occasional moments of repose. Then she sits, staring into space, clearly lost in languorous memories. The faint, fugitive smile that hovers about her lips suggests the gentle melancholy of one hearing Mozart played beautifully. Suddenly she leaps to her feet. "I know it will work," she says. "All we have to do is remove that wall, plug up the windows, and extend the porch."

It's undoubtedly fortunate that she has the thrust and the energy of a well-guided missile. Otherwise she wouldn't get a lick of work done, because everybody who comes to her house, whether to read the gas meter or to collect for UNICEF, always stays at least an hour. I used to think that they were one and all beguiled by her Irish accent. But I have gradually gleaned that they are telling her the story of their invariably unhappy lives. "Do you remember my lovely huckleberry man?" Mother will ask. "Oh, *yes* you do—he had red hair and ears. Well, his brother-in-law sprained his back and hasn't worked in six months, and we're going to have to take a bundle of clothes over to those children." Or, again: "Do you remember that nice girl in the Scranton Dry Goods? Oh, yes you do, she was in lamp shades and she had gray hair and wore gray dresses. Well, she's having an operation next month and you must remember to pray for her." Mother's credo, by the way, is that if you want something, anything, don't just sit there—pray for it. And she combines a Job-like patience in the face of the mysterious ways of the Almighty with a flash of Irish rebellion which will bring her to say—and I'm sure she speaks for many of us—"Jean, what I am really looking for is a blessing that's *not* in disguise."

She does have a knack for penetrating disguises, whether it be small boys who claim that they have taken baths or middle-aged daughters who swear that they have lost five pounds. She has a way of cutting things to size, particularly books, which she gobbles up in the indiscriminate way that a slot machine gobbles up quarters. I sent her a novel recently because it had a Welsh background and because the blurb on the jacket declared, "Here is an emotional earthquake—the power and glory of a great love story combined with the magic of childhood." Later, I asked her if she liked it. "Not really," she said. "It was nothing but fornication, all seen through the eyes of a nine-year-old boy." The first time I had a collection of short pieces brought out in book form, I sent an advance copy to Mother. She was naturally delighted. Her enthusiasm fairly bubbled off the pages of the letter. "Darling," she wrote, "isn't it marvelous the way those old pieces of yours finally came to the surface like a dead body!"

I knew when I started this that all I could do was list the things Mother says, because it's not possible, really, to describe her. All my life I have heard people break off their lyrical descriptions of Kitty and announce helplessly, "You'll just have to meet her."

However, I recognize, if I cannot describe, the lovely festive air she always brings with her, so that she can arrive any old day in July and suddenly it seems to be Christmas Eve and the children seem handsomer and better behaved and all the adults seem more charming and—

Well, you'll just have to meet her.

The Communication Arts:
Writing to a Boy
Away at School

Do you remember the Lord Chesterfield who wrote those noble, true-blue *Letters to His Son* that all the rest of us had to read in high school? Well, you won't believe this, but it turns out that Chesterfield practically never laid eyes on that kid, which, undoubtedly, was good for his prose and maybe even for his blood pressure. But the fact remains that the boy, in spite of all the splendid advice that was lavished on him, amounted to rather less than a hill of beans. He was an eighteenth-century dropout is what he was.

I know it seems downright tacky of me to be going on about the failures of other parents when, as it happens (and happens and happens), three of my five sons are guaranteed to walk off with the car keys (sometimes as far as Washington, D.C.) each time they borrow the car. I suppose the truth of the matter is that I wish to be reassured that there is no necessary connection between good letters and good behavior.

And that's a relief. Because I am aware that the letters *I* wrote to the boys when they were at prep school (one of them is still there, hello, dear) were—for sheer, droning dullness—in a class by themselves. (Which reminds me that down through the years it has been hinted to me that my *boys* should be in a class by themselves, but I have always dismissed these suggestions in the spirit of fun in which I know they were made.)

I guess I began to find it difficult to write to the boys at about the time I realized that while they definitely wanted to get mail, they didn't necessarily want to *read* letters from Dear Old Mom. Apparently it gives a boy status to find mail in his box, it gives him pleasure to wave it under the noses of his peers (who may or may not be orphans), and it costs him absolutely nothing to throw it unread into the closet that contains his Biology II books, also unread. This will be understandable to those who grasp the great truth that girls will always wish to be asked to dance, even by boys they don't wish to dance with.

The boys themselves once indicated a partial solution to the correspondence problem, and it's a tribute to my character—however faint and flickering—that I didn't seize upon it. There was a period when all students were required (forced) to write home every Sunday. Or at least they were required to address an envelope to their parents and stamp it. The resulting mail was full of fascination. Sometimes the entire message (on a large sheet of paper or two large sheets of paper) would be "Please send more stamps, will write again next week, love." On certain other occasions we have received a corrected Latin exam, notes for a term paper on Robert Penn Warren, and once a letter from me—if you follow that. However, I never retaliated by sending them an old Gristede bill or even a coupon for a free introductory jar of Night Cream.

Nonetheless, I thought it was an excellent system. It meant that every Tuesday morning you would be assured that your child was alive and, if not well, at the very least hadn't broken both wrists. Also, he had not forgotten his home address, which, in terms of mental health, is supposed to be very important.

Having confessed that I never learned the art (the craft?) of writing to a boy in prep school, I may say that in the course of fifteen years I have picked up a few ideas, ideas I am perfectly prepared to pass on to those of you who find that once you have written "Dad and I are just fine" you've pretty much run out of steam. (By the way, even *that* opening is better than the sweeping "Everything around here is just fine," which leaves you nowhere to go at all.) It's too bad that that kid isn't interested in your bronchitis or the fact that the Chevy broke down on the Triborough Bridge and had to be towed home. But he isn't. He also doesn't seem to care who you had dinner with or what you had for dinner. This in spite of the fact that his own letters dwell exclusively on cuisine ("The food here stinks. Mystery meat four times this week. Pleas send pretsels.").

The real solution to the correspondence problem is perfectly complicated, but it does work. It may not fit into your needs or even into your apartment, but the thing to do is purchase a lot of animals and you will find yourself prized as a pen pal. A horse is probably out of the question; New Rochelle is not Marlboro country. But apart from cats and dogs, and word may have reached you about this, there are all kinds of smaller beasts like hamsters and turtles and mynah birds and fish (tropical or domestic), plus various other little creatures that have to be fed or walked or have their tanks cleaned or be taken to the vet.

This animal husbandry is all pretty wearing but it is, as they say in the trade, good copy. Now, where animals are concerned, even a softened cynic like myself can become quite mushy about certain dogs or cats. But I never met a fish I liked, or a hamster, for that matter. Yet even these miserable specimens can provide a rich lode of material for a letter to a fourteen-year-old boy. (James Michener could probably get eight hundred pages and a Literary Guild Selection.) So, instead of passing on a lot of boring information about the refrigerator which broke down totally just two months after it went out of warranty and will have to be replaced at a cost of three hundred and eighty dollars, how much better to pass on the simple message: "Guess what? Lady Teazle has had her kittens!" Or you might be able to report that Chuck (the mynah bird) can now say "That's all, folks!" This is not to suggest that Chuck is approaching the virtuosity of Alistair Cooke, but since previously he has not said one damn thing I take it as something of a milestone and perhaps even a prediction— which will be all right with me. Or, to give you still another bulletin: "The fish are biting." They may even be biting each other; I think there was one less in the tank this morning. Of course, I could have counted wrong since, as you know, they swirl by pretty fast and it's easy to count the same fish three times, or not at all.

One thing I have definitely learned is the futility of asking questions in my various missives. I mean, I used to be dumb enough, and curious enough, to ask things like: "What did you do with your father's stapler? Hammer? Electric pencil sharpener? Also, what did you do with the ball-point pen I had chained to the wall next to the telephone?" If he even bothers to give you an answer to these wistful queries, it will come in the shape of further questions: "What hammer? What pencil sharpener? What telephone?"

I don't mean to suggest that *all* of the questions the children ask in their letters are idiotic. Far from it. Some will touch a chord in a way that is almost existential in its perception of being.

For example: "Did you happen to see the pair of skis I left on my bed?" Did I see them? *Did I see them?* Well, at long last I have something to write to that boy about. But I don't think I will. It would be intemperate, if not X-rated. And while I have never heard that those thoughtful teachers censor the mail up there, I still wouldn't want to take the chance.

The Beautiful People
and How They Stay That Way

If you've seen me lately, you will wonder how I have the nerve to be dispensing beauty secrets. Just remember the old adage: those that can't, teach. In any case, you may *have* to learn all the latest beauty tricks from someone like me who has the time to bone up on the subject. The naturally ravishing are much too busy attending galas or being ravished. Even in beauty parlors, where some of us do extensive research in magazines that have stood the test of time (having been published six months ago), these gorgeous creatures don't even bother to crack a *Vogue*. They just sit there wiggling their freshly enameled fingernails in the air, like puppies begging for a Liv-a-Snap.

I say they are not growing. And they miss so much. Listen, if I weren't the voracious reader that I am, I wouldn't be in a position to tell you Paul Newman's beauty secret. Ah, that does surprise you, doesn't it? You supposed he was a fine actor and a good Democrat who just naturally looked terrific. Yes, that's exactly what I thought, until one of Newman's fellow actors went blabbing to a columnist. It seems that Newman keeps that complexion so vibrant by plunging his entire head into a bucket of water for twenty minutes, while breathing through a snorkel. He does this every day. If my figures are correct (multiply twenty minutes by seven, multiply the result by fifty-two, divide by sixty, then divide by twenty-four, or, if you break down along the way, send for your son with his instant calculator), Paul Newman spends more than five days a year with his head in a bucket of water. Sure it's tough, but I never promised you a rose garden.

Before someone comes right out and asks me, I will confess that I haven't yet tried the Newman Method. However, I did buy a new bucket. I certainly wasn't going to put a foot, much less my head, in that crummy bucket we keep in the garage. Furthermore, that bucket didn't really look big enough to me. You wouldn't want to skin your nose while toning up your complexion. (The snorkel didn't represent any additional expense since one of the boys already had one.)

Inasmuch as I am clearly prepared for the great experiment, you will wonder what delays me. Actually (excuses, excuses) I just don't seem to know when to do it. Obviously I'm not going to do it right after I've had my hair done. I'm crazy, but I'm not careless. And it's fairly evident that I'd have to get it done immediately afterward (every day). But somehow I just can't see myself running into Mr. Joseph's Salon with my dripping wet hair and some wild tale about Paul Newman.

Even that, I suppose, could probably be worked out. The crux of the matter is this: I'm chicken. Since the subject of my general instability has already been the source of much unwelcome humor around our house, I would hardly allow my husband or my children to observe me as I knelt on the rug and submerged with my snorkel into a pail of water. And I'd be afraid to attempt it alone. What if I got stuck? What if the snorkel didn't work? Think of the story in the local paper, "Matron Drowns in Bizarre Accident," or worse (there are a lot of wags on the local paper), "Mother Kicks the Bucket."

Anyway, there are easier ways to look sensational. An exquisite model recently interviewed in depth declared that she owed her special luminosity to milk of magnesia. No, no, she didn't drink it. She spread it on her face.

My research would seem to indicate that I am one of the few people left around who are still buying conventional cosmetics. Most women, if you can believe what you read, are using groceries. In the last couple of months I have read suggestions for facial masks made from oatmeal, egg whites, egg yolks, honey, mayonnaise, and yogurt. And my favorite: a mask composed of olive oil and vodka. The olive oil is an excellent lubricant and the vodka, in case you didn't know, is bracing. This one seems full of possibilities to me. If you keep licking away at the vodka and olive oil, you will, beyond question, *feel* better. And, if I may make one small suggestion, you could add a little chopped parsley and call it dinner.

Notice that I am nowhere mentioning women like Candice Bergen or Ingrid Bergman, who were born beautiful and just stayed that way. I think it is more helpful for the rest of us to confine our investigation to those ladies who, by their own admission, have to work, work, work to be so attractive.

In her autobiography, Doris Day tells us that once a week she covers her entire self (from the scalp right down to her little toes) with vaseline petroleum jelly. Then she puts on an old flannel nightgown and goes to sleep. Perhaps anticipating the lifted eyebrows of the bemused, she makes it very clear that she sleeps alone while jellied. What I want to know is *where* she sleeps. In a bed? Suppose she turns over in the middle of the night. In her slippery condition wouldn't she skid right out of the bed, knocking over lamps and alarm clocks and possibly damaging herself, wiping out the improvements? Maybe she sleeps on the floor. They say that's good for the back muscles. Of course we must remember that Doris Day can afford to buy a hospital-type bed with those crib slats that you can pull up. But then she'd have to store this crazy bed somewhere for the other six nights. Personally, I find it a nuisance even to store my small facial sauna, which I have used twice since I bought it in 1972. Just twice, and it cost fourteen dollars. Well, that's the kind of helter-skelter, devil-may-care attitude that has left me in my present condition, about which the less said the better.

All right, I'll go soak my head.

The Child as Houseguest

Now that I'm all grown up, I'll tell you what I want to be. A mother-in-law. For those interested in somber statistics, I will confess that I have been a *mother* for thirty years, a circumstance—I assure myself—that is hard to believe. We will dismiss as irrelevant the way I look in the early morning since I never appear *anywhere* in the early morning except, most occasionally, in the operating room of a hospital. (Of course, there they come and get you and sedate you and put you on a cart and wheel you down, which, we are agreed, makes it a lot easier.) But never mind my appearance. There are eight of us in this family and I'm the only one, so far, who's managed to get married—except, of course, for my husband.

It may be thought that my desire to be a mother-in-law has, perhaps, something to do with my wish to dandle a grandchild on my knee before I am too arthritic even to dandle. Not so, or, at least, not really. I don't think I'm a sentimental person. Certainly the salesperson in The Crystal Collage Gift Shop doesn't think so. I was hunting for my BankAmericard last week and she noticed the picture of a charming little boy in my wallet. "Which of your boys is that?" she wanted to know. And she seemed genuinely bewildered when I explained that the picture just happened to be the one that was in the wallet when I bought it.

However, I do admit that I find nothing in this world more joyous than the spectacle of an almost brand-new infant (five months is about perfect) who has just been bathed and sprinkled with Johnson's baby powder and snapped into a clean pink wrapper with his gauzy hair swooshed up into a little peak. No, I mean it. Nothing so lifts the heart—not getting good reviews on a play, not losing ten pounds, not even hearing the dentist say, "Well, we don't seem to have anything to do *here*."

But you can love something, yearn for it even, and realize it's no longer for you. Another example of the same thing would be Robert Redford.

By the time you're fifty—and why do I bring *you* into it, by the time *I'm* fifty—I'm not really looking to collect more children, however beguiling. I'm trying to unload. I don't mean get them out of the house. Except for one small girl, they *are* out of the house. Three of the boys are away at school (prep school, graduate school, medical school), and two are (oh, the wonder of it and I accept congratulations) actually employed and living in quarters of their own. But they don't belong to anybody else yet, they haven't been snatched, claimed, or taken over permanently by an alternate sponsor.

I don't know why young people don't seem to get married anymore. Unlike the Messrs. Gallup and Harris, I wouldn't recognize a trend if it sat down beside me. I do gather from the polls that theologians think it has something to do with the pill, while sociologists attribute it all to post-Watergate cynicism. Personally, I think the manufacturers of Brownie mixes have a lot to answer for. A boy hardly needs anybody else messing around in his kitchen these days.

Our friend Walter Slezak used to say, "Children eventually become letters and then the letters disappear," and I believed that. In fact, I got quite choked up about it. But I have learned that the facts are quite otherwise. In my experience, children *don't* disappear. They become houseguests. Lacking nests of their own, they turn up as often as meatloaf, arriving with the exuberant good cheer and frantic manner of tourists determined to see all of the Vatican Museum in twenty minutes. Certainly they don't want to be any trouble: "No, no, you sit down, Mom, I'll get my own sandwich." Presently a series of more or less connected observations can be heard from the deep recesses of the refrigerator. "I don't see anything besides this boiled ham. Are we out of mayonnaise? I'll tell you something, this lettuce has *had* it." Now this particular child lives in Philadelphia. What does he mean, are *we* out of mayonnaise?

It's not that I want to retire from parenthood like a bank teller gets to retire from bank telling. I don't want a gold watch or other retirement benefits. All I really and truly want to do is shut up. And don't tell me I *could* shut up; that's been explained to me. But if this is still their home, or at least where they store their old guitars, and I am still their mother, I am, much to my dismay, going to *sound* like a mother.

Recently one of my sons was being given the benefit of my expertise on nutrition ("Cold spaghetti for breakfast and chocolate-chip cookies for supper? That's crazy!"). Now he was perfectly polite (they're all polite) but he was staring heavenward with that tinge of melancholy and ennui that I myself assume whenever the announcer says "Stay tuned, we'll be back right after this message." Believing myself to be on the side of the angels and Julia Child (if that isn't redundant), I said to him, "If I don't tell you, who will?" His answer is worth repeating: "Hopefully, nobody." But how can I be silent? There is darkness to be lit, there are shoals to be avoided, and we no longer have Eric Severeid to lend a guiding hand.

No, other voices must be heard. But, you may ask, would an average, typical, pretty girl of twenty-three do better than I? She certainly would. How I shall rejoice some rainy night when I hear some other responsible person say to just one of my loved ones, "My God, you're not going out in *this* weather, in *that!*" or, to repeat another phrase rather abused around here, "Okay, you don't want to have it cut, but couldn't you *wash* it?"

Having said that children are like houseguests, let me count the ways in which houseguests differ from children:

(1) Your authentic, invited houseguest does not call you collect at midnight and announce, "Hey, Andy and I will be there for dinner tomorrow night, right? . . . No, that was *Albie*, who had an identity crisis because his father was a psychiatrist. Andy is really a terrific guy, he just can't eat anything with egg in it. See ya!"

(2) Your A-1 houseguest does not usually bring along his dirty laundry.

(3) He seems to fit in better with the family. More than that, he writes such charming thank-you letters. Our friend Charles was here for five halcyon days not long ago. His conversation is bewitching, he wears his hair becomingly short, he is as tidy as a Trappist. When he returned home he wrote, "Darling Girl, nothing will ever be the same here at Wuthering Depths, but I have my Gallo port and my memories. . . ." Of course, one doesn't look for this kind of felicity within the family. But wouldn't you think someone could scribble a couple of lines on a postcard: "Gee, it was great to see the whole gang again, and gosh, Mom, I've missed your hot biscuits." Now it should be clear to any rational person that my biscuits, which come frozen in a cardboard tube, are—and this is being as literal as you can be—nothing to write home about. But I am tired of being a rational person. I want to be showered with idiot compliments like those women in the TV commercials who, apparently, enthrall everyone in the immediate environment with their shrewd use of some new fabric softener.

Why can't those kids lie a little, now that they're adults?

"I Do Most Solemnly Swear"

I have this jumpy feeling that New Year's resolutions are best made in the necessary privacy of The Morning After. Or that could be the entire *day* after, depending on the duration and quality of the preceding night's revelries. Your average revel is frequently attended by more than sixteen people, which is too many; and you don't even get to talk to Old Charlie, which is why you went in the first place. Then the liquor flows like wine and, since dinner may not be served until eleven o'clock, most people are not even aware that the wine is now flowing like water, which is absolutely unavailable.

This is why, on New Year's Day, you need privacy and sympathy and tea and something that will put more pain reliever into the bloodstream in seconds. If you're going to turn over a new leaf, you want to be quiet, and all alone *away* from the telephone. To get privacy, all you need to do is pick up an object, any object, a box, a shoe (anything but the baby or your mother) and announce, "I'm taking this up to the attic." Nobody will think this in any way odd, since it's clear that at least half of that junk that's been on the floor since Christmas will have to go somewhere before Monday.

Once in the attic, surrounded by silent trunks and old playpens with missing slats, you can think. You can ask questions. Why were you born? Why did you ever agree to go to a party in New Jersey when Bill gets lost even driving to Connecticut? Is there enough leftover turkey to serve seven people if you cream it and add tuna fish? What on earth would Craig Claiborne say about *that?* And one more thing: Why do your children *always* begin a conversation just as you start dialing the telephone? By now you should be in the proper state of mind to mend your ways and make your list.

Having been so generous with my excellent advice, I must now confess that I began my own resolutions not in the attic but, quite prematurely, in the basement of a department store. It was the week before Christmas and the days had definitely dwindled down to the precious few, when I dashed—actually, I was sort of loping, like a kangaroo or the Bionic Woman—into Bloomingdale's to buy an omelet pan. Maintaining my usual caution, I avoided the omnipresent mirrors as I scurried through Make-up and Hosiery on the main floor. So it was in what I considered the total safety of Pots and Pans that I caught sight of myself in a full-length mirror. How shall I describe this? Well, for one thing my hair seemed to have blown into spikes, making me look like a frightened cat in an animated cartoon. And then, for another thing . . . oh, never mind.

What I really want to know is why they have mirrors in a hardware department? Do some people wish to see how they look holding a meat thermometer? In any event, the salesperson was out back hunting for my concept of an omelet pan ("Not a frying pan, the sides should be kind of bendy"). Thinking myself to be alone, I said, evidently out loud, "I swear I shall never go into Bloomingdale's without getting my hair done or I may end my life by slitting my wrist with the sharp edge of my charge-a-plate." There was a clang as a pan dropped and the very pretty young girl grabbed my arm and muttered, "Oh my God, lady."

Resolution Two. Since I believe, with Fletcher Knebel, that "It is now proved beyond doubt that smoking is one of the leading causes of statistics," I will quit smoking next year or I will not quit smoking. But I won't discuss it.

Three. I will stop telling the plots of television commercials to perfect strangers. But listen. Did you see the one in which this woman is in a supermarket making a telephone call? You can tell it's a supermarket because you can see all of the counters and her shopping cart is full of groceries. What she is saying on the telephone (with *nobody* watching that cart) is "Helen, I've been wondering. What do *you* use for occasional irregularity?" Now, I just can't leave it there. I want to know more about Helen. I want to know about Helen's husband. Does he say "Who was that on the phone? Janice? Where was she? She was in the A & P and wanted to know *what?*" Okay, I'm stopping. I've stopped.

Four. I will not try to be reasonable with my little girl. It just confuses her.

Five. I will not try to be chic, ever—because I see that for me this is a doomed endeavor. Last January, for reasons that seemed quite sensible at the time, I agreed to appear on the "Tomorrow" show. For the occasion I selected a rather billowing flowered caftan, which I then modeled for my Loved Ones. My oldest son took one look and remarked, "I don't know, I think I liked it better on the sofa." Thus rebuked, I hastened to Saks where I bought a rather slinky red dress with ruffles around the neck and down the front. Since the chronology here is important, I must explain that the show was aired on Monday night. On Tuesday morning *Time* magazine arrived, with an actress on the cover wearing the same, identical dress. And what's wrong with that, you'll ask. I'll tell you. The cover story was about soap operas and, running right across my red dress and my ruffles was this caption: "Sex and Suffering in the Afternoon."

Six. I will not force my younger children to watch educational television programs because that doesn't seem to work out either. Recently there was an hour-long show about Johann Strauss, the "Waltz King," on my favorite channel and I gathered the unpersuaded to watch it with me. Well, the Vienna Symphony sounded fine, if a little dim (that may have been our set), and the ballet dancers were lovely if perhaps not quite in sync with the music. But the children didn't seem to notice. Actually, we were getting through it pleasantly until we got to the big closing number—"The Blue Danube," naturally—in which the orchestra and the corps de ballet were joined by what was, I guess, the male chorus. The members of this group looked like slightly overweight businessmen who'd just come from the office. They shuffled in more or less at random, and they sang somewhat haphazardly. Even so, the children would probably have accepted the whole thing if their father, wandering through the room at the moment, hadn't muttered "Who are they—the season subscribers?"

Seven. Before I read a magazine, any magazine, I will search out and destroy all those little advertising postcards that promise to send me fifty issues for thirty-eight cents or is it thirty-eight issues for fifty cents? I mean, I already *am* a subscriber, for heaven's sake.

Eight. I will remember that there are no foolproof ways of reforming yourself, and I will be wary even of composing lists. A man I know (he's in advertising, in case that's relevant) was advised by his therapist to make two lists. One was to include the things he admired about himself. The other was to enumerate his failings, character defects, rotten habits, and so forth. Well, it turns out that the "bad" list practically wrote itself. In no time at all he had pages and pages of misdeeds so deplorable that one feels he needed only a little help to produce a best seller. But when he came to write the "positive" list, he could recall only one thing he was proud of. He wrote, "I don't litter."

I litter.

Index

In all cases, the page numbers refer to the magazines in which these pieces originally appeared.